Money and Markets in the Americas: New Challenges for Hemispheric Integration

Money and Markets in the Americas: New Challenges for Hemispheric Integration

Edited by
**James A. Dorn and
Roberto Salinas-León**

The Fraser Institute
Vancouver, British Columbia, Canada

Printed in Canada.

Canadian Cataloguing in Publication Data

Main entry under title:

Money and markets in the Americas

Revised papers from a conference held in Mexico City, May 25-26, 1994.
ISBN 0-88975-155-2

1. Monetary policy—North America—Congresses. 2. Monetary unions—North America—Congresses. 3. North America—Economic integration—Congresses. 4. Mexico—Economic policy—Congresses. I. Dorn, James A. II. León, Roberto Salinas. III. Fraser Institute (Vancouver, B.C.)
HG3902.M66 1995   332.4′566′097   C95-911160-3

Contents

About the Editors

James A. Dorn is Vice President for Academic Affairs at the Cato Institute, Editor of the *Cato Journal*, and Director of Cato's Project on Civil Society. He also directs Cato's annual monetary conference. Dorn is coeditor of *The Search for Stable Money, Economic Liberties and the Judiciary, Dollars, Deficits, and Trade*, and *Economic Reform in China*. He has taught at the Central European University in Prague and Fudan University in Shanghai, and is a Professor of Economics at Towson State University and a Research Fellow of the Institute for Humane Studies at George Mason University. His articles have appeared in the *Financial Times*, the *Washington Times*, the *Boston Herald*, and the *Dallas Morning News*. He holds an M.A. and Ph.D. in economics from the University of Virginia. From 1984-90, he served on the White House Commission on Presidential Scholars.

Roberto Salinas-León is the Executive Director of the Centro de Investigaciones Sobre la Libre Empresa and Academic Director of the Instituto Cultural Ludwig von Mises, both in Mexico City. He is also an Adjunct Professor of Political Economy at the Escuela Libre de Derecho and an Adjunct Scholar of the Cato Institute. He is an editorial writer for many newspapers and business journals in Latin America and a commentator on the daily radio program "Libre Comercio" ("Free Trade") on Radio VIP. Salinas has testified before the U.S. Congress in support of the North American Free Trade Agreement. He holds a Ph.D. in philosophy and political science from Purdue University.

Foreword

THIS PUBLICATION IS ONE OF A SERIES from the North America 20/20 project of The Fraser Institute. Funded by a grant from the Lilly Endowment Inc. of Indianapolis, the purpose of the project was to explore the impact of hemispheric trade relations by fostering research on the subject throughout North and South America. Under the auspices of the program, research was undertaken by more than 100 scholars in 9 countries.

This book reflects the collaboration of The Fraser Institute with the Cato Institute of Washington, D.C., and the Centro de Investigaciones Sobre la Libre Empresa, A.C. of Mexico City. The papers in the book were originally presented at a symposium in Mexico City in May 1994, sponsored by the three organizations. The purpose of that meeting was to consider current monetary arrangements in the region, as well as to explore alternative arrangements which might be superior.

The conference and the advice emanating from it predated the Mexican currency crisis but anticipated many of the key issues surrounding that crisis. The papers dealing with Mexico have been updated to reflect intervening developments. Other papers have been added to make the volume more comprehensive. Taken together, they constitute a valuable investigation of various aspects of monetary arrangements in the hemisphere, and offer concrete proposals for avoiding in the future some of the recent problems.

The book also explores the possibility and desirability of a currency union in the region and the outlines of a monetary constitution. All told, the book rounds out the discussion of the topics that are important to consider in a free trade area, and it makes a fine addition to the other books that have been published under the auspices of the North America 20/20 program.

The authors of the various papers published here have worked independently, and their views may not correspond singly or collectively with those of the members or the trustees of The Fraser Institute. The Institute is pleased to publish this book in the hope that it will thereby hasten the discovery of better, more effective monetary arrangements in the hemisphere.

Michael A. Walker
Executive Director
The Fraser Institute

Editors' Preface

THIS COLLECTION OF ESSAYS is the intellectual result of papers commissioned for the Cato Institute's 12th annual monetary conference, "Monetary Arrangements in the Americas after NAFTA," which was held in Mexico City in May 1994 and was cosponsored by the Centro de Investigaciones Sobre la Libre Empresa (CISLE) and The Fraser Institute. Many of the themes developed at the conference anticipated the policy debates generated since the collapse of Mexico's exchange rate system in December 1994—particularly proposals for monetary reform, the focus on monetary accountability, and the demands for greater monetary integration among the three NAFTA partners.

The book centers on the fundamental issues confronting countries that experience regional trade liberalization and on the types of monetary and financial polices governments should follow in order to maximize trade opportunities derived from lower barriers to external markets. The devastating financial crisis generated by the peso devaluation has placed those issues in the forefront of public policy debates. On the one hand, a consensus has emerged for the need to fashion initiatives that target various items of monetary policy across different borders, especially foreign exchange rates, as structural complements of trade liberalization. On the other hand, interpretations of such policy initiatives differ widely—for instance, whether devaluation should be wielded to stimulate exports, whether exchange rate stability should be pursued come what may, and whether a North American monetary union should be formed to realize benefits from full dollarization of the trade bloc.

The peso devaluation and its financial repercussions in the international financial system led us to include several new essays (chapters 5, 7–10, and 18), as well as to substantially revise the original set of contributions. We think the final product is representative of the ideas first expressed at the conference; but we also feel the book sheds valuable new light on the debates triggered by the peso collapse. For this we thank our contributors who waited patiently for over a year before seeing their intellectual efforts in print.

Many people have worked hard to make this book a reality. We would like to express our gratitude to CISLE's research assistants—Daniel Muñoz, Margarito Cruz, and José Enrique López—who helped to coordinate the essays from the Latin American contributors and helped update the data in these essays. In addition, we would like to thank the editorial efforts of Mary O'Grady, former Visiting Fellow at CISLE and now with the *Wall Street Journal* as editor of the "Americas Column," as well as Ian Vásquez, director of Cato's Project on Global Economic Liberty, and Kristin McCahon, Director of Publication Production at The Fraser Institute. Their input was essential to the completion of this project.

We are especially grateful to Ed Crane, president of the Cato Institute, for making it possible to hold Cato's annual monetary conference in Mexico City. The conference represents the second joint project undertaken by CISLE and Cato in Mexico, and we hope its success provides an incentive to realize more intellectual joint ventures of this kind.

Above all, we would like to express our gratitude to Michael Walker, a champion of free markets and common sense, for The Fraser Institute's financial backing and logistical support for the conference and the book. Michael was instrumental in developing a first-class program of speakers and obtaining the contributions of such prominent policy makers as Michael Wilson and John Crow. We thank him for the opportunity to publish the proceedings in this volume and for his tireless efforts to develop a proper public understanding of the monetary aspects of hemispheric integration.

Roberto Salinas-León
Mexico City

James A. Dorn
Washington, D.C.

CHAPTER 1

Introduction: Stable Money and a Market-Liberal Order

James A. Dorn[1]

> Widespread prosperity cannot be engineered from the central planner's rulebook. Higher real incomes do not flow from the ink of the currency printing press. Restricting the free flow of goods and investment may protect the few, but at enormous cost to the many.
>
> —*Lawrence B. Lindsey*

The market-liberal revolution

THE TRANSITION FROM THE STATIST MODEL of development to a market-liberal model is one of the most important events of the 20th century. The collapse of communism in Eastern Europe in 1989 and the abandonment of the ossified Soviet system of central planning sent

---

1 James A. Dorn is Vice President for Academic Affairs at the Cato Institute and Professor of Economics at Towson State University. He is a Research Fellow of the Institute for Humane Studies at George Mason University.

shock waves throughout the world—reminding people of the empty promises of Marxists and the prosperity of markets.

Mexico's decision to abandon its autarkic development strategy and open its markets to competitive pressures was yet another indication of the market-liberal revolution that is occurring throughout the global economy.

The North American Free Trade Agreement (NAFTA), which became law in early 1994, created the largest trading bloc in the world. Trade liberalization between Canada, the United States, and Mexico has the potential to spread to the rest of the hemisphere. The pace of economic integration, however, will depend on following a principled approach to trade policy and adopting institutions that support rather than hinder the market-liberal order.

Money and markets

Markets depend on private property rights and a rule of law, but they also depend on sound money. Monetary disequilibrium disrupts trade and investment and creates conditions for political turmoil. The uncertainty stemming from high and variable inflation, or from sharp swings in the growth of money and credit, upsets business and personal planning—since unanticipated changes in the value of money affect relative prices and profits and make economic calculation more difficult.[2]

When the future value of money is uncertain, resources have to be devoted to hedging against changes in the value of money. Mistakes will be made, and those mistakes can seriously disrupt economic life. Excessive increases in the quantity of money relative to the demand for money, for example, can stimulate business and trade until expectations fall in line with reality. As monetary excesses are corrected, businesses and financial institutions find that their planned profits turn into losses

---

2   For a discussion of the theory of monetary disequilibrium, see Dorn (1983) and Yeager (1986). The pioneering work of Clark Warburton is especially notable (see Yeager 1981).

and nonperforming loans. The "highs" of inflation become the "lows" of recession.[3]

The stop-go nature of monetary policy, which is characteristic of discretionary central banks issuing fiat money, means that an excess supply of money can easily turn into a deficiency. It is uncertainty about the actions of monetary authorities, and hence the future value of money, that endangers the transition from a closed to an open economy. Without monetary stability, there can be no price stability, no financial stability, and no exchange rate stability. And without confidence in the value of money, the soundness of financial institutions, and the exchange rate, there can be little confidence in markets and prices. The temptation then is to revert to government regulation and move away from market liberalism and toward market socialism.[4]

The excessive growth of the monetary base in Mexico in 1994 and the contraction in 1995 are the latest example of stop-go monetary policy.[5] Where the Bank of Mexico goes next no one knows, and that is precisely the problem confronting not only Mexico but many developing countries. The question is, how can monetary stability be achieved

---

3   The costs of business failure, lost opportunities, and financial instability caused by inflation are often neglected (see Schwartz 1995). According to Schwartz, "A regime of monetary and price stability is the route to financial stability. Such a regime avoids the quantifiable and unquantifiable costs of price instability in distorting economic performance" (ibid.: 25). Even moderate inflation can be costly (see Marty and Thornton 1995).

4   Politicians are all too apt to look for scapegoats, such as "foreign speculators," when a financial crisis occurs, instead of accepting responsibility for failed policies—especially monetary and fiscal policies—and for failing to deepen market reforms. Milton Friedman (1995: 4) brings this point out with regard to the peso crisis: "Speculation neither caused nor accelerated the crisis in Mexico. The only thing it did was to help recognize the problem.... The collapse is only attributable to deficient policy. The crisis could have been avoided and should have been avoided by a devaluation of the peso at least two years before and, at the same time, by the installation of a monetary policy regime to further reduce inflation."

5   See Meltzer (1995, especially Figure 3). Data from Haver Analytics show that Mexico's monetary base (currency held by the public plus bank reserves) grew at an average annual rate of 20.4 percent during 1994, an election year.

and thereby keep Mexico and other Latin American countries on the path toward market liberalization and privatization? Is monetary union the answer? Or would Mexico be well advised to adopt an Argentine-type currency board to achieve price stability? What type of monetary constitution is appropriate for the Americas? Those and related questions about the future of money and markets in the Americas are the focus of this volume.

The question of monetary union

The papers in Part I deal with the question of monetary union, that is, does a North American free trade area (FTA) require monetary integration to realize the full benefits of economic integration? The clear answer is no. But even if monetary union is unnecessary for economic union, is a common currency area desirable in North America? In principle, the use of a common currency would lower transactions costs and expand market exchange, but the divergence in economic policies, the difference in economic conditions, and the lack of wage and price flexibility (especially in Mexico) indicate that North America is not an optimum currency area. Moreover, without political consensus, there is little prospect of a North American monetary union with a supranational monetary authority.

To achieve monetary stability and safeguard the long-run value of their currencies, members of NAFTA should adopt policies that provide for domestic price stability, price liberalization, and deregulation. A regime of freely floating exchange rates for North American currencies would then discipline those countries that violated the principles of free trade and sound money that underlie a market-liberal order. Institutional competition is to be preferred to creating another bureaucracy, a North American central bank, which may hinder economic integration. These are the main conclusions from chapters 2–5.

In chapter 2, **Alan Walters** reiterates the point that a common market or FTA does not necessitate a common currency. Likewise, a monetary union does not require a common market. Since a monetary union eliminates the exchange rate as an adjustment mechanism, a North American monetary union would require greater wage and price flexibility to avoid prolonged unemployment during balance-of-payments crises. The temptation is for policy makers to turn to capital controls and protectionism to maintain a fixed exchange rate rather than to further liberalize markets. Moreover, if Canada and Mexico chose to join a dollar bloc, their futures would depend on "Washington shenanigans."

In chapter 3, **Jerry Jordan** examines the costs and benefits of monetary union. A successful monetary union is likely if member countries have a strong commitment to price stability, experience similar economic shocks, adopt institutions that provide for competitive markets, and are politically integrated. In countries or regions that experience different macroeconomic conditions and face regulatory hurdles to resource mobility and price liberalization, as in the case with the North American countries, any attempt to form a monetary union is doomed to failure. Instead, Jordan suggests a regime of floating exchange rates and independent domestic monetary and fiscal policies along with trade liberalization. Those countries that follow sound monetary and fiscal policies and adopt market-enhancing institutions will have strong currencies and attract foreign investment, as opposed to those that do not. Markets will discipline governments that fail to follow the principles of a market-liberal order. In the process, there will be a spontaneous movement toward institutions that promote price stability and increase the wealth of nations. Competition among national currencies thus ensures that economic forces will bring about institutional change in favour of markets, as opposed to futile attempts to create a common currency without a common polity.

Rogelio Ramírez de la O, using logic similar to Jordan's, argues in chapter 4 that a North American currency area would not at present be feasible. In particular, Mexico's labour and capital markets need to be more competitive and similar to those in the United States before monetary union would be beneficial. His advice is "to avoid creating bureaucratic institutions where their justification is not well established." Meanwhile, the goals of a monetary union—money of stable value and exchange rate stability—can be obtained by adhering to "sound macroeconomic policies."

In the final chapter of Part I, **Jean-Luc Migué** draws on public choice theory and the political theory of federalism to elaborate on the case for competing national currencies. He prefers a type of monetary federalism to the politically contrived and centrally planned type of monetary union that proponents of a North American currency area envision. For Migué, a system in which individuals are free to choose among freely floating national currencies within a free-trade area is equivalent to "competitive federalism applied to monetary matters." Under such a system, policy makers operating within a constitutional democracy have an incentive "to deliver the kind of performance people want." Currency substitution will tend to force bad policies out and let good policies in. In the long run, the market will discover the best monetary arrangement.

Lessons from the peso devaluation

The events leading up to the December 1994 devaluation of the peso and the ensuing stagflation offer important lessons on how to avoid derailing the transition to a market economy. Successful transition requires adherence to a consistent set of policies that embody the principles of sound money, open markets, privatization, and depoliticization of economic life. Sound money requires not only credible monetary institutions but rule-bound fiscal and political institutions, so that people have confidence in the long-run stability of both economic and political life. The papers in Part II discuss the loss of confidence in Mexico's policy makers that stemmed from their failure to curb excessive spending in 1994 and limit monetary growth to a noninflationary path. The mishandling of the peso crisis by the Ernesto Zedillo administration further eroded confidence, while the $50 billion bailout package, assembled by the United States and the IMF, merely postponed the day of reckoning and did little to help ordinary citizens. If Mexico wishes to return to the path of prosperity, Mexican leaders must reembrace market principles, not grab at short-run solutions for long-run problems. Moreover, political reform must accompany economic liberalization. Those are the key lessons discussed in chapters 6–10.

In chapter 6, **Luis Rubio** provides an overview of the ideological transformation of Mexico's development policy from a state-led development strategy to a market-led strategy. Before the 1980s Mexico clung to the idea that economic autarky and state planning were the best means for developing economic potential. An authoritarian political regime was consistent with that development strategy. The failure of orthodox development planning led to a revolution in development economics. In 1985 Mexico began to shift in earnest to a market-liberal path by privatizing state enterprises, opening markets, and cutting the size of government.

The move toward economic liberalization, however, threatened to displace special interest groups who gained from Mexican mercantilism. By 1988 it became clear that lasting economic reform would require political reform. The Salinas de Gortari administration deepened market reforms and initiated political reform, but the reform process in both cases was too slow. During the 1994 election year, politics took precedence over sound economic policy and led to increased public spending and excess money creation. By December the devaluation was inevitable as capital fled the country and the Bank of Mexico's foreign reserves were insufficient to support the pegged exchange rate. The challenge for the Zedillo administration is to restore confidence in market-led development and to open the political process to greater competition as well.

In chapter 7, **Luis Pazos** considers the various events leading to the December 20, 1994, devaluation of the peso, in which the peso-dollar band was widened under the crawling peg. He has no doubt that the political uprising in Chiapas in January 1994 and the murder of Luis Donaldo Colosio in March contributed to the loss of confidence in the peso. But the major factor leading to devaluation and to the ensuing economic chaos was the failure to pursue sound economic policy. Pazos blames that failure on "the hubris of many technocrats who believed they could trick the markets."

Mexico's march from stability to stagflation is analyzed in chapter 8 by **Roberto Salinas-León**. The tragedy is that the peso crisis could have been avoided if Mexico had stood by "the principles of confidence, fiscal discipline, and market certainty that had led to the highest foreign investment boom in Mexico's modern history." Instead of restraining the growth of the monetary base in 1994 and raising short-term interest rates to stem the capital outflow, the Bank of Mexico increased the annual growth rate of high-powered money from less than 1 percent in

1993 to more than 20 percent in 1994. And part of that increase was due to the financing of government debt, including off-budget credit extended to state development banks. Other policy errors added to the crisis, especially the overreliance on short-term debt to pay for an excess of imports over exports, the failure to adequately reform the pegged exchange rate regime, and the absence of a positive program to extend privatization and market liberalization and thereby offset the loss of confidence caused by the devaluation. According to Salinas-León, the proper role of the central bank should be to achieve price stability, not to micromanage the exchange rate to achieve a current account surplus. The major issue of the Mexican fiasco is, not whether Mexico ought to join a monetary union, "but whether a monetary framework can be fashioned consistent with the permanence of a sound and stable currency."

In chapter 9, **Jonathan Heath** considers the debate over Mexico's economic policy in 1994 and who is to blame for the peso crisis. Two points are of interest: First, Mexico's reported fiscal deficit for 1994, which was only 0.3 percent of GDP, did not include "financial intermediation," that is, the net credit position of state development banks. Had that information been included, as it was before 1993, the government's deficit would have been reported as 4.7 percent of GDP—a significant amount and a factor in explaining the increase in Mexico's current account deficit in 1994. Second, if the Bank of Mexico had not extended credit to the government and had not allowed an excessive growth of the monetary base, the crisis might have been averted or at least minimized. The Bank of Mexico gained autonomy in April 1994, but the central bank law stipulates only that the government not request funds directly from the bank; there is no provision against the bank's independently granting credit to the government. The bank's efforts to achieve price stability are therefore compromised under the present law. Heath contends that the lack of information on the real fiscal deficit in 1994 and the absence of up-to-date information on the growth of the monetary base made it difficult to determine what policy actions to take at the time and who or what was responsible for the crisis. In his view, there is enough blame to spread around; he would not pin the crisis on any one factor.

Lee Hoskins and **James Coons** do pin the peso crisis on a single factor, the failure of monetary policy. In chapter 10, they use new data to support the conclusion that "the fundamental cause of the 1994-95 peso crisis was an inflationary monetary policy...largely driven by electoral politics." The Bank of Mexico sought to keep interest rates from rising to unacceptable levels during an election year and maintain the pegged exchange rate.

Once domestic and foreign investors anticipated inflation and a devaluation, official reserves began to decline. To avoid devaluation, the central bank should have cut the growth of the monetary base and allowed a sharp increase in interest rates. By failing to do so, the bank bowed to political pressures and was forced to widen the exchange band, that is, to devalue the peso. Mexican policy makers were punished by the international capital markets, as pesos were converted into dollars. According to Hoskins and Coons, therefore, the main cause of the peso crisis was not capital outflows but "the underlying instability of monetary policies."

To revitalize the Mexican economy, Hoskins and Coons recommend that Mexico not rely on aid but further remove barriers to trade. They take a market-based approach to solving the peso crisis and see the bailout plan as simply putting ordinary Mexicans deeper in debt without fixing the fundamental problem. What needs to be done, they argue, is to provide for (1) price stability; (2) monetary credibility; (3) a freely floating exchange rate, so policy errors become visible immediately, instead of being concealed behind "the veil of a peso peg"; (4) market-driven debt negotiations under a rule of law, so that private creditors and sovereign debtors can work out mutually beneficial terms during a debt crisis without putting taxpayers at risk; (5) U.S. withdrawal from the IMF and World Bank; and (6) "a full embrace of free-market principles."

Proposals for monetary reform

How can the value of money best be protected from governmental abuse? The record of discretionary central banks in a world of fiat monies is one of persistent inflation. The stop-go nature of monetary policy and the poor performance of central banks, especially in developing countries, offer a challenge to think about alternative monetary arrangements that are more likely to deliver sound money. The papers in Part III investigate the importance of stable money for a free-market system and consider proposals for monetary reform in the Americas.

In chapter 11, **John Crow**, a former governor of the Bank of Canada, argues that, to be credible, central banks must have a clear mandate to achieve price stability and be held accountable. Giving the bank multiple targets is a mistake that diverts attention from the primary goal of providing a noninflationary path for nominal GDP growth. If the bank is prevented by law from financing government deficits and has a single goal of maintaining price stability, monetary authorities will be accountable because the public will recognize the bank's failure to achieve a clearly stated mandate. When independent central banks deliver domestic price stability, financial stability and exchange rate stability will follow. On the other hand, "if monetary policy does not provide a solid domestic anchor, the adverse effects from domestic financial uncertainty are more likely to make the exchange rate an additional source of instability"—a lesson Mexico should now have learned.

Although NAFTA liberalizes trade in goods, it falls short of fully liberalizing financial services. In chapter 12, **George Selgin** explains why and makes a case for real free trade in banking. U.S. and Canadian banks can now enter the Mexican market, and Mexican and U.S. investors can acquire ownership of Canadian banks. There are still limits to foreign ownership of Mexico's largest banks, but the real limits to free trade in banking are (1) the prohibition against U.S. banks' establishing branches in Mexico and Canada and (2) the doctrine of "national treatment," which requires that Mexican and Canadian banks operating in the United States be subject to U.S. banking regulations rather than more lenient home-country regulations. By adhering to the principle of national treatment, NAFTA "precludes competition among national regulatory authorities, allowing inefficient and burdensome regulations to persist." Real free trade in banking, argues Selgin, would allow consumers to choose the ownership mix and regulatory regime they prefer, as well as generate a safer and sounder banking system in North America.

Juan Andrés Fontaine accepts the monetarist view of inflation but rejects a rigid monetary rule. In chapter 13, he draws on the Latin

American experience with inflation, especially the Chilean experience, to show that nearly everyone now agrees that inflation is primarily a monetary phenomenon and that to stop inflation it is necessary to constrain the monetary and fiscal powers of government and practice free-market principles. After rejecting fixed-quantity rules (such as a constant money-growth rule) and fixed-price rules (such as a fixed exchange rate rule), Fontaine settles on what he calls a "flexible feedback rule" or "bounded discretion." He would tie the hands of central bankers but not tight enough to forestall "rational discretion." His independent central bankers are rule bound, but the rules allow some flexibility to adjust to particular events in the search for stable money.

Chile has had an independent central bank since 1980, but that independence, plus the commitment to price stability, was strengthened by the Central Bank Law of 1989. By following a feedback rule, the bank has been able to reduce inflation from historic averages of 30 percent per year to single digits. The feedback rule relies on real interest-rate targeting to achieve a desired path for real GDP as an intermediate target of monetary policy—with the ultimate goal being zero expected inflation. Although there are difficulties in implementing such a rule, Fontaine contends that "political independence, well-defined objectives, and transparent criteria for policy have provided a good framework for monetary stability."

Fontaine also considers the case for free banking and competing private currencies, which F. A. Hayek (1978) proposed as an alternative to government fiat money. He finds "the privatization of central banking...a very appealing idea." But he is hesitant "to leap into this unknown water" without further study. Nevertheless, he recommends three reforms to increase monetary freedom: (1) "abolish exchange controls and authorize the free circulation of foreign monies for the payment of goods and services, including taxes"; (2) "minimize central bank regulations on the private issuing of money substitutes"; and (3) follow Chile's example by allowing "the issuing of CPI-indexed securities and deposits."

In chapter 14, **Steve Hanke** and **Kurt Schuler** propose a currency board system as a proven way for developing countries to achieve monetary stability and promote economic growth. With a currency board, the domestic currency is fully convertible at a fixed exchange rate into the reserve currency. There is no scope for discretion or for financing fiscal deficits. A currency board imparts confidence and credibility to the home-country currency by directly linking it to a stable currency like the dollar. As long as U.S. monetary policy keeps inflation low, the value of the board's currency will be stable, and interest rates will converge toward those in the United States. Argentina adopted a currency board-like system in April 1991 and has brought inflation down from 2,000 percent to less than 10 percent. Hanke and Schuler think other Latin American countries could achieve greater price stability if they got rid of their failed central banks and shifted to a currency board arrangement.

Currency boards, however, are no panacea. **John Greenwood**, who was instrumental in designing the Hong Kong currency board, notes, in his comment on the Hanke-Schuler paper, "Simple currency board arrangements are not immune from corrupting influences; their mandate and their instruments can be transformed over time." To prevent the politicization of money, he emphasizes the importance of "a strong monetary constitution" and a sound public understanding of the social benefits of a currency board.

Jack Carr and **Kam Hon Chu** provide a detailed discussion of the idea of a monetary constitution in chapter 15. They examine alternative monetary rules and argue that the best rule would be a simple quantity rule that fixed the growth of a monetary aggregate with the objective of providing long-run price stability. The problem is how to enforce such a rule or any rule that binds the central bank. Central banks dislike being rule bound, and politicians like to have some control over monetary affairs. In Canada, for example, the central bank announces inflation targets, but there is no legal mandate for price stability as the sole objective of monetary policy. Moreover, the targets can be changed by a government directive—so there is no enforceable monetary rule. To be credible, the monetary rule would have to be incorporated into constitutional law, and other changes in the economic constitution may be necessary (for example, a balanced-budget amendment).

Regardless of the specific rule chosen, the Americas would benefit from adopting monetary constitutions that depoliticize money and provide a stable framework in which markets can function efficiently to satisfy consumers' preferences. As Carr and Chu point out, "A monetary constitution which takes the form of rules establishing and limiting the power of the central bank appears to be the best way to achieve both monetary and financial system stability."

In addition, they note that financial stability can be enhanced by eliminating or significantly reforming deposit insurance, an institution that increases risk taking and penalizes prudence at the taxpayers' expense.

Future policy directions

The full benefits from trade liberalization under NAFTA depend on adherence to market-liberal principles—to private property rights and freedom of contract protected by a legal framework based on a constitution of liberty and a monetary constitution that prevents the state from eroding the value of money. How bright the future is under NAFTA will depend on whether policy makers take a principled approach to free trade or take the path of least resistance and fall into the trap of managed trade and market intervention.

The papers in Part IV examine the future role of the dollar in the global economy, the steps that still need to be taken to realize the long-run potential of NAFTA, the problem of stabilizing the peso and restoring economic growth, and the question of how best to expand trade liberalization in the Americas.

In chapter 16, **Lawrence B. Lindsey**, a member of the Federal Reserve Board, emphasizes that the future of the dollar will depend crucially on whether U.S. policy makers adhere to the goals of price stability and market liberalization. Erratic monetary policy, financial instability, and protectionist policies that block the free flow of goods and capital would weaken the status of the dollar as an international currency. Competition among the major currencies dictates that policy makers keep an eye on international capital markets when choosing among policy options. Countries that fail to meet the market test will find their currencies losing out to countries that follow credible policies.

A loss of confidence in U.S. economic policy will result in a loss of confidence in the dollar and a loss of seigniorage (that is, the profits from money creation). As the supplier of the world's major international currency, the United States has an important stake in expanding world trade. As Lindsey writes, "The more vibrant the international economic order, the more demand for the country's currency, and the more benefits which flow to the issuer."

The voluntary dollarization of Latin America is an indication of the relative strength of the dollar as a store of value, a unit of account, and a medium of exchange. Currency competition will help discipline policy makers in Latin America to lower inflation and keep markets open. According to Lindsey, "Dollarization is a transfer of power from political decision makers to the individual citizens and market participants of the hemisphere's countries." Institutions that promote U.S. monetary stability can therefore benefit both the United States and those countries that allow citizens to freely hold and exchange U.S. dollars.

Michael Wilson, former Canadian minister for international trade, was actively involved in the Canada-U.S. Free Trade Agreement and was responsible for the NAFTA negotiations. In chapter 17, he argues that the competitive forces unleashed by market liberalization in North America will produce better goods and better money—provided Canada, the United States, and Mexico are consistent in following free-market principles. Moreover, he points out that "the benefits of trade liberalization come fast and best to those firms and workers prepared to adjust and take advantage of opportunities that free trade offers."

Wilson recognizes the shortcomings of NAFTA and the need for further liberalization, especially in financial services. He thinks that a monetary union is neither economically nor politically feasible and that the best way to achieve sound money and stable exchange rates in North America is by having each country pursue price stability as the primary goal of monetary policy.

A rules-based approach to trade liberalization in the hemisphere appeals to Wilson. He believes it is best to work within the NAFTA framework rather than negotiate separate bilateral trade agreements. And he accepts the idea that "adherence to NAFTA is only feasible for those countries that have made a major and sustained commitment to market-based economic reform."

When Mexico devalued the peso in December 1994, it was an admission of failure not only for macroeconomic policy but for the crawling peg exchange rate regime. Fixed but adjustable exchange rates are an instrument of government intervention and are contrary to market-liberal principles. When exchange rates are neither permanently fixed nor freely floating, the price of foreign exchange is bound to become politicized. The adjustable peg meant that Mexico's misguided monetary and fiscal policies in 1994 were prevented from immediately showing up in a depreciation of the peso. When the devaluation came about, the underlying pressures that had been suppressed came to the fore, and there was a much sharper fall of the peso than would have occurred with a floating-rate system in which there is a continuous adjustment process.

Although the peso was allowed to float after the devaluation, the float is a "dirty" float, and the exchange rate has continued to slide because of the lack of a solid anchor for the peso. There is still no credible, long-run commitment to price stability as the primary aim of monetary policy or to any clear-cut monetary rule; there is no effective monetary constitution in Mexico.

That is why, in chapter 18, **Roberto Salinas-León** advocates a currency board for Mexico. He draws on arguments used by Hanke and Schuler to make a case for moving to a fixed exchange rate regime that would restore credibility and confidence to the peso and encourage investment and growth. With greater price stability, interest rates would fall, and the precarious state of Mexico's banking system would improve. The beauty of a currency board for Mexico, in Salinas-León's view, is that it "rules out discretionary monetary policy," which has been Mexico's Achilles heel.

Salinas-León recognizes that the currency board route is not the only route to price stability. If the Bank of Mexico followed in the footsteps of New Zealand and were made accountable for a single mandate of price stability, then it is possible that a regime of floating rates and rule-bound monetary policy would lead to the same confidence a currency board would produce. In such a case, "the political choice between a board and a floating regime would constitute a distinction without a difference."

While Mexico's ruling elite clings to the status quo and is reluctant to give up control of the exchange rate, the Mexican people desire a stable monetary regime. They "know all too well," writes Salinas-León, "that the peso desperately requires transparency, simplicity, and complete depoliticization." If so, prospects for real monetary reform may be better than they appear at first glance.

In the final chapter, **Edward Hudgins** makes the case for expanding NAFTA to all countries in the hemisphere that want to adopt market-liberal principles. The further liberalization of trade and economic integration of the hemisphere will have long-lasting benefits and, in Hudgins' view, "will drive monetary considerations." He holds that individuals have a right to free trade—to noninterference in the use of their property rights, as long as they respect the equal rights of others. Thus, free-trade areas ought to be formed whenever possible.

Trade liberalization reduces the power of government and should be encouraged from a market-liberal perspective, even if there is some trade diversion. The natural course of trade is to expand, when free to do so. The challenge is for governments to open markets and for the United States to "be a trade entrepreneur and seek out countries that are engaging in market reforms . . . and offer them free trade areas," writes Hudgins. What America should not do is to export its failed regulatory policies to developing countries seeking to dismantle their statist regimes in favour of a market-liberal order. A market-based approach to regulation, Hudgins contends, would offer developing countries more scope for growth and prosperity than adopting the command-and-control approach that has characterized the regulatory regime in developed countries.

Latin American countries should consider institutional changes, including a system of tort law, that help safeguard the life, liberty, and property of their citizens—without creating another layer of bureaucracy to further politicize economic life, notes Hudgins. Moreover, leaders should "oppose attempts to impose American regulatory burdens on their economies as the price for freer trade." In his view, "regulatory competition in this hemisphere would be good for Latin American countries and the United States as well." Most important to Hudgins, however, is that all countries in the hemisphere remove remaining barriers to free trade so that individuals can enjoy greater economic freedom and the opportunity to achieve a higher living standard.

Conclusion

The liberalization of trade under NAFTA will provide new opportunities to expand markets in the Americas. Increased competition is good for trade and good for consumers. Increased competition is also good for institutional change: those institutions that are consistent with a market-liberal order will tend to crowd out those that are not. The privatization of state assets, the opening of capital markets, the recognition of the futility of exchange rate pegging, and the move toward more stable monetary and fiscal regimes are the results of market-led development replacing state-led development. The challenge will be to create an ethos of economic liberty in the Americas that will extend the market-liberal revolution to all countries in the hemisphere and around the globe, so that people everywhere can enjoy the benefits of free trade.

To be successful, the economic integration of the Americas requires not only free markets but sound money. The peso crisis is only the latest example of how misguided monetary policy can wreck havoc on economic life and disrupt society. The danger is that a monetary crisis can cause a financial panic, and government may react by imposing wage and price controls, and perhaps capital controls. Even in the United States, in the early 1970s, when inflation was less than 4 percent but rising, the government reacted with wage and price controls, which resulted in stagflation, the creation of a new federal bureaucracy (the Department of Energy), and bottlenecks in the market system.

Latin American countries cannot afford to sacrifice their future for the false promises of a controlled market. What they need is a free, open market, and to ensure that, they need to maintain the value of their currencies by adopting some type of monetary constitution that safeguards the long-term value of money. Only then will they achieve financial stability and reduce exchange rate volatility.

The essays in this volume show the close link between stable money and stable markets and provide a framework for thinking about how best to reform the discretionary monetary regimes that now dot the economic landscape in the Americas. Although the authors do not agree on any one solution, they do agree that transparency, credibility, and accountability are essential if people are to have confidence in the monetary regime.

The future of economic integration in the Americas will depend, in large part, on the choice of monetary institutions. In making that choice, policy makers would do well to respond to consumers' preferences for sound money and keep in mind the principles and proposals elaborated on in this volume.

References

Dorn, J.A. (1983) "The Search for Stable Money: A Historical Perspective." In J.A. Dorn and A.J. Schwartz (eds.) *The Search for Stable Money: Essays on Monetary Reform*, 1-28. Chicago: University of Chicago Press.

Friedman, M. (1995) Quoted in *The Mexico Report* (16 June): 4.

Hayek, F.A. (1978) *The Denationalisation of Money: The Argument Revisited*. Hobart Paper 70. London: Institute of Economic Affairs.

Meltzer, A.H. (1995) "A Mexican Tragedy." *Harvard International Review* (forthcoming).

Schwartz, A.J. (1995) "Why Financial Stability Depends on Price Stability." *Economic Affairs* (Autumn): 21-25.

Marty, A.L., and Thornton, D.L. (1995) "Is There a Case for 'Moderate' Inflation?" Federal Reserve Bank of St. Louis *Review* (July/August): 27-37.

Yeager, L.B. (1981) "Clark Warburton, 1896-1979." *History of Political Economy* 13 (Summer): 279-84.

Yeager, L.B. (1986) "The Significance of Monetary Disequilibrium." *Cato Journal* 6 (Fall): 369-99.

Part 1:
The Question
of Monetary Union

CHAPTER 2

Do Common Markets Require Common Currencies?

Alan A. Walters[1]

Common markets, economic unions, and free trade areas

THE EMERGING POPULARITY OF TRADING BLOCKS of one sort or another seems to be a consequence of the alleged success of the European Community (which we must now learn to call the European Union). Certainly if we judge success by the anxiety of outsiders to join the EU, then it must be seen as impressive. Of the possible joiners, only Switzerland, Iceland, and Norway have firmly resisted the temptation. Austria, Sweden, and Finland are virtually in the EU, while the ex-communist central European countries, not to mention Turkey, are vigorously

---

1 The author is Vice Chairman and Director of AIG Trading Groups, Inc., Director of IDEA Ltd., and Chairman of Counter Cyclical Investment Fund. He served as Chief Economic Adviser to Margaret Thatcher.

pursuing membership. But it is important to note that the EC is (or one should more accurately say "should be") a common market and, if the reservations of the United Kingdom are discounted, the EU is on the way to becoming a political union, as well as an economic union, with a federal structure—the United States of Europe, no less.

A free trade area, like NAFTA, differs from a common market. The essence of a common market (or customs union [CU]) is not simply that goods can move freely without tariff or other hindrance within the community, but also that there is a common external tariff. This enables goods imported into one country freely to enter another in the community of nations. NAFTA, however, allows countries to have different external tariffs. The free trade conditions extend only to domestic goods and not to imports through different external tariff regimes. Thus in NAFTA any imports under a low external U.S. tariff which are re-exported to Mexico, with a higher tariff, will be checked at the Mexican—U.S. border and will have to pay the additional duty. The rules about "domestic content" become all important in charging for these inter-FTA trades.

I do not know whether the NAFTA will ever progress to a NACM (North American Common Market), but clearly it is a long way off. Making NAFTA work will take many years. But will it progress like the EC? Will it develop, not only as a common market, but also as a regional currency arrangement, like the "snake," the Exchange Rate Mechanism (ERM), or a monetary union?

NAFTA, common markets, and monetary unions

One interesting aspect of NAFTA is that no one seems to have seriously mentioned the development of a monetary union. Nor have there been any negotiations for even a formally administered pegged exchange rate system for Canada and Mexico. The governments and central banks of these two countries clearly take into account the dollar exchange rate in their monetary policy, but there is no sense in which they are tied to particular rates. True the Mexican authorities did have an informal "crawling peg" until it all fell apart in December 1994. But this is quite different from the principles of convergence that have been enunciated and assiduously peddled in the European Community. We must note, of course, that the birth of the EC at the Treaty of Rome was under the aegis of Bretton Woods and the system of pegged exchange rates combined with exchange controls and, until 1960, inconvertibility of all major currencies.

After the United States went off gold, the European countries were very wary of floating rates and quickly mackled up the "snake" followed by the establishment in 1978-79 of the ERM, which in an albeit emaciated and emasculated form is still with us today. The rationalization for pegging exchange rates was ostensibly to "create a sea of stability" in European common market countries, de facto on the Deutschemark. A subtext, however, was the fear of "competitive devaluation" which was thought to have had "beggar-my-neighbour" consequences in the interwar years. Manipulation of the real exchange rate could be a substitute for tariffs and export subsidies. Preventing or inhibiting nominal exchange rate movements was thought to be at least some defense against the exporting of unemployment through competitive real devaluations and the dog-eats-dog policies of the 1930s.

As we now know, the system of pegged nominal rates did not prevent quite large movements in real exchange rates, and, of course, it presented gifts to speculators who had all the time in the world to anticipate a collapse in or a substantial movement in the peg. For most of the life of the ERM, the reluctance to move parities gave the low-inflation countries, mainly Germany, the competitive edge and current surpluses vis-à-vis the other community countries more or less continuously.

Thus, it is likely that the pegged currency system for a common market itself induced the distortions in real exchange rates that it was designed to cure. Various suggestions have been made for making the pegged system more flexible so that it automatically adjusts the nominal exchange towards the "fundamental real equilibrium exchange rates" or FREERs. It is however difficult to define FREERs in theory and impossible to measure them in practice, so it is not surprising that they have remained the playthings of policy wonks rather than practical instruments of policy.

Fixed exchange rates and currency unions

It must be noted that the characteristic rigidity of nominal rates and the distortion of real exchange rates with the associated capital movements is true for a pegged exchange rate system—sometimes called, oxymoronically, "a fixed-but-flexible system." An absolutely fixed system is quite another matter. And there is virtually no difference between exchange rates that are absolutely fixed and a currency union which is characterized by a single currency. For example, the Hong Kong dollar has been fixed at 7.8 to the greenback since October 1983, with no thought of a change in the parity. The exchange rate is transparently fixed and guaranteed by the institutional mechanism of the currency board. If one offers a U.S. dollar to the board, then the board will pay 7.80 Hong Kong dollars for it and vice versa. With completely free capital flows, the short-term rate of interest in Hong Kong cannot much differ from the rates in New York. The central bank of Hong Kong is effectively the Fed.

If there were no Hong Kong note issue and if the Hong Kong authorities adopted the U.S. dollar as legal tender and as the customary form of payment, then there would be a complete one-currency type of currency union (as existed for many years in Liberia). The difference between a currency board and a union is first, the seigniorage—in the currency board it is largely credited to the Hong Kong government, whereas in the one currency union case the United States pockets it—and second, the doubts whether Hong Kong will remain fixed to the dollar as the PRC takes over. Hence, one may expect that long-term interest rates will carry a political risk factor and exceed those in the United States, which is unlikely to be taken over by the PRC in the foreseeable future. For the rest of this paper, however, I shall assume that currency boards and monetary unions are identical.

Common markets, free trade areas, and monetary unions

One conundrum which arises is whether the reverse of the question raised in my title is true: do common currencies require common markets? The answer is "of course not!" During the many years of the old gold standard, there was effectively a common currency through free gold convertibility, yet substantial trade barriers existed between the countries. And there are many countries that have common currencies (e.g., Liberia) where there were large import duties in spite of the circulation of the dollar.

The corollary is clearly "do common currencies make it more or less difficult to adhere to an open trading regime such as that required in a common market?" This is an important question, largely because I believe that open trading regimes are one of the foundations of economic prosperity and the linchpin of so many successful strategies. If a common currency makes it difficult to keep the doors open, then it is a powerful count against a monetary union.

The general theory of adjustment of fixed and flexible exchange rates is well known. Within a currency union a small country has its tradeable goods prices fixed; all adjustment has to be done through price changes in the nontradeable goods sector. These movements of absolute prices in nontradeables, with tradeables anchored, induce resources to move into and out of tradeable goods to achieve an equilibrium in the current account. Price changes in nontradeables may be thwarted by institutional arrangements—normally that is a nice way of saying that powerful trade unions may preclude or delay such adjustments. And even in the absence of powerful unions, the fixed exchange rate regime requires a flexible fiscal policy, with all sorts of dubious linkages, somehow to help effect the adjustment. That is the story with the exchange rate fixed. In contrast, with no monetary union and a variable exchange rate, there is additional flexibility. The devaluation of the exchange rate raises the domestic price of tradeable goods even though their dollar value remains unchanged. The flexibility of the exchange rate makes it easier to adjust to external or internal changes in circumstances (or "shocks" as we usually, but misleadingly, term them). This suggests that flexible rates would be more consistent with open regimes since the country could simply allow the exchange rate to take the strain and need not resort to the Big Bertha of trade restrictions.

So far as I am aware there has been no comprehensive systematic study of this issue. Superficially the Bretton Woods experience of a monetary union and the associated reduction in protection up to 1973, when the currencies floated, suggests that the fixity of exchange rates did not induce greater protectionism; on the contrary. But this is misleading. Until 1960 all the currencies were inconvertible, and even after 1960 there were substantial exchange controls on domestic residents. Furthermore the vicissitudes of 1960-67 saw massive increases in "emergency" protection—such as increases in across-the-board tariffs in the United Kingdom, Italy, and France—as well as more stringent capital controls to protect payments positions. Nevertheless, in spite of the increased protection, sterling, then a most important currency, was devalued in 1967, and Bretton Woods was all but over. Another example is the fact that the ERM in its early years in the first half of the 1980s (that is to say before the Single European Act became effective from 1987 on) was clearly associated with increased protection within the Community.

I leave this important issue unresolved. I now pass to the general question raised in the title.

Do common markets (or customs unions) require common currencies?

The importance of this question arises largely from the fact that the top-level bureaucrats of the EU have asserted that the answer is unequivocally "yes." Messrs. Delors and Bangermann and Sir Leon Brittan have all asserted that in order to complete the Economic Union of Europe, a monetary union is required. In his new book, *The Europe We Need*, Sir Leon has again asserted that it will be hard to maintain a single market unless there is a single currency (Brittan 1994). And if these big whigs are correct, then surely it has some import for NAFTA and other trade blocs. Of course, you may say "some, but not much." Europe is different from North America. Although Germany is the dominant economic power in Europe, there is no sense in which it dwarfs its neighbours. In North America, however, the United States towers over Canada and Mexico. One may debate about the form of a single currency of Europe—e.g., the ECU or perhaps the Deutschemark—but, in the event of a currency union in North America, there is no contest: it is the dollar with the Fed as its central bank. Nevertheless the core of the policy issue remains the same whether in NAFTA or EU.

Messrs. Delors, Brittan, and Bangerman have not advanced any arguments about optimal currency areas to support their thesis. Nor is there any allegation of simultaneity in cyclical oscillations, so that the same monetary policy is optimal for all union countries. They have put forward the old arguments of (1) reductions in transactions costs, (2) reduced exchange risks, and (3) economizing on information. It is undoubtedly true that some direct savings will follow from having one currency: exaggerated calculations and predictions of such savings for Europe are to be found in the Delors Report of 1989. In terms of the Delors et al. assessment, it is difficult to see why the elimination of such small costs is so essential to the completion of the single market. The ultimate test of a single market is, of course, price equality, allowing for local taxes and transport costs. On this test numerous studies, widely reported in newspapers, have shown that the Community fails dismally. (It was recently assessed that the cost of an automobile in the most expensive city in Europe was more than 50 percent greater than that in the cheapest.) Eliminating the small change of exchange operations seems to be of trivial importance.

Of course this is not the only reason for pursuing a monetary union. I would suggest that we examine the usual explanation for political policy—the pursuit of power. A monetary union would give great power to the central bank of Europe and to its political masters in Brussels. For with the centralization of monetary control would come the concentration of fiscal policy in the federation rather than in its constituent states. We can only guess at the magnitude of the fiscal transfers from rich to poor constituent states that will be needed, but the size of the transfers which we have seen in the German union gives one some idea. The bargaining by the poor "south" of the Community (Spain, Portugal, Greece, and Ireland) for larger welfare funds gives warnings of the size of the federal budget to come. The interstate differences in income per capita in Europe are much bigger than those in the United States. (And the interstate differences in income in NAFTA are even larger—which explains in part the fact that no one appears to have seriously suggested an economic and monetary union for NAFTA countries.)

I conjecture that the real reason behind the impetus for a monetary union in Europe is that it will inevitably imply a political union. Indeed Germany has often said that, before one can make real progress on a monetary union, much more political integration of Europe is required. Monetary union is the "soft underbelly" of political union. For obvious reasons, which I discussed in a review article in *National Interest* (Spring 1994), people are much more susceptible to saying "yes" to a monetary union than they are to a political union with all the substantial loss of sovereignty that must ensue. It was a wise tactic of the European Commission to pursue primarily the goal of monetary union in the Maastricht treaty.

Evidence of monetary unions

First, a preliminary point: in discussing monetary unions I shall assume that the unions do not adopt a commodity currency, such as gold, silver, or a basket of commodities. The unions operate a fiat money system. It is clear that with a gold standard, there can be—there have been—monetary unions without common markets or customs unions. But since no free trade area, customs union, or economic and monetary union at present or on the cards has a commodity standard, we have no need to conjecture on their consistency.

In the historical record, there have been associations of customs unions with monetary unions. Probably the best example is the (first) unification of Germany. In the Prussian-led Zollverein in 1834, the statutes called for a common coinage. But although the customs union was effective, because of the many objections of the states, there was no common currency until 1871 when the Reichsbank was established to supervise it on a gold standard. For near 40 years the Zollverein had many distinct currencies.

England and Scotland long enjoyed not merely a customs union but an economic union, with free flow of labour and capital, for more than a century before the imposition of the English coinage on Scotland from 1844 on. The Scots had a monetary and banking system quite different from that centred on London. It has been argued by Lawrence H. White

(1984) and George Selgin (1988) that the "free banking" arrangements in Scotland were more effective in producing a stable financial environment than the Bank of England in London. But the point is that for more than 100 years the customs union was not thought to require a monetary union. Furthermore, the Scots were apparently quite content (at least as White records there were few complaints) with not having a monetary union inside Scotland. The Delors et al. thesis would, of course, preclude any "free banking."

Did the absence of a common currency somehow crucially hinder the development of Scotland? Obviously there is no definitive answer. In my reading of history since 1601, I cannot recall any historian even mentioning such an allegation. Scotland prospered mightily in the 18th century and the first half of the 19th century.

Finally, we have the case at hand today. NAFTA was negotiated on the foundations of an FTA between Canada and the United States. The flow of trade between Canada and the United States is the largest between any two countries in the world. The overwhelming majority of U.S.-Canada trade is free from tariffs or trade restrictions. (Indeed, some Canadians have suggested that there are more restrictions between Canada's provinces than there are with the United States.) There is also a completely free flow of capital and virtually free mobility of labour. In other words, there is a near economic union. Yet, so far as I know, no one has suggested that to complete this union, one would require that there be a common currency (presumably the Canadian dollar would disappear and Canadian residents would use greenbacks). At present, the two currencies circulate to some degree in border areas and are fully convertible, largely because it is in traders' interests to make them convertible.

Instead of the upheaval of a formal demise of the Canadian currency, the Canadian dollar could be easily attached to the U.S. dollar by means of a currency board. This would give the same economic effects as a union. But again this possibility was not seriously considered as part of, or as a sequel to, the free trade arrangements for the area. While the large disparities in income per capita may well preclude a monetary union with Mexico, this explanation clearly does not hold for Canada and the United States.

We are left then with the fact that, notwithstanding favourable preconditions, no one in North America has seriously considered the Delors-Bangermann-Brittan thesis that monetary union is essential for a single market. Of course we in North America may lack the penetrating insights of these famous three Europeans, but that seems dubious. More likely the Canadians believe that they need the extra degree of flexibility that an independent dollar gives to policy and that the additional transaction costs are not sufficient to offset the advances of such a degree of independence. Perhaps also the Canadians are not willing to subjugate all monetary policy to the Fed in the belief that the Fed will be concerned with conditions in the United States rather than the state of the Canadian economy (and there are marked structural differences between the two).

Furthermore the Fed may pursue stupid policies, as they have done in the past, and the Canadians would not wish to be forced to follow, as the wag that dogs the tale.

Whereas in Delorsian eyes, the European Central Bank would be run by veritable philosopher kings in the interest of all Europe, nicely balancing tradeoffs for the good of all. The monetary policy of the ECB has been defended as clearly superior to the sum of the monetary policies of the separate constituents. (And, of course, in addition there are the savings in transactions costs.) To the Eurosceptic and even to those who fully support the single market, as distinct from its monetary, fiscal, and political union trappings of Maastricht, this is a great deal of faith to place in an institution that does not yet exist and for which we have the vaguest of blueprints.

Conclusion

The first conclusion is that an FTA or CU does not require a monetary union to "complete" it. Nor does a monetary union require an FTA or CU. The second conclusion is that there is some case for arguing that a monetary union makes it more difficult to maintain a FTA or CU, since all the adjustments have to made in prices and wages rather than through the nominal exchange rate, and the fixed exchange rate may be considered more important to maintain (a la franc fort) than the open market. The third conclusion is that monetary union in its various forms should be judged on its own merits, and I assume that the main option for Canada and Mexico is to join a U.S. system dominated by the Fed.

The major rationale for fixing the peso and Canadian dollar to the U.S. dollar must be because Mexico and Canada believe the Fed will give a more stable and growth-oriented monetary policy than their separate central banks. Monetary policy in Mexico and Canada is thus freed from domestic politics, but not from Washington shenanigans and mutual recriminations. (It is important to note that the alternatives are a free exchange rate or a fixed one. The European Monetary System has demonstrated that pegged or "fixed but flexible" rates are destabilizing and untenable.)

Although I have concluded that NAFTA does not require a monetary union, I have clearly not made much if any progress in deciding whether a floating or fixed regime is best. Such a decision depends on judgements of institutions and structures far beyond the scope of this essay. But does anyone doubt where my sympathies lie?

References

Brittan, L. (1994) *Europe: The Europe We Need*. London: Hamish Hamilton.

Selgin, G. A. (1988) *The Theory of Free Banking*. Totowa, N.J.: Rowman and Littlefield.

Walters, A. (1994) "Success Story." *National Interest*, no. 35 (Spring 1994): 93-97.

White, L. H. (1984) *Free Banking in Britain: Theory, Experience, and Debate, 1800-1845*. Cambridge: Cambridge University Press.

CHAPTER 3

Economic Forces versus Monetary Institutions

Jerry L. Jordan[1]

F OR BETTER OR WORSE, PEOPLE HAVE ALWAYS liked to organize things. Even ancient, primitive tribes sought to organize their activities in order to improve their quality of life. A natural assumption is that if individuals simply cooperate with one another, more will be accomplished. The arrangements we refer to as "government" are a set of rules and organizations constraining the activities of individuals, presumably for the benefit of all.

People voluntarily come together in firms to pool accumulated capital and contribute their labour to produce goods for consumption or exchange. Similarly, political arrangements become a form of "social capital"—networks of relationships created by past efforts. However, just as a firm with an unprofitable strategy or obsolete product cannot withstand the stiff winds of market forces, government institutions and agencies also face competition. To survive, both firms and government

---

1 The author is President and Chief Executive Officer of the Federal Reserve Bank of Cleveland.

organizations must be "living organisms," capable of adapting to change. When policy design ignores the actions of resourceful, intelligent, opportunity-seeking individuals, it risks being overwhelmed by events beyond the control of even the most authoritarian government bodies.

As we ponder the question of monetary union, we should keep in mind the essential elements of survival of any arrangements in a dynamic global environment. What we have learned from the broad array of experiences with government involvement in economic affairs during the 20th century is that successful policies have been those that enhance the effectiveness of markets. Those institutional arrangements and organizations that were erected to resist the onslaught of economic forces have crumbled in a heap of obsolete notions about the powers of government.

Economic Forces and Political Institutions

Economic forces

Many forces have been at work over the 20th century—certainly political, social, and religious forces have helped to shape the course of events for these 100 years. Here, however, my focus is on those I call "economic forces." These include technological changes and innovations; productivity increases; lower information, transaction, transportation, and communication costs; the phenomenon sometimes referred to as downsizing; and, of special note as the century draws to a close, the true value added from the rise of knowledge-based industries, as opposed to activities that exploit resources.

In the previous century and at the beginning of the 20th century, we tended to measure the wealth of nations in tons and numbers: Tons of iron ore, coal, and metals produced, the numbers of logs cut, tons of wheat grown, and so on, combined to make a statement about the output or wealth of countries. But that is no longer appropriate. In today's world, those things produced by companies such as Microsoft—the world's leader in software—and other human-capital-enhancing enterprises have assumed more importance in determining the relative well-being of nations. Consider the poverty of some of the nations most rich in natural resources—Africa, Brazil, and Russia—versus the prosperity of countries like Japan and Switzerland, whose natural resources are quite sparse.

Political institutions

Let me elaborate on what I mean by the term *institution*. Generally, an institution (or organization) can be defined as a set of humanly devised constraints. As such, the term includes governments, corporations, and families, but our attention at this conference is on government monetary institutions. In an increasing number of countries, these institutions operate in a broadly defined market environment, affecting men and women who are "searching and groping for opportunities" and who are faced with "resourceful coping with circumstances and environment encountered," as Karl Brunner put it so well (Brunner 1986).

Political institutions come in two varieties. The first is government organizations—ministries, bureaus, departments, agencies, and central banks—and international organizations such as the IMF, the World Bank, and the Bank for International Settlements. Even the United Nations and NATO could be included here.

The second variety of institutions in a political context is *rules*—meaning contracts, generally accepted accounting principles (GAAP), labour laws, laws of incorporation, the judicial system, and the enforcement of property rights. Rules also include various types of economic controls, such as wage, price, credit, interest rate, exchange, and capital controls, or even margin requirements. One would also include restrictions on financial industries such as loan loss reserves, capital adequacy standards, debt limitations, credit allocations, and leverage ratios.

Some of both of these types of institutions—the organizations that are created and the rules that are laid down—are intended to improve the workings of markets. Others, however, are geared to inhibit or alter the working of markets because the benefits of intrusion are perceived to be greater than the costs. That is the case when political or social objectives seem to be more important than economic efficiency. Such objectives as income redistribution—a political decision to give priority to sharing wealth, rather than creating wealth—result in institutional arrangements that reduce the efficiency of markets. The classic conflict of democracies is between an environment that fosters equality of opportunity versus a structure that seeks equality of outcome.

In selecting the degree of organization characterizing society, there are *tradeoffs* between determining structure and preserving individual freedom. The threatening aspect of organizations and rules occurs when well-meaning policymakers start to believe that the solution to a problem always involves creating more organizations or rules. That is, there is a tendency for the public to demand solutions, so it is natural for policymakers to look to political methods of resource allocation instead of market methods.

Interplay of forces and institutions

Some of what I call economic forces are irresistible forces, while some political institutions presume to be immovable objects. Even those political institutions that are intended to improve the workings of markets, and are designed to have a great deal of inherent flexibility, evolve in the latter direction.

In a pure market economy, there would be no institutions that we would call immovable objects. In a total command economy, on the other hand, *all* institutions would take on this characteristic. Ultimately, however, they would prove not to be immovable in the face of the irresistible economic forces in a global economy. The command economies of the former Soviet Union serve as the 20th century's monument to the fatal conceit of central planning. The architects of new rules or organizations usually understand the need to create institutions that are capable of adapting to changing conditions. This is true not only of constitutions for governing, but also of the various agencies of government with specific missions.

When markets and institutions conflict

People desire a stable framework for their activities. Without a modicum of certainty, people will not undertake investment in human capital, relationships, and physical capital.

The now-classic example of "The Costs of the Absence of Good Law" is provided by Hernando DeSoto (1989), who discusses the resulting lack of investment in housing stock and production in Lima, Peru. DeSoto describes the former situation of "informal" (read illegal) housing in Lima. Property rights did not exist, and there was no recourse if the state or another individual confiscated property. As a consequence, people invested in TVs, cars, and movable goods—not in pipes, drains, sewers, and roofs. When property rights were more clearly delineated and enforced, housing investment was much improved: For the same class of occupants, formal housing was worth nine times as much as squatters' housing. Absence of property rights discouraged other types of investment as well, because informal housing could not be used as loan collateral.

Similar problems plagued the informal production sector in Peru. Again, DeSoto shows that with no legally binding contracts, investment in production was low and critical suppliers could renege on promises at the last minute, forcing inefficiencies. Informal textile producers, for example, tended to overdiversify suppliers: Instead of buying 1,000 buttons from one firm, they bought 200 from five. Moreover, property insurance was out of the question.

Latin American monetary reforms provide more lessons in how the market disciplines policy:

1. Argentina attempted a currency reform in 1979, but did not reduce the fiscal deficit, and the reform failed. Chile instituted fiscal reform in the late 1970s and succeeded.
2. In 1985, Bolivia slashed state controls, opened up the economy, and balanced the budget on a day-by-day basis. Inflation fell from 23,000 percent in 1985 to 9 percent in 1993.
3. Argentina, in mid-1991, balanced the budget, deregulated the economy, and began privatizing state industry.

These events show the importance of preserving economic decision-making in markets. If governments presume to make allocation decisions, both in the currency markets and in private capital flows into and out of a country, markets can impose harsh discipline. In cases where monetary policy directly caused hyperinflation, fiscal policy was the underlying culprit. When the government sector was too large and attempted to do too much, it could not finance itself with taxes and resorted to inflationary finance.

In harmony with markets

Good examples of political institutions and economic forces working in tandem are the "Asian Tigers"—the nations of Taiwan, Hong Kong, South Korea, and Singapore. A recent World Bank report (1994) gives much credit to these countries' free-market pricing of labour, capital, and goods, and for creating stable macroeconomic frameworks that also let the markets work. While these nations have used government subsidies and political credit allocation, to a considerable extent they have relied on market outcomes to judge their success. For example, South Korea tried to build a heavy chemical industry in the 1970s, but government support was withdrawn when the effort failed.

Famines also highlight the contrast between using institutions that utilize markets and institutions that resist them. The organizational response to famine is to fly in massive amounts of food. This solution creates refugee camps, pulls people off the land, and occasionally alleviates the problem at high social cost—all of which begs the question of the institutional arrangements that gave rise to the famine in the first place.

In contrast, A.K. Sen (1993) shows how the conditions that avoid the circumstances that create famine are democracy and a free press. The unimpeded flow of information via a free press means that people know what is happening, and democracy means that the people are relatively free to act on that information. Sen states, "no democratic country with a relatively free press has ever experienced a major famine" (p. 43). The market disciplines policymakers.

Legacy of conflict

Much of the history of 20th century reflects what I think of as the "contest of ideas"—democracy and capitalism locked in a struggle with dictatorship and socialism. Essentially, it has been a contest for the minds of the people of the world as to the best ways to organize economic and political affairs.

This century has produced two watershed decades in terms of the government's role in the economy—the 1930s and the 1980s. During the worldwide economic depression of the 1930s, the intrusion of government in economic affairs increased massively. If governments did not outright nationalize and directly control resources in a command structure, at a minimum they set up regulatory agencies to decide what was to be produced, where it was to be produced, how much could be charged for products and paid to workers, and what interest rates could be charged or paid.

In the several decades following the 1930s, the role of the nation-state in economic affairs became ever larger. Much of the underlying conceptual framework was based on what I think of as the "stagnation thesis," as set forth by John Maynard Keynes (1936) in *The General Theory*. Its premise is that even economies that are based on private property, and that rely on market forces to allocate productive resources, tend to stagnate at less than full potential in the absence of government initiatives to cause growth. Notions about "market failure" and "insufficient aggregate demand" permeate the literature.

In other words, a view widely held through much of the past century—one that may even continue to be held today by many people—is that governments cause growth. The so-called economic "policies" of government are viewed not only as appropriate, but even as necessary for influencing economic activity.

The rival conjecture from the 1930s, which had little following for most of this century, was the "inherent resiliency proposition" associated with thinkers such as Ludwig von Mises, Friedrich A. von Hayek, and William Hutt. It holds that an economy that relies on a price system to allocate resources in a market environment, and that protects private property rights, tends to be inherently resilient. That is, it naturally gravitates toward full utilization of its productive resources without government pump priming. Whenever shocks of various types—oil price increases, droughts, wars, or perverse government policies—knock the economy down, growth naturally begins anew as the negative effects dissipate.

Two common attributes of the contest of ideas in the 20th century are: (1) political and economic institutions tend to become rigid over time, mainly because organizations created and operated by people become resistant to any change in the status quo; and (2) the fundamental economic forces—technological innovation, declining information and transaction costs, increasing economies of scale and scope of production, and globalization of goods, financial, and asset markets—are *dynamic and global*. Terms such as "global village," "borderless world," and "twilight of sovereignty" express this view. Organizations impose constraints on the not-formally-organized sector, composed of resourceful, intelligent people who seek ways around the constraints. Market forces can overwhelm the constraints, or yield unintended consequences.

There is a positive way to state this point. Essentially, markets discipline policy. With the free flow of information, goods, labour, and capital, bad policy is eroded in the marketplace. The challenge for the future is to set up institutions that use market discipline in a *positive* way.

The ultimate implication of the conflict between irresistible economic forces and the political institutions that take on the characteristics of immovable objects is that institutions must change, or they will fail. Joseph Schumpeter (1950: 82) wrote, "The essential point to grasp is that in dealing with capitalism we are dealing with an evolutionary process. . . . Capitalism, then, is by nature a form or method of economic change and not only never is but never can be stationary."

Schumpeter's observation applies equally well to all of the institutions that define the parameters of our global economy. Propelled by technological change and chance economic events, these institutions undergo a continuous process of change. Those qualities that enhance economic well-being tend to survive, and those that do not eventually disappear. People develop institutions—laws, rules, conventions, and customs—to define and enforce property rights and, more generally, to reduce the costs of economic exchange. The various laws, rules, conventions, and customs that define money, protect its purchasing power, and govern its use are examples of such institutions.

Monetary rules and organizations

International monetary developments in the past couple of years can be explained in terms of these general ideas about institutional transformation. What appear to be conflicts between global monetary integration and regional monetary autonomy are artificial, resulting largely from vested interests in maintaining local government monopolies over the issuance of the national media of exchange. History demonstrates, however, that national currencies inevitably compete in the international financial arena.

Following Hayek (1976), approaches to international monetary relations that foster competition among alternative currency units and vehicles for asset management are more likely to enhance world welfare, compared with systems like Bretton Woods that mandate change directed by supranational governmental bodies, which tend to ossify over time.

Economists think of money as primarily an institutional convenience for greatly reducing the costs of transactions. Overall, a stable monetary unit allows greater specialization in production and wider choices in trade, thus enhancing the associated economic benefits. Building on these ideas, many economists and political scientists erroneously contend that monetary integration over a greater geographical area would confer significant gains on the residents of that area.

Monetary integration can take two institutional forms: The first is complete monetary union with a common currency and a single central bank. That has been the ultimate objective of the European Monetary Union. A second and weaker form of monetary integration is fixed exchange rates, such as experienced under the gold standard or the Bretton Woods System, as well, of course, as under the European Exchange Rate Mechanism. The conditions under which either form is viable need to be addressed.

Although a system of fixed exchange rates could confer significant benefits on participants in terms of reduced transaction costs, it also imposes specific costs in terms of monetary sovereignty and macroeconomic adjustment. The external value of a national currency ultimately reflects the relative internal purchasing power of that currency. So, to maintain an exchange rate, participating countries must coordinate their monetary policies to generate similar inflation rates. Monetary sovereignty—or autonomy—is incompatible with fixed exchange rates. Inflation convergence is crucial to a pegged exchange-rate regime.

Under certain circumstances, however, the costs of integrating monetary policies across countries can exceed the benefits. Countries are most likely to form a successful monetary union with other countries if: (1) all regions within a monetary union have the same preferences for inflation, reflecting similar theoretical or conceptual views of monetary policy; and (2) all regions within a monetary union experience similar macroeconomic conditions.

While common experiences with economic shocks are a desirable condition to enhance the likely success of monetary integration, they are not necessary. Regions of the United States often experience different economic conditions, especially in response to energy-price shocks, defense spending increases or decreases, and so on. What *is* crucial is that other avenues for adjustment between regions are available so that exchange rate changes are not the issue.

In the 1980s, the United States had a bicoastal economy: California and New England were booming, while depressed conditions existed throughout much of the middle part of the country. In the early 1990s, the tables have been turned: We have seen severely depressed economic conditions in California and a continuing recession in New England, while the Rocky Mountains and the Midwest have been, by comparison, considerably stronger.

If it were not for the political integration and the associated high degree of resource mobility (investable capital resources as well as labour resources), then it would be more tempting for various regions within the United States to contemplate devaluation of their currencies in such an environment. In the 1980s, for example, devaluing the Texas dollar or the Michigan dollar against the California or New England dollar would have seemed an attractive option. Similarly, the severe recession in California in the early 1990s might have led some to believe that devaluing its dollar against the Ohio or the Rocky Mountain dollar would be sensible. But because of political unity and resource mobility, these options were not considered.

The recent history of our global monetary systems suggests that attempts to achieve monetary integration by way of fixed exchange rates are not likely to succeed in the absence of political integration. In part, this results because regions of the world that experience disparate economic conditions and low resource mobility can adjust to economic shocks more efficiently by allowing their exchange rates to fluctuate. Furthermore, monetary integration cannot proceed in a credible manner, even among regions in which it is feasible, unless governments first adopt domestic institutions that credibly assure their commitment to maintaining domestic price stability.

Institutions, including those that determine the use of national currencies, inevitably compete, leading to the emergence of efficient wealth-enhancing institutional forms. To create greater international stability and integration, we should encourage such competition. This requires, above all else, the free movement of resources through the elimination of artificial restraints on the movement of capital, goods, services, and labour. A free flow of resources fosters a convergence of institutional forms across participating governments as they compete for these resources by providing stable economic and political environments. Countries whose governments fail to provide such an environment will lose resources as markets vote on policies. The resulting convergence of monetary and fiscal regimes will achieve the highest sustainable rate of real growth in an environment of monetary stability.

Conclusion

When some observers look at the divergent forces at work in various regions of the world, there seems to be a conflict. For example, in examining the efforts under way to achieve European Community objectives—economic integration and perhaps ultimately political integration among 12 or more European nations—in contrast with the political and economic *dis*integration of the former Soviet Union, it might appear that these trends are going in opposite directions. On the contrary, I find common elements in both developments.

In the case of Europe, the move toward political and economic integration involves a large number of specific steps to *reduce* the role of the participating nation-states in economic affairs. In other words, actions are being taken to improve the workings of the markets within Europe—to strengthen property rights and to eliminate a host of rules, regulations, and obstacles to the free mobility of goods, labour, and capital.

In contrast, in the former Soviet Union we see that political and economic disintegration is also a process of tearing down the highly centralized command-and-control socialist economy. It is a process of searching for ways to make markets flourish in the 15 or so republics of the former Soviet Union, as well as in the eastern European countries of the former COMECON.

Viewed in this way, the moves toward economic and political integration in Western Europe and disintegration in the former Soviet bloc are both market-driven. Both seek to foster a strengthening in private property rights and to ensure that the price system is the primary mechanism for allocating resources to their most productive uses. Both look toward greater mobility of goods, labour, and capital.

In this final decade of the century, it seems that the clearest trend around the world is to reduce the role of the nation-state in economic affairs. Deregulation, denationalization/privatization, and tax reduction/tax reform are all part of a process of economic regeneration—to restore the wealth-creating capability of markets. Resources, especially investment capital, move quickly to those regions that are making the most progress, while resources move away from those regions making little or no headway. This competition of political institutions—both of the organization type and the rules type—is a part of what I consider a healthy process of reinstituting 19th century economic liberalization. The result will be a freer and more prosperous world, with the ultimate autonomy not in the nation-state, but in individual choice.

Attempts to achieve monetary union without political integration are not likely to be successful. Certainly, monetary union is not a necessary condition for achieving free movement of goods, labour, and capital. Furthermore, competition among alternative national currency units can impose a healthy discipline on policymakers. That competition, in turn, promotes relative price stability and a wealth-enhancing environment. Finally, institutional arrangements such as enforceable property rights are much more essential to economic development than are politically created and controlled organizations, no matter how well-intentioned their missions.

References

Brunner, K. (1986) "The Ambivalence of Political Structure: Illusion and Reality." In K. Brunner and R.E. Wagner (eds.) *The Growth of Government: A Symposium.* Center Symposia Series No. CS-19, University of Rochester, Graduate School of Management.

DeSoto, H. (1989) *The Other Path: The Invisible Revolution in the Third World.* New York: Harper & Row.

Hayek, F. A. (1976) *Denationalization of Money: An Analysis of the Theory and Practice of Concurrent Currencies.* London: Institute of Economic Affairs.

Keynes, J.M. (1936) *The General Theory of Employment, Interest, and Money.* New York: Macmillan.

Schumpeter, J. (1950) *Capitalism, Socialism, and Democracy,* 3rd ed. New York: Harper & Row.

Sen, A.K. (1993) "The Economics of Life and Death," *Scientific American,* May: 43.

The World Bank (1994) "The East Asian Miracle: Economic Growth and Public Policy." Oxford: Oxford University Press.

CHAPTER 4

A North American Currency Area: Is It Feasible?

Rogelio Ramírez de la O[1]

THE DISCUSSION ABOUT A NORTH American Currency Area (NACA) appears to be gaining ground, based on the notion that freer trade in the area requires the elimination of uncertainty about exchange rate fluctuations. This insight has received important attention since the currency collapse of the peso in December 1994. But even before the currency crisis, analysts had suggested that Mexico might broaden its capital investment inflows by eliminating expectations of sudden and undesirable exchange rate fluctuations through an formal arrangement like a NACA. This is, for example, the proposal by Darryl McLeod and John Welch (1991), although contrarian arguments have also been offered (Waverman 1994). The discussion on this topic promises to be a fruitful one, since the exchange rate regime of Mexico has become a

---

1   The author is the President of Ecanal, S.A., an economic analysis firm based in Mexico City.

central topic of discussion on the part of academics, policy makers, and international investors.

This chapter discusses the justification for and feasibility of a NACA from a Mexican viewpoint and draws on the recent history of exchange rate policy in recent years. The discussion is focused on two issues: (1) the justification for a NACA, and (2) the requirements for a successful currency area.

The justification for a currency area

A standard definition of a currency area is an area within which different exchange rates bear a fixed relation with one another, based on a system of rules that imply multilateral support for a currency under given circumstances and a certain convergence of economic policies. Paul Masson and Mark Taylor (1992) define such an area as free from capital controls and with only one monetary policy. Robert Mundell (1961) established that labour and capital must move freely within regions of the area, and that, in the absence of free mobility, a shift in demand in one region relative to another may lead to unemployment if the exchange rate is rigid.

The literature on currency areas establishes that there are many advantages for a country to become a member of the area, mainly for gaining greater credibility for its anti-inflation policy. But it is also established that this requires adopting a monetary policy consistent with that of the country with the strongest currency. Analysis and evidence are inconclusive on the need for a similarly compatible fiscal policy, but large effects are recognized on output and employment with implications for fiscal policy. Such effects suggest that coordination of fiscal policy between members of the area is desirable, but this issue brings further complications to the specification of rules for the members of the area.

The case for a currency area can be constructed in terms of maximizing gains from trade and in terms of gaining a higher degree of financial stability than would otherwise be possible. The trade-enhancement argument, as expounded by Paul De Grauwe *et al.* (1992), is that exchanges between two countries with different currencies always faces greater uncertainty than between two countries with the same currency.

A currency area permits countries to obtain gains from a common currency while still allowing them to keep their own national currencies. The currency area would accordingly set limits to the movement of exchange rates and provide rules on permanent adjustments or realignments and support mechanisms for currencies at critical periods. Exporters and importers in the area would therefore benefit from lesser uncertainty about future settlements of trade obligations. A currency area would consequently reduce transaction costs for member countries.

This argument is generally accepted, but is not a sufficiently powerful condition for greater trade. Trade is not the only economic activity facing uncertainty, and currency fluctuations are not their only cause. In North America, the absence of a currency area has not prevented a high growth in trade. In fact, growth in trade has systematically surpassed the growth in income. Similarly, the recent high growth of trade between Eastern Europe and the West has not been impeded by the existence of many currencies. In fact, currency movements have facilitated trade growth over the medium term in so far as they reestablish good economic fundamentals and competitiveness. By adjusting a currency to a realistic level, a country eliminates uncertainty about potential financial pressures against that currency.

For example, trade flows between Mexico and the United States increased rapidly for the period 1989-93 despite the absence of a currency area and even in the presence of a crawling exchange rate up until 1991 in Mexico. Trade also grew under the influence of Mexico's economic restructuring based on reduced public sector deficits and inflation, as well as rapid trade liberalization. It is difficult to see how trade could have risen more rapidly, for in 1993, even as Mexico's rate of GDP growth was only 0.7 percent, its deficit on current account reached -6.6 percent of GDP, while manufacturing exports were increasing by 18.5 percent in current dollar terms, and goods exported by in-bond *maquiladora* industries (mostly to the United States) rose 17 percent.

Mexico's trade liberalization became a major force behind the rapid increase in imports. The government also de-regulated important industrial sectors, such as the auto industry, which resulted in rapid growth in trade and allowed firms to specialize. Since a large part (probably 80 percent) of the auto industry trade is intrafirm trade, deregulation helped to reduce uncertainty, which, independently of the exchange rate, contributed significantly to trade growth.

It is difficult to establish the independent effect of a smoothly crawling peso over international trade flows when deregulation and trade liberalization are also considered. A plausible argument is that greater certainty over the crawling peg influenced trade indirectly, as it strengthened economic conditions. But such conditions were equally strengthened by deregulation, trade liberalization, and the elimination of fiscal deficits. The boom in imports is associated probably to a rapid appreciation of the real exchange rate (which was unexpected), but also to modernization and lower trade barriers. Thus the deficit on current account rose from -2.3 percent of GDP in 1990 to -6.6 percent in 1993. As for Mexico's exports to the United States, they grew at high rates owing to a rapid reconversion of output in the auto industry to focus more on exports, and in 1992-93 owing to the low level of domestic demand.

The advantages of currency areas, which imply a certain degree of rigidity on exchange rates and monetary policy, are also of different value at different times and circumstances. For economies that emerge from long periods of inflation and financial pressures, a currency area represents a different value than for more stable economies— for example, in Western Europe. Economic adjustment of previously closed and inefficient economies usually takes several years judging by the experience of Latin American and Eastern European countries. During this period, several adjustments to their currencies may be necessary. This is because structural adjustments usually cause large shifts in relative prices and labour costs while uncertainty over the possible success of programs almost makes it compelling to have flexible exchange rates. The large amount of foreign exchange needed to give credibility to exchange rates in such circumstances renders pegged or fixed rate systems unrealistic in most cases.

Financial stability

The argument of a currency area enhancing financial stability runs as follows: a currency area provides support for a weak currency as it reduces its variability against the strong currency and thus facilitates investment and growth by a greater degree than it might otherwise be possible. The area consists of a currency peg or a known fluctuation band for the weak currency relative to the strong one. In practice, this means that the weak currency country borrows the credibility and the reputation of monetary policy of the strong-currency country (Artis and Currie 1983). The peg allows it to have lower interest rates than would be necessary were this country pursuing stabilization policies on its own. An enhanced version of this argument stresses that a country following a stabilization program will need high real interest rates and tight fiscal policies to establish a good reputation before it can embark on a program of economic growth. A more credible currency would therefore shorten the time in which these policies have to be applied and growth sacrificed.

This argument has considerably more weight than the trade-enhancement argument previously examined. Frequently, countries embarking on stabilization programs are forced, because of lack of credibility, to adopt fixed or quasi-fixed exchange rates, the most dramatic example of this policy being Argentina in 1991. Nonetheless, as an exchange rate is established for the purpose of such plans, domestic costs keep increasing for some time at higher rates than international costs. This causes a steady appreciation of the real exchange rate. Such an appreciation is difficult to avoid as it partly responds to inflationary inertia, shifts in relative prices justified by a more open trade regime, or lack of sufficient credibility of the anti-inflation policy most frequently reflected in excessive increases in wages. How a currency area helps countries in these circumstances must be discussed in two parts: one is the contribution of exchange rate credibility to economic stabilization immediately following a period of high inflation. Another is the consolidation of an anti-inflation policy and culture in public institutions once stabilization has brought inflation under control.

A currency area can do little to help a country in the initial stabilization effort, as its macroeconomic policy is unlikely to enjoy a good reputation to make the currency area feasible or even credible. In this case, the most powerful arguments against a currency area would come from the monetary authority of the strong-currency country, unwilling to intervene too often in favour of the weak currency. One exception is

Germany, where the Bundesbank accepted, albeit reluctantly, to participate in a scheme that gave the East German currency all the backing it needed at an unrealistic exchange rate. But this is an exceptional case, and in any event, the bad experience with unemployment in East Germany might in fact serve to prevent similar schemes in the future. Other reasons for not considering a currency area seriously in such a situation is that stabilization programs usually take several years before they bring inflation under control. Such programs and structural reforms which usually accompany them, alter the structure of relative prices in a significant way. A fixed exchange rate or a rate in a currency area unable to fully adjust to changes in relative prices might soon become overvalued and cause distortions. Eventually, it may require a relatively high rate of interest to be sustained by capital inflows or it might need to advance further into a full monetary union. The problem of unemployment *à la* East Germany is likely to emerge, however, if such a union were politically feasible. It is difficult for countries, therefore, to avoid the cost of economic stabilization or even reduce such cost by any significant amount by a currency area.

In the second stage of stabilization, once a country has recorded good fiscal balances and established a sound monetary policy, then there are considerable gains to be made from a currency area through lower interest rates. This, however, requires a convergence of inflation rates and monetary policies between the countries involved. As evidenced in Europe, even countries coming down from reasonable inflation rates have found it difficult to assure macroeconomic convergence. Among other reasons, this is because monetary policy coordination is insufficient when there are important shifts in fiscal policy. For example, a country may adopt a policy to keep interest rates slightly above those of the strong country in order to keep its exchange rate at pre-announced levels. But this policy becomes more difficult to maintain if interest rates in the strong country rise following a shift to fiscal expansion. The weak-currency country eventually faces the dilemma of maintaining its exchange rate or attacking domestic unemployment.

Other reasons that make it difficult for countries to synchronize macroeconomic policy are practical in nature: different election calendars, different levels of structural unemployment, or a different timing of the business cycle. In Europe, such circumstances have frequently played an important role in upsetting foreign exchange markets. One was the removal of exchange controls by some members of the Exchange Rate Mechanism (ERM) in 1990, which brought pressures on their currencies and set a level of interest rates higher than expected. Later on, the enormous cost of German reunification lead to substantial increases in interest rates and unemployment in other European countries, rates which would not be justified otherwise by their own macroeconomic conditions. In fact, such countries had plenty of room for interest rate reductions.

Mexico's financial system would substantially improve with a fixed exchange rate or a dollar currency area, given our intense international transactions with the United States. But, in the presence of substantial economic adjustment, even in a period of consolidation rather than initial stabilization, a currency area would surely impose high costs. The reason is that consolidating the anti-inflation program does not assure stable relative prices when the country has embarked on continuous economic modernization affecting the basis for resource allocation, demand, and trade. The latter would result mainly from the North American Free Trade Agreement (NAFTA) and decisions by economic agents following the greater certainty of a new trade regime and lower trade barriers. One of the most important factors to consider in this regard is the steady and high growth in Mexican wages to be expected from greater integration with the United States, with the corresponding effect of increasing U.S. exports to Mexico.

During the period of stabilization (1989-93), there was a rapid increase in Mexican manufacturing wages, expressed in U.S. dollars and compared with a crude estimate of average productivity in manufacturing (resulting from the ratio of output to employment changes). The latter measure is likely to over-estimate productivity growth, given the cyclical reduction in the labour force consistent with the 1989-93 stabilization program. The real appreciation of the exchange rate was largely a consequence of rising labour costs. This is one of the factors that induced a correction in the exchange rate regime resulting from the unsustainability of permanently high deficits in the current account. We should be cautious of proposals for a currency area in the presence of these indicators, independently of the fact that in the long run increasing economic integration may create conditions for closer financial cooperation which might resemble some of the features of a currency area.

Since Mexican manufacturing wages are still one fifth of U.S. wages (unadjusted for productivity), labour costs in Mexico are likely to rise in a period of sustained economic growth and greater integration with the United States. This is so because labour in Mexico is abundant, but skilled workers are scarce. Thus, it is my opinion that wage inflation will be a permanent threat for Mexico's future unless training programs for labour and education create new structural conditions in the labour market.

The reality of greater economic integration in North America advises us to be cautious rather than enthusiastic about a currency area or a pegged exchange rate. In addition, the structural labour problems are not the only ones to cause future large shifts in relative prices. Environmental standards must also be raised in Mexico and their effect on industrial costs shall be substantial. The stability to be gained for the financial sector from a currency area would therefore become a disadvantage for manufacturing industry and some services, and competition with U.S. producers is sure to intensify.

With regard to the argument concerning lower interest rates, one should note that expected reductions in interest brought about by a pegged exchange rate are far from being established in any solid way either in theory or by empirical evidence. Lessons from Europe are that a country pursuing tight fiscal policies may need to extend the application of such policies even after, and sometimes long after, it has reduced inflation to very low levels. Part of the explanation for this seemingly paradoxical result lies in the background of low economic growth in which this policy is often applied. For political reasons governments may have to relax this tight policy and give a signal that growth, rather than the exchange rate, is the top priority. Such uncertainty creates a discount against the forward exchange rate which calls for higher interest rates in case the government decides to stick to the same policy. As interest rates mount and gross international reserves rise, economic growth deteriorates. The paradoxical outcome is that the country in question cannot capture the benefit of lower interest rates.

Countries willing to capture the benefit of credibility from the currency area may have to go a lot further from the area and into an explicitly fixed rate as Argentina did in 1991. Thus, a fix may be preferable to a wide band, if the fix results in greater credibility and lower interest rates. The usefulness of the currency area for the financial sector of a country like Mexico is also diminished when that country maintains a steady and sound macroeconomic policy that becomes increasingly convincing to foreign investors—as Mexico did during the 1989-93 period. It is illustrative, for example, how at the beginning of 1994 investors in Mexico were apparently satisfied with a rate of interest on 28-day government Treasury Certificates (*Cetes*) as low as 9.4 percent in pesos, even with a prospective current account deficit of more that $28 billion and with presidential elections in sight. It is unlikely, however, that a currency area with the United States would have reduced rates to the same level as those in the United States, unless there were a complete currency union. And even in such circumstances, pressures on interest rates might persist if the financial sector in Mexico remains restricted to foreign banks or if there is higher unemployment and a perception of higher political risk.

Requirements for a successful currency area in North America

From the standpoint of monetary and financial policy in Mexico, a currency area for North America which grants credibility to the peso is a highly attractive idea and seems feasible, largely because Mexico has had traditionally a peg to the U.S. dollar in order to encourage financial savings and control inflation. Moreover, the exchange rate regime can be adapted without much difficulty to a formal peg under a currency area where rules are explicit. The support offered by the U.S. government to Mexico to prop up confidence in the peso, both shortly after the Colosio assassination in 1994 and through the massive $52 billion loan guarantee package assembled in the aftermath of the peso crisis following the devaluation, is revealing of a degree of financial cooperation which may evolve naturally into a formal currency area. In such an area, the exchange rate system would need to be a narrow fluctuation band becoming soon an unambiguous fix in order to provide firm signals to financial markets.

But this argument does not necessarily mean that a currency area is the optimum system for the peso exchange rate nor that the natural evolution of financial cooperation must be forced up to yield quick results in terms of a new exchange rate system. The system, to be feasible, would require full convergence of macroeconomic policies and of institutions influencing monetary developments and policy. It would, consequently, require an independent central bank as well as a medium-term financial framework assuring the adherence to a sound fiscal policy. It is doubtful, however, that this latter condition can also be asked of the U.S. government, where the structural budget deficit is high, and the government faces increasingly serious problems over time, such as future obligations of the pension system. Thus, a possible expansion of U.S. fiscal deficits to be financed by borrowing might impose the need for Mexico to keep a tighter monetary policy than would otherwise be necessary.

There is little doubt that this type of system can be implemented, but its durability will depend on structural conditions which are un-likely to be met in Mexico for some years. The essential factor is that total capital mobility and the transformation of Mexican institutions influencing wage costs and the regime of competition must become very similar to those in the United States. This means that Mexico must change its labour institutions, a reform that the current Zedillo admin-istration is not yet politically willing to take, despite awareness of how badly it is needed. It would also require a degree of liberalization in the markets for goods and assets which is now impeded by the presence of public and private monopolies or oligopolistic structures in a much greater degree than tolerated in the United States. Barriers exist today that prevent free entry of any investor into important sectors, such as oil, electricity, telephones and basic telecommunications, banking, and others.

In the absence of such structural changes, Mexican costs will con-tinue to rise at rates above those in the United States, and the fixed exchange rate will most likely become too strong to deliver high eco-nomic growth and employment in Mexico. The removal of structural barriers faces deep political problems, and the possibility of removing them is a political unknown. Thus, to formalize a peg system there is little problem from a monetary standpoint, but there may be problems regarding fiscal policy and asymmetries between Mexico and the United States. At a more fundamental level, however, a system that functions as an authentic currency area is not feasible within the foreseeable future given the lack of similarity between institutions of Mexico and the United States that influence costs and prices. In addition, there is an expected substantial adjustment in Mexican labour costs and other relative prices brought about by NAFTA.

It is sometimes suggested that many of the impediments mentioned above could be addressed effectively by North American monetary institutions backed by the appropriate legislation. This is true, but the argument itself does not eliminate the need for currency realignments when the exchange rates are far from those needed to ensure good economic fundamentals. It also brings too largely into the discussion the need to create new institutions when NAFTA has already given birth to its first institutions and there has been little time to evaluate their performance. At any rate, cautiousness suggests to take one problem at a time and to avoid creating bureaucratic institutions where their justification is not well established.

Conclusion

A North American Currency Area, defined as a system of mutual support for stable nominal exchange rates, is less attractive than it seems at first sight for Mexico. This is so because the fundamental benefits from this system can be obtained from a pursuing of sound macroeconomic policies, even if, admittedly, they will take a longer time than within a currency area—particularly after the erosion of investor confidence following the peso devaluation. But by the same token, once economic stabilization and adjustment to NAFTA are consolidated (which will take several years), the benefits for the financial sector of lower interest rates will naturally follow. It is uncertain that even with a currency area such differentials can be eliminated without an ambitious structural and institutional reform in Mexico.

Potential benefits to the financial sector of a currency area are large, but they are not necessarily extensive to the real sector of the economy in the presence of barriers to entry into specific sectors, including the banking industry. In fact, much of the appeal that a currency area has for financial agents stems from the expectation that interest rate differentials will continue to exist and that substantial profits are to be realized for some years from financial intermediation and investment banking, as well as from investment in public debt. Nonetheless, these advantages are outweighed by the relative disadvantages which this system can bring about for the real sector until a comprehensive structural reform is completed.

Whether this reform is in itself feasible merits a separate discussion, but the important difference in institutions lies in the different degree of liberalization in markets for goods, labour, and assets between Mexico and the United States, and in political forces and culture.

This suggests that only an imperfect currency union can be created within the foreseeable time. This would be a bad idea, given the substantial economic adjustment still to take place in Mexico, partly as an adaptation to NAFTA. The most important, but not the only, potential problem, is represented by high wage growth, which calls for caution regarding not only a currency union, but also regarding any rigid exchange rate system.

An imperfect currency union would provide immediate positive effects, but would eventually contribute to higher than necessary deficits on the external accounts of Mexico (given the real exchange rate appreciation which it would cause), and higher interest rates than would be required in a more flexible policy environment. This would inevitably be reflected in high unemployment and political tension, which might break the political consensus for the currency union. It might also damage the consensus for free trade with the United States.

Mexico has pursued sound macroeconomic policies and can continue to do so, even despite the crisis generated by the currency collapse, but it will need to give specific attention to microeconomic issues, specifically deregulation of the labour and asset markets. To the degree in which these efforts are delayed or not fully successful when at the same time exchange rate policy follows nominal targets, the government must continuously examine the situation in the markets and be ready to effect changes as necessary. Experience since 1987 with a peg, close to the conditions of a unilateral target but with substantial explicit support from the U.S. government, suggests that the system may be too rigid for handling external shocks, even when backed by a strong fiscal position. This suggests that a floating regime may be preferable at least until major structural reforms are completed. The gains to be obtained from greater financial integration with the United States will continue to accrue on the basis of sound macroeconomic policies, not on the basis of a currency union per se.

References

Artis, M.J., and Currie, D.A. (1983) "Monetary Targets and the Exchange Rate: A Case for Conditional Targets," in W.A. Eltis and P.J.N. Sinclair (eds.) *The Money Supply and the Exchange Rate.* Oxford: Oxford University Press.

Cardoso, E. (1990) "Capital Formation in Latin America, "NBER Working Paper No. 3616. Cambridge, Mass.: National Bureau of Economic Research.

De Grauwe, P.; Gros, D.; Steinherr, A.; and Thygesen, N. (1992) "In Reply to Feldstein," *The Economist,* 4 July.

Feldstein, M. (1992) "Europes Monetary Union: An Article." *The Economist,* 13 June.

Giavazzi, F., and Giovaninni, A. (1990) *Limiting Exchange Rate Flexibility: The European Monetary System.* Cambridge, MIT Press.

Masson, P.R., and Taylor, M.P. (1992) "Common Currency Areas and Currency Unions: An Analysis of the Issues." Center for Economic and Policy Research (London), Discussion Paper Series No. 617, February.

McLeod, D., and Welch, J.H. (1991) "North American Free Trade and the Peso: The Case for a North American Currency Area." Mimeo.

Mundell, R. (1961) "A Theory of Optimum Currency Areas," *American Economic Review* 51 (November): 509-17.

Waverman, L. (1994) "Post NAFTA: Can the USA, Canada, and Mexico Deepen their Economic Relationships?" Paper presented at the Conference on the Future of Western Hemisphere Economic Integration.

CHAPTER 5

The Political Economy of Monetary Arrangements in North America after NAFTA

Jean-Luc Migué[1]

THE EFFICIENCY RANKING OF MONETARY INSTITUTIONS depends on the political-legal rules governing the behaviour of agents in those institutions.[2] Arrangements classified as efficient in one legal setting will be ranked differently under alternative rules. When monetary arrangements are evaluated in conventional normative discourses, a particular political order is of course implicitly assumed. For instance, in Europe and North America, normative monetary economists prescribe actions as if the state or the collective agency under harmonized

---

1   The author is Professor of economics at the Université du Québec.

2   I draw my inspiration from the Buchanan framework in setting the analytical background. See, for example, Buchanan (1993: 404-10).

exchange rate arrangements, is all-powerful and benevolent. Monetary prescriptions are offered on the assumption that politics does not matter and that multiple-country agencies aim for efficiency in monetary policies. If government is a benevolent entity, then the conventional approach may yield useful normative advice as to interest and exchange rate policies. But if such a model of government is not descriptively accurate, then the ordering of monetary arrangements that emerge may be misleading. My purpose is to contrast the conventional approach with that which describes the politicized environment in which monetary decisions are effectively processed.

This paper proceeds from the assumption that both within national constitutional rules under present multiple-currency conditions and within rules foreseeable under coordinated- currency regimes, public decisions regarding interest and exchange rates are politicized. In other words national central banks and a hypothetical North American Fed are constitutionally unconstrained regarding the range of policies they may choose to adopt. Within this most likely constitutional setting, monetary arrangements characterized by multiple currencies and multiple decision centres will involve a lower waste of economic value than any currency harmonization alternative.

Alternative monetary arrangements

Three alternative monetary arrangements can realistically be conceived. First, some supra-national harmonization agency may be empowered to set monetary policy without specific constitutional constraints. Second, as envisaged by the Maastricht Treaty, North America might evolve toward full currency union, with monetary decisions assigned to some central Fed. Finally, national governments may retain their present autonomy under floating rates while being constrained to adjustment by the discipline of currency competition. The position taken in this paper is that decentralized monetary decisions are to be preferred in political democracy, because the very structure through which political decisions are made prevents the attainment of the type of monetary policy that might be defined to be optimal in the idealized setting of benevolence. Alternatively, constraints imposed on national authorities by resource mobility and individual freedom to locate one's assets in the most stable currency provide a realistic instrument to discipline national governments.

The first two institutional frameworks result in identical politically determined outcomes and as such cannot realistically deliver efficient outcomes. Both rest on the assumption that monetary policy will be platonically determined to maximize continental income. Rent seeking as empirically observed throughout the history of national monetary practices is ruled out. Decision making under institutionalized coordination of monetary policy does not differ from public choice under single-currency regimes. It remains central in nature and as such goes against the federalist logic. Whether tax, budgetary, or monetary standardization emanates from a central parliament, as under Maastricht, or from the interaction of national authorities, it still suppresses competition between governments as long as it uniformly applies to the entire common market. In the dichotomy of mechanisms conceivable as instruments to regulate exchange and interest rates, harmonization arrangements belong to the central voice process rather than the exit mechanism.

Monetary coordination in an idealized world

In the ongoing debate in Europe and North America, economists define optimum currency areas in normative terms, which implicitly recognize the interdependence between the rules of politics and the pattern of outcomes generated by the behaviour of persons who act within those rules. For a group of independent nations, a single currency is appropriate when: (1) the economic fluctuations that characterize individual members of the area are similar, and (2) labour is highly mobile among the countries in question. When shocks synchronously hit every country, the desirable monetary policy is the same everywhere, so that little can be gained from separate policies. Movements in exchange rates within the area become inappropriate. Differentiation in monetary policy also becomes unnecessary if labour freely and effectively moves from countries with high unemployment to those with high demand for labour. Because potential gains in transaction costs (including greater stability) are realized under a single currency regime, national governments in those conditions have nothing to lose from sacrificing such policy instruments as interest and exchange rates.

Identifying the optimum monetary arrangements for North America in this framework becomes a mere empirical question. I shall leave it to more quantitatively oriented analysts to determine what level of parallelism in economic fluctuations is sufficient and whether the three members of NAFTA come close to meeting that normative requirement. On the other hand regional shocks and differential cyclical movements cannot be ruled out in as diversified an area as the North American economy. The rarefied conditions of symmetry are never met in the real world. Normative analysts are not at a loss for all that. They argue that, compared with a regime of floating rates, only currency union or its harmonization ersatz can limit rate volatility and uncertainty. Their not so secret weapons: inter-national fiscal transfers. This immediately suggests the weak spot in this logic: a monetary coordination mechanism is not appropriate because within realistic institutional settings, it implies an idealized decision process unlikely to be descriptively accurate. Even assuming symmetry between all regions of the North American economy, supra-national determination of policies would not deliver an efficient outcome as long as monetary decisions are governed by politics rather than constitutionally set rules.

Yet this centralist vision has become mainstream teaching among economists. In assessing the proposed unified European currency, many argue that such a plan could result in very serious strains, unless some type of EU-wide tax-transfer scheme is put in place.[3] Their idealized model is the United States of America where the federal government absorbs, in reduced taxes and increased transfers, up to 40 percent of any decline in a typical region's income. In contrast the European Union, they lament, merely cushions 0.5 percent of the impact of an adverse shock.

Barry Eichengreen's (1991: 24-25) assessment of the savings and loan crisis in the United States more vividly illustrates the confusion. In a perfectly perverse use of language, Eichengreen designates by the

---

3   See, for example, Sachs and Sala-i-Martin (1991).

label "fiscal federalism" the arrangement whereby depositors in Texas received $20 billion in deposit insurance, while the U.S. Treasury collected only $ 1.3 billion in taxes from S&Ls in that state. Two implicit assumptions are contained in this judgment. First, federalism is measured not by the extent of decentralization and competition but by its opposite, the power of a central authority to neutralize competitive forces. Second, it is wrongly assumed that the government of a non-federal state could not have done even better in terms of redistribution in favour of some regional interests.

The policy and institutional implications of this view are that moving to a full currency union à la Maastricht is the way to deliver the benefits of greater economic stability, inasmuch as vast inter-regional fiscal transfers, only possible under centralized currency regimes, can guarantee a workable, stable system. This conclusion is, to say the least, disturbing. It is also incorrect.

Monetary arrangements with politics

Political rules under a centralized regime guarantee that there will be discrimination in the treatment of persons and regions. The inclination to discriminate holds for monetary policies as it does for all other activities of governments.

Full monetary integration, whether inside single countries or in Europe and North America, does not suppress the cost of regional or national inconsistent policies. A currency union or a collective agency combined with compensatory payments merely shifts the cost of adjustment to the more conservative and prosperous regions of the union. Analogically the Maritime provinces (declining regions) can pursue costly policies within the Canadian currency union because they are subsidized to the tune of billions of dollars for their failure to adjust. Downward pressure exerted on the Canadian dollar by secessionist threats reduces the living standards of all Canadians, not merely of Quebeckers, as a result of deteriorating terms of trade and higher interest rates. In both cases the adjustment cost is shifted to other Canadian provinces by the action of the central monetary monopoly.

Inter-regional disequilibria are not corrected. They are merely subsumed under the false equilibrium of political handouts.

The alternative of currency competition

What is the alternative? What are the institutional implications of this federalist vision for Europe and North America? A realistic regime most likely to deliver stability combined with responsibility and freedom from coercive transfers is currency competition. Freely floating currencies circulating together in a common market, with or without an ERM-style mechanism, are nothing else than competitive federalism applied to monetary matters. Individuals and businesses can hold assets in any currency they choose. Incentives are applied on national authorities to deliver the kind of performance people want. Irresponsible micro- and macro-economic policies cause dissatisfied individuals to switch to other currencies, as costly policies make the economy less attractive.

The process by which discipline is imposed on national authorities under multiple currencies is familiar: The high mobility of capital and other resources within common markets carries a penalty for regions with riskier currencies in the form of higher interest rates and lower standards of living. Deteriorating terms of trade would be a drag on their living standard. Weak exchange rates rather than central handouts would befall regions that lost investors' and consumers' confidence as a result of costly policies. At the same time, declines in their living standard from their devalued currency, not shifts of the burden of their bad policies, would enable poorly governed regions to maintain export and production in adversity. Canada has experimented with this medicine in the last 15 years or so. In the end, each nation assumes the burden of its choices.

Once politics is introduced into the arrangements equation, a pegged-rate regime occupies the middle road between a currency union and freely floating rates. The risk of recurrent ERM- style crises remains. On the other hand, monetary crises, as are occasionally experienced in Europe, are themselves signals to national governments that their micro and macro policies have been inconsistent with exchange rate stability.

Either they adjust or they do not. In all circumstances they bear the cost of their decision. A coordinated currency regime with compensatory payments would in no way facilitate the adjustment and would not deliver the benefits of greater economic stability. It would merely shift the adjustment cost from irresponsible and inefficient countries to more conservative ones.

In any circumstances, since there is no way of knowing in advance the optimal size of a currency area, one can only rely on the market process of discovery to arrive at a determination. If the advantage of a single European or North American currency as a way of minimizing transactions costs are so overwhelming, such a system will spontaneously evolve as the choice of Europeans and North Americans. In the meantime, free competition in currencies offers individuals protection against irresponsible national policies. As was the case under the old gold standard, conservative and prosperous countries are sheltered from the dangers of a North American or Eurofed and other institutionalized handouts to weak and inefficient regions.

A single common market does not imply a common currency nor coordination arrangements, any more than it calls for a common social policy or a common language. North America would do well not to emulate Europe and turn its back on arrangements designed to encourage rent seeking by national members.

Monetary federalism

In the conventional debate in federal states and in Europe, federalism is associated with the strengthening of the central government's powers, while the search for autonomy and decentralization is linked to narrow secessionist movements and anti-European options. Supporters of devolution are immediately labelled anti-Europe and "nation-builders." Yet the opposite is closer to the truth. Federalism is decentralization. As a form of government, federalism is the opposite, not of decentralization, but of the unitary state. The partisans of devolution are the real federalists.

The logic of federalism operates in any political structure where the power of political (including monetary) authorities extends to less than the size of the economy in which resource movement is unimpeded by trade barriers. Its competitive action can be at work within national economies in decentralized federal states or among countries associated in common-market arrangements with limited central powers.

Whether the central layer of authority is made up of elected officials as in federal states and in the European Union or of multinational coordination bodies is analytically immaterial. The determining characteristic of a federalist structure is that most responsibilities are entrusted to decentralized authorities, which have no power to legislate for the whole area where trade is free. Such arrangements enhance the ability of resource owners to move their goods, their capital or themselves away from detrimental tax and regulatory measures. In its impact on public choice, free trade places national governments in the approximate position of a province or a state vis-a-vis the national economy in a federal state.

This competitive model comes into play without it being necessary to limit legally or constitutionally the legislative power of the member governments of free trade areas, provided the mobility of resources is not hampered. In a decentralized system, exit not voice is the ultimate instrument at the disposal of individuals to discipline the government.

By the same logic, the competitive model only comes into play if national decisions are not superseded by a vast central power covering the same fields at the supra-national level. Centralization is analytically defined as the assignment of growing power to the authority that rules over the entire common market via taxes, spending programs, and regulation, including monetary regulation. As such, centralization neutralizes the competitive process of federalism by making the mobility of resources inoperative and useless. What use is the freedom to leave a country, what use is the choice that individuals and business have to purchase their goods from outside suppliers, or to move their assets into another currency, if the central authority can regulate and tax the economy at the common-market level? Individuals and groups bound by country A no longer have the option to escape its restrictions by emigrating to country B, or by moving their capital into a more attractive currency, as the federalist solution is thwarted by the cartel implemented at the central level. The mobility of resources is made useless as a mechanism to shield resources from unfavourable legislation and as an avenue for productive adjustment.

Harmonization versus monetary federalism

Both in federal states and in the nascent federal structure of Europe, the public debate runs on the assumption that the duplication of monetary functions is a waste. At the minimum, arrangements between autonomous jurisdictions should provide for institutionalized policy harmonization. Standard textbook assessments underline the distortions likely to ensue from non-harmonized national tax and monetary policies. From the formal theory of optimal taxation, one learns that national governments in common markets should not impose significantly different taxes because supply and demand in open economies are price elastic. This would imply high distortions. Differential changes in short- and long-term growth call for fiscal transfers as macro-economic adjustment remedies. It therefore seems appropriate that central authorities should levy taxes and set interest and exchange rates. Harmonization, defined as the action of converging toward similar tax structures, similar expenditures programs, and similar monetary action with compensatory payments, is the alleged minimal solution to such distortions.

But the logic supporting monetary coordination is no less disturbing than the argument behind full currency union. Political forces unleashed by a coordinating agency are not basically different from those under a single currency. Harmonization is alleged to be desirable because it makes it harder for taxpayers and regulated agents to shift their purchases, their savings, and their persons to more clement jurisdictions and more stable currencies. By contrast, easy-to-switch activities in national economies can escape taxation and reduce wealth losses to residents in irresponsible currency jurisdictions. In a word, decentralized regimes induce economic distortions, because in their attempt to avoid unfavourable tax and regulatory treatments, residents can shift their resources to less heavily taxed and more stable jurisdictions. In the orthodox, conventional discourse, those consequences are undesirable.

In the more realistic view of governments as redistributors rather than producers of wealth, harmonization is to be avoided inasmuch as it serves as an excuse for suppressing tax and currency competition. In the institutional-legal framework likely to emerge in North America after NAFTA, harmonization is a recipe for rent-seeking expansion.

Centrally setting monetary priorities and goals does away with competition by removing any advantage the population might have of moving to another region or of seeking higher return on their assets in a neighbouring country.

The truth is that policy harmonization does not require centrally coordinated action. When it serves the national interests of member states, harmonization between programs, taxes, and monetary regulations is more likely to occur spontaneously as a result of competitive market pressures arising from the inter-regional mobility of resources. Through the invisible hand of inter-currency competition, national monetary decisions tend to converge across the common market, especially those affecting capital, the most mobile factor. Harmonization is thus deplorable or desirable depending on whether it is imposed from the top by a collective agency or whether it proceeds from decentralized choices. The first version cartelizes member states, the second expresses freedom and competition. Duplication of a government function such as monetary policy by national authorities may prove beneficial; duplication by a supra-national authority threatens competition and is detrimental.

Currency harmonization: a force toward balkanization

An idea widely held by politicians, bureaucrats, and some economists has it that only a strong supra-national authority can safeguard the common market against the narrow protectionist and unstable forces of local and national interests. History and analysis teach a totally different lesson. If the central government of existing federations is any guide, a central monetary authority in North America would use its enlarged monopoly power over the free trade area to balkanize the overall economy in erecting the equivalent of barriers between member states. The power of a central monetary authority to balkanize a common market vastly outmatches the ability of member central banks to do so.[4]

---

4   For an application of this line of analysis to the Canadian federation, see Migué (1994: 107-30).

Economics provides a strict theoretical measure of the concept of international balkanization. It is the extent by which a government intervention dissociates the market or tax price of regional services from their production cost. Inasmuch as prices are determined at the common-market level, outside the national territory, such distortions can mostly be caused by a central intervention acting over the whole community. A supra-national authority can more easily shift the burden of a policy to non-national victims. By virtue of their inability to affect outside prices, member states by themselves are in no position to shift the cost of their inefficient decisions (monetary or otherwise) to other members of the common market. Because they have no choice but to assume the burden of their policy options, national governments constantly face resource mobility constraints on their ability to distort prices and balkanize the economy.

The collective agency operates under far leaner constraints, inasmuch as it possesses the power to rule over the entire economic union. And the distortion is no less real when exchange and interest rates, rather than sectoral market prices such as agricultural products, are distorted. In fact balkanizing a common market is equivalent to erecting tariffs, quotas, and protectionist subsidies between the member states of a common market.

Inter-regional price distortions through central handouts

One instrument available to a supra-national authority to pursue its discriminatory pricing goals is fixed exchange rates combined with payments to national governments or transfers to business and people in countries experiencing shocks or slack labour demand. Assume that some North American collective agency puts in place a fiscal transfers scheme such as regional investment grants or some coordinated tax structure to absorb shocks in one of the national economies. This lowers the price of publicly supplied services below their cost in lagging regions and raises it above elsewhere. Productive resources in prosperous areas have now the incentives to move away from jurisdictions burdened by their higher share of the subsidy or tax cost. Similarly producers and residents in subsidized territories are encouraged to stay in their less productive employment by what has become in effect a public service cartel at the common-market scale. Offering grants across countries or standardizing tax structures is like cross-subsidizing regionally rather than at the industry level. Standardization can be viewed as a form of tie-in sale whereby people in prosperous regions are coerced into sharing the product of their efforts with people in low-demand areas. Only a central authority possesses the monopoly power necessary to practice discrimination.

This means that policy uniformity and central handouts hamper the specialization of resources. They act as national protectionist barriers. Unemployment outlays, regional tax credit, development grants, equalization payments and shared-cost arrangements are some of the instruments familiar to analysts of traditional national federations under domestic currency union. Viewed in this light, centrally coordinated programs act as sources of dissociation between regional prices and regional costs. They result in the balkanization of the common-market economy: they are essentially trade barriers.

In a true federalist structure, such violation of the true price-cost ratio across areas of a common market, would cause the mobility process to be set in motion. National member states of the common market which devalued their currencies to stimulate exports or raised taxes to subsidize declining activities would soon find out that resources are being repelled from their territory. Not so under the centralist arrangement assumed above. By virtue of the coordinated transfer mechanism implemented at the common-market level, adjustment forces are neutralized.

Inter-regional price distortions through central regulation

All forms of coerced international uniformization in matters of taxation, expenditures, and regulations reduce the ability of local economies to adjust to temporary or permanent changes in demand and supply conditions, and as such are sources of balkanization. Currency union or harmonization are no exceptions to the rule. The irony of currency harmonization is that while its associated fiscal transfers would result in lower resource mobility and excess population in declining areas, harmonized social, economic, and monetary regulations would imply reduced investment and population in those countries. Individual countries invariably experience different shocks in the supply and demand for their products. With wages and prices adjusting slowly, output and employment movements cannot be mitigated by the induced changes of the currency's value in various circumstances.

It is significant that a movement toward collective currency harmonization would exert the same local impact as the NAFTA side deals with their provision for more uniform environmental standards and common working conditions. First, the common standards cause production costs to rise throughout the common-market territory. Second, they are likely to be set by the demand of interest groups in the most developed and prosperous urbanized regions. The ability of lower-income, lagging areas such as Mexico to compete with the most productive ones would be reduced in the same proportions. High unemployment regions would be denied the power to compete with prosperous ones through lower wages, lower taxes, or fewer environmental amenities.

Consider the impact of imposing common working conditions and collective bargaining rules throughout the common market. By raising labour costs in greater proportions in lagging areas, those measures would act as specific taxes on labour in less productive countries. Similarly, extending common environmental standards to Mexico would raise the cost of doing business in that location and cause declines of capital inflow into the country that needs it most. Defying all common sense but not surprisingly, opposition to the North American Free Trade Agreement came largely from Canadian and American environmentalists and organized labour, who fear the expansion of opportunities in Mexico. While some may view the NAFTA side deals as harmless in that no central bureaucracy has been empowered to impose standards uniformity,[5] it in principle has opened a Pandora's box with consequences similar to those foreseeable under currency harmonization schemes. In serving as tariff barriers on the inflow of capital into the less prosperous countries, regulation by any form of supra-national arrangements could

---

5   This position is argued in Taylor (1993).

act as a dominant factor in the balkanization of the North American economy.

Cartels of national governments

Centrally determined monetary policies would foster resistance to necessary national adjustments in another way. By releasing member states from the consequences of their decisions, central subsidies and regulations encourage national governments themselves to show little concern for adopting adjustment policies. Equalization payments, cost-sharing programs, and central regulatory measures mostly serve to shield decentralized administrations from the consequences of their own cost-increasing policies. All three instruments result in national policy costs being shifted to other parts of the common market. The more inefficient national governments are, the more they are compensated. This is nothing less than an exercise in economic absurdity.

Should Europe or North America engage in the centralist monetary path idealized by conventional wisdom and embodied in Maastricht, member states would find themselves freer to indulge in distorting practices, because harmonization schemes would stand ready to shift the cost of their policies to outside taxpayers or consumers and to neutralize the federalist adjustment process. Decentralized governments have an incentive to collude. To enforce collusive agreements, the offices of some central, "higher" authority are required in the form of common trade barriers against the outside world, stabilization taxes and programs, revenue and cost sharing and regulation at the common-market level. As evidenced by the Common Agricultural Policy, the lion's share of the European Union budget and regulations mainly serves to shelter member states from the consequences of their own decisions.

Conclusion

The conclusion to be drawn from past and planned practices of centralized structures is unambiguous. If the distortion of prices among member states is accepted as a valid measure of protectionism, then coordinated initiatives which impose the uniform treatment of regions in matters of taxation, expenditures, and monetary regulations are distortionary and protectionist in nature. All central interventions with variable local incidence are the equivalent of implicit regional customs tariffs, regional quotas, or discriminatory subsidies to regional consumers and producers. They all inhibit the specialization of the community's resources and restrict trade. To argue for a centrally managed currency from the requirements of economic integration within common markets is to make an erroneous evaluation of historical facts.

Social planners have tended to hold that planning under monopoly supply removes the costly duplication associated with market competition. History and analysis teach the opposite lesson. The centralist vision overestimates the potential benefits from centralized decision making and it underestimates the rewards likely to result from competition. In the political-legal order likely to govern any central management of exchange and interest rates in North America, it is hard to argue for a change in the present multiple-currency framework.

References

Bean, C.E. (1992) "Economic and Monetary Union in Europe." *Journal of Economic Perspectives* 6 (Fall 1992): 31-52.

Buchanan, J.M. (1993) "The Political Efficiency of General Taxation," *National Tax Journal* 46 (December 1993): 404-10.

Eichengreen, B. (1991) "Is Europe an Optimum Currency Area?" NBER Working Paper No. 3579, January.

Migué, J.L. (1994) "The Balkanization of the Canadian Economy, A Legacy of Federal Policies." In Filip Palda (ed.), *Provincial Trade Wars: Why the Blockade Must End*, pp. 107-30. Vancouver, B.C.: The Fraser Institute.

Sachs, J., and Sala-i-Martin, X. (1991) "Fiscal Federalism and Optimum Currency Area : Evidence for Europe from the United States." NBER Working Paper No. 3855, October.

Taylor, J. (1993) "NAFTA's Green Accords: Sound and Fury Signifying Little." Policy Analysis No. 198, Cato Institute, November.

Part II:
Mexico, Markets, and
the Peso Devaluation

CHAPTER 6

Stability and Stabilization in Mexico: A Historical Perspective

Luis Rubio[1]

THE MEXICAN ECONOMIC REFORM of the 1980s began, and was pursued, with a zeal similar only to the efforts that led to protectionist policies decades before. This constitutes one of the most visible paradoxes of Mexican politics. For decades, the political system had one objective: stability. In the economic arena, stability was identified with relative isolation: it was assumed that a closed economy could not be subject to the fast-paced changes of the world economy, and hence that it would guarantee stability and the easy flow of benefits to the privileged few that were members of the political status quo. The prevailing economic theories of development of the time, particularly in the im-

---

1   Luis Rubio is a political scientist from Brandeis University, and the General Director of CIDAC (Research Centre for Development), an independent research institution devoted to the study of economics and public policy issues.

mediate aftermath of the Second World War, not only supported such a view, but conferred upon it a sense of respectability. Several decades after, the costs of this ideology proved to be very high—both in terms of diminished rates of growth and lesser income levels.

In theory, "protecting" an incipient industrial base is *superficially* appealing. However, the issue is *not* (and should not have been) *protection from imports*. The issue, rather, is to follow the best process to obtain integration into the world economy. An open economy guarantees this, by definition. The Asian success stories found a way to remain integrated into the economy while at the same time sheltering their firms from outright external competition: forcing them to compete in the international arena through exports, while maintaining their domestic turf subject to domestic competition only. From this perspective, there was a profound difference with what was done in Mexico and in most other Latin American economies. While Latin American economies built impressive walls to "protect" their economies, the Asian nations (Japan and the so-called tigers) sought to make their economies internally competitive and target global export markets. The combination of competition in the domestic market plus permanent growth of exports allowed those economies to grow dramatically, while being completely attuned to the evolution of new technologies and to the world economy at large.

The Mexican economy followed a different course. Economic development and the pursuit of "social justice" were basic tenets of post-revolutionary philosophy and, together with political stability, were the central goals to be pursued in the economic realm. These goals might have been pursued in any number of ways, including the "Asian strategy." Yet this was assumed to be incompatible with the *additional goal of political stability*, since the latter was also identified with the interests of the members of the political bureaucracy. This curious form of political stability required a basis in corruption that would have been virtually impossible to forge in an open economy. Besides, post-revolution governments argued that their ultimate goal was to turn Mexico into a developed society and that such a course required a virtual duplication of what industrialized nations had done a century before. This kind of strategy was incompatible with *any* incursion into the world economy. Hence, as part of the mythology that was created to build a consensus on the development policy, industrial strategies such as those followed by Taiwan and Korea were said to be unbecoming to Mexico because those countries were developing an economy built around *maquiladoras* (in-bond industrial operations) rather than on "real" industry. Thirty years later the impressive success of those nations in per capita growth and industrial strength made a mockery of Mexico's political mythology.

Thus, Mexico's development grew under the shadow of *two myths*: the myth of *autarchy* (i.e., the viability of a strategy based on virtually absolute independence) and the myth of the *infant-industry hypothesis* (i.e., protecting incipient industries from global competition will make them competitive in the future). Mexico's geographic location made any choices more difficult than they might have been for other nations. Mexico's complex history with the United States made it politically necessary for Mexican governments to develop policies that diminished any contact between the two neighbours. That policy had the positive effect of attracting foreign investment from other sources, mainly Europe and Japan, but also hindered the consideration of any policy that was assumed to increase contacts and exchanges with the United States. The result was an economy incapable of competing successfully in the international arena, yet one that helped attain decades of fairly high economic growth. In the end, a structural crisis ensued. Despite the unique political considerations in conceiving and implementing a development policy, Mexico was not alone in pursuing such closed-ended economic strategy.

The evolution of a development strategy

For decades, the Mexican economy developed under the intellectual auspices of the Economic Commission for Latin America (ECLA), a United Nations agency charged with the mandate to help develop the Latin American nations in the aftermath of the Second World War. Up to the 1930s, Mexico had been an exporter of various types of raw materials and an importer of all sorts of manufactured goods. Though some industry had begun to grow and develop since the late 1800s (such as beer and steel), Mexico's industrialization began when imports became unavailable as the war effort in the Allied nations consumed all that was produced. At the time, there were no available imports, so nobody even suggested the need to change the prevailing trade regime. Substitution of imports became a natural and logical response to the international environment. This, in turn created a new domestic constituency with an inward-looking focus of government policy.

Thus, by the late 1940s, the situation had changed drastically. Ten or 15 years after Mexico became an incipient manufacturing nation, a strong constituency for import-protection, government subsidies, and a lax taxing system had become a reality. Hence, precisely at the same time as the industrial nations were working on a structure for international trade and currency stability, Mexico shut its doors to the outside world. Exports of raw materials and agricultural goods financed imports of machinery and intermediate goods for industry. It appeared to be a perfect strategy.

In stark contrast with the way Japan and the "Asian tigers" (particularly Korea and Taiwan) structured their economies, Mexico followed the pace of Latin American countries and rejected the very idea of exports of manufactured goods. A difficult history with the United States during the mid 1800s, in which Mexico lost half its territory, created a deep suspicion of the United States, and thus a strong desire not to become "dependent." Independence was thus equated with lack of close economic ties with the rest of the world. The fact that imports of industrial intermediate goods and raw materials were being made possible by exports of traditional goods was not recognized, for some mysterious reason, as having the effect of linking Mexico to the rest of the world just as well.

As long as the domestic market kept on growing and the balance of payments remained viable, the Mexican economy thrived. In fact, Mexico was able to sustain a 6.5 percent average rate of growth for 35 years with less than 3 percent inflation in average. By the late 1960s, black clouds began to appear in the horizon. Agricultural exports began to decline through the 1960s as a result of population growth and declining land productivity. In the early 1970s, Mexico would have experienced a balance of payments crisis had it not been for the profligacy of the international banks that resulted from the 1973 Arab oil embargo. The latter, together with significant oil discoveries in Mexico itself, allowed Mexico to postpone the day of reckoning for another decade. Exports of oil plus foreign indebtedness made it possible to finance all necessary industrial imports without having to compete in the international arena or care about efficiency or productivity—the very factors that were transforming world production after the 1973 first oil shock.

In 1982, after accumulating an unsustainable $80 billion dollars of debt, Mexico defaulted on its obligations and began to experience the worst depression in its history. Inflation sky-rocketed and economic growth ceased. By the mid 1980s, Mexicans had become impoverished after an accumulated per capita *negative* growth of about 15 percent. Reforming Mexico's economy became an imperative. And the Mexican government went full force with structural reform.

The politics of reform: from debt to full-fledged liberalization

After two years of interminable economic mismanagement, in December 1982, the newly elected Miguel de la Madrid administration launched an economic program to deal with the increasingly chaotic economic situation. Its first aim was to stabilize the economy and reduce inflation (which was reaching annualized levels above 400 percent). The draconian program that the new administration adopted succeeded in reducing inflation to 80 percent in 1983, while halving the fiscal deficit (to 8.5 percent of GDP). Likewise, it overturned the trade deficit, generating a surplus in the first year of that administration.

The Immediate Program for the Reordering of the Economy (PIRE) was successful but short lived. While confronting the critical situation head on, the program was based on assumptions that were proven wrong. First, the program aimed at reducing or overturning the fiscal and trade deficits. It succeeded on both counts, but through policies that could not initiate economic recovery: it lowered the fiscal deficit essentially by reducing (or, rather, by virtually eliminating) investment spending, by increasing taxes, and by containing current expenditures, mostly wages. The government achieved the goal of reducing the deficit, but at the very high price of postponing economic recovery. Its main aim, at least in practice, had been not to affect the bureaucracy or the network of political interests around the government. In other words, *everything was done to reduce current spending as little as possible.* The worst part of this strategy is that a policy of containment cannot last: budgetary restrictions were always met by political pressures to increase spending, which ultimately paid off. A similar principle was applied in the case of the trade deficit: imports were severely constrained, while exports were never fostered. Lack of imports, particularly of capital goods, just like lack of investment in infrastructure, spelled only one inevitable consequence: economic stagnation.

Foreign debt seemed the obvious culprit. In order to justify the draconian program of adjustment, the government blamed the foreign banks. The latter were easy targets not only because of their natural unpopularity, but because, to a large extent, the assertion that servicing debt was being done at the expense of domestic spending was literally true. At that time, no politician was willing to discuss the possibility that it was the structure of the economy that had to change, not for the sake of servicing debt, but in order to attain a sustainable recovery. Also, foreign bankers assumed that they had done no wrong, despite the obvious fact that many (if not most) of their loans had been made for "general purposes"—that is, to projects that had ceased to have financial viability because of the collapse of oil and steel prices. On both sides, it was a time prone to blame somebody else.

For the first time in Mexico's modern history, Mexicans experienced a depression in 1983 (a decline of the GDP of 5 percent), accompanied by a decline in the purchasing power of the average salary of more than 45 percent. Unemployment levels increased, though not significantly, since most of the impact of the recession, in terms of employment, was borne by the underemployed (people who are structurally unemployable in the modern economy for lack of very basic skills). But the income effects, ironically, fell mostly on the middle classes, which were the largest beneficiaries of subsidies (to staples, to drinking water, to public transportation, and so on).

Despite a modest economic recovery in 1984, the PIRE collapsed early in 1985. Inflation ceased to decline and levelled off at about 50 percent, while once again the economy was in deep recession. Within the administration, infighting over economic policy was permanent. Some argued for repudiating foreign debt obligations while others advocated a profound economic reform. One interminable area of dispute was trade policy—precisely where the more radical reformist coalitions began to make their first successful strides. More importantly, the connection between trade and debt was critical: to the extent that the countrys trade policy remained restrictive, debt was permanently unserviceable; by the same token, an open trade regime could gradually reduce debt in relative terms.

The economic argument was an easy one to make, but the debate was political and bureaucratic in nature. Those in charge of trade policy benefited enormously from the discretionary powers embodied in a restrictive trade regime. Furthermore, their constituencies (bureaucracy and the industrial sector) supported them because they feared foreign competition and because they all benefited from a relationship that generated wealth for a few, at the expense of the welfare of society. Over time, as the economy deteriorated and the country experienced another exchange-rate crisis in mid-1985, the absolute rejection of any kind of reform and liberalization was overturned with one of the most ambitious reforms undertaken by a developing country. One could speculate what would have happened had the trade bureaucracy been willing to accept the very modest liberalization that reformers had been pushing. In 1985, however, this argument became mute, for the process of liberalization became more far reaching than the reformers themselves imagined.

The PIRE was superseded by a series of policies that, put together, stood for an extraordinary transformation of Mexico's economy. In mid-1985, a different approach to economic policy was adopted: government-owned corporations were privatized, old regulations that fostered monopolies were dropped, and public finances were squeezed. Most significantly, government departments and entities were eliminated, thus bringing about real and sustainable reductions in government spending. In fact, over the last six years, the government has privatized close to 1,000 companies out of a total of 1,200, while the budget has been cut by close to 10 percent of GDP—more than double the original (and much tougher) Gramm-Rudman budget reduction package in the United States.

The new set of policies were tantamount to an economic revolution. The old policies responded to well-established constituencies that benefited from the existence of monopolies, monopolistic practices, and discretionary powers in the bureaucracy at large. The new policies responded to a novel conception of the world and to clear political calculations that the "old order" was unsustainable. The reformers recognized both that Mexico could not remain partially isolated from what was happening in the rest of the world, as well as that economic stagnation would eventually destroy the traditional political system. A new order would thus require a very strong and growing economy, as well as a very competitive one in the world markets, so as to raise the incomes of the population. In the absence of these conditions, the days of the "old order" were counted. Thus, even if reform entailed a gradual political change that would inevitably alter the old cozy environment and affect existing vested interests, it was preferable to the prospects of instability. For the coalition sustaining the government in power, the potential costs of not changing were overwhelming when compared to the short-term dislocations that the process of change might produce.

Placed in the context of the historical moment in which those decisions were being made, both the vision and the commitment of the De la Madrid administration became paramount. It was precisely at that same time that president Alan García in Peru was repudiating its debt, with no apparent consequences. The populist tune of the Peruvian government was hard to contain in Mexico. The Mexican government was pursuing an orthodox adjustment program, while Peru's followed the easy way out: no debt payments and rapidly growing public spending. Until it became obvious that the latter was not a viable way to resolve the country's economic problems, it was difficult in Mexico to successfully advocate austerity, competition, and reform. By 1990, when Peru's economic situation had become terrifying, Mexico was already on the path to recovery. On the other hand, in spite of the reformist vision, the political calculation soon proved to be extremely tight.

To the De la Madrid (1982-88) administration, as well as to the later Salinas de Gortari administration, economic recovery constituted a political imperative. The high rate of demographic growth posed an economic demand on the government dramatically different from countries with stable populations, such as Venezuela or Argentina. In the case of Mexico, the fact that over 50 percent of the population is under 15 years of age and that, because of the population pyramid, about a million new jobs need be created every year for the next 15 years, poses a unique conditionality on government policy. In short, economic growth and job creation are political imperatives: they constitute necessary responses to avert a potentially uncontainable process of social instability. The fact that many hindrances to economic recovery were being dismantled was of little relevance to the majority of Mexicans, which could not care less about the subtleties of policy arguments. For the average Mexican, reform was largely an inconsequential issue. Very few understood the issues at stake, while the majority were interested in the benefits of economic growth, not the policy behind them. In fact, the government made little effort to explain what reform was, why it was necessary, and what the true scale of the financial crisis of state-owned corporations was. But the problem went much further. For decades, most Mexicans had been indoctrinated about the benefits of state-led development, and the nature of reform was anathema to that mind-set. Furthermore, those that stood to lose from the reform process, particularly government bureaucrats, immediately realized the thrust of reform and began to exploit the tradition of state-led development to their political advantage in the elections of 1988.

In 1988, Carlos Salinas de Gortari became president after a very close election. After four years of economic reform, the benefits had yet to appear to the population at large. The new administration understood that there was a missing political link in the equation of reform. The PRI party had been running the country for almost six decades and its stakeholders had been the foremost beneficiaries of that reign. And reform implied affecting this set of vested interests above all other interests. From this perspective, by the time Salinas assumed office, reform had been eroding the power base as it continuously strapped its constituencies from privileges, subsidies, and the like. Many of the traditional constituencies of the PRI were opposed to reform and many of them ended supporting the candidacy of Cuauhtémoc Cárdenas, the former leftist PRI member that opposed reform.

For the new administration, the political logic of reform had never been so clear. The reform process had gone too slowly to garner any benefits, while it had allowed its opposition to organize and fight against it. Hence, there were two obvious lessons stemming from the 1988 elections. One was that reform could not succeed unless it went against the vested interests that hindered it. Miguel de la Madrid had attempted to avoid direct hits against those interests, in the hope that the benefits of reform would accrue, making their opposition irrelevant. The other lesson derived from the elections had to do with the political system. A closed and protected economy had been matched by an inner-looking political system that sought to control and organize society, very much in line with the thrust of economic policy. As the economy began to be liberalized, it became obvious that a new political arrangement would eventually be needed, one that matched with the new economic reality of competition.

The Salinas administration wasted no time. Reform was a political urgency. For the De la Madrid administration, the political calculation behind reform had been based on the political costs of maintaining the status quo versus the theoretical costs of dislocating the vested interests opposed to reform. However, for the Salinas administration, the issue was no longer academic. The political costs had been paid in the presidential election of 1988. This made structural reform the only alternative to bring about economic recovery.

Thus, Salinas launched a four-pronged strategy. The first part was to attack vested interests impeding reform. In his first months in office he prosecuted corrupt union leaders and prominent businessmen, thereby signalling what he aimed to accomplish and what his opposition could expect. The second part of the strategy was to accelerate and deepen reform. He undertook a massive program of deregulation and elimination of hindrances to investment Also, he pursued the anti-inflationary program launched by his predecessor, which succeeded in reducing inflation from 160 percent to 7 percent in 1994. Third, he launched a new negotiation with the foreign banks to reduce the debt burden. Finally, he worked to develop a new constituency for reform, a strategy that involved consensus-building, social spending, and the expansion of the traditional stakeholders of previous governments.

The problem of consolidating reform

For more than two decades, Mexicans learned to live with uncertainty, knowing full well that policy could shift with the wind. During much of that time, inflation was the main trait of the economy, although also a novelty in Mexicos experience. After years of this deadly mixture, government credibility became a scarce commodity. For reform to succeed, Salinas had to find a means that could guarantee its viability beyond a reasonable doubt.

Mexico's government thus confronted a series of dilemmas that had to be resolved for reform to succeed. These dilemmas had to do with standards of living, with eliminating the last vestiges of inflation, with settling trade disputes with the United States (the nations largest trading partner), and with overhauling the political system. Each of these rubrics entailed enormous risks, and demanded clarity of vision. At stake was not only the reform process, but the political viability of Mexico's current system of government.

Naturally, one thing was making the decision to reform the economy; quite another was making it work. For five years, the economic indicators were consistent and showed a slow but constant improvement. Yet reform would only be relevant (and politically viable) to the extent that it delivered higher standards of living. Without the latter, the concept of reform would become meaningless. Hence, the first dilemma confronting the government had to do with making reform deliver its promised benefits.

For several decades, the Mexican economy grew systematically at over 6 percent per year. Most, if not all, sectors of economic activity grew at a similar pace. The economy was protected from imports, so domestic demand tended to be more or less even for all sectors. It did not matter whether a businessman invested in one sector or the other; the fact remained that the odds of success were overwhelming. The same applied to workers in any given activity. Very few firms went bankrupt. Saving jobs was critical and subsidies were usually available. The assumption for most businesses was that they could succeed in any area, so many diversified into implausible sectors. This assumption collapsed in the wake of trade liberalization.

This change, obvious in any society where competition has generally been the rule, is extraordinary for a society accustomed to evenness. The post-reform scenario is one where growth and employment are determined not by government spending, but by each firm's ability to remain competitive in both domestic and foreign markets. One aspect is inevitable: some sectors and firms will succeed, while others will not. This is not natural to an economy that, due to huge trade barriers to the outside world, had to manufacture everything domestically regardless of quality, cost, or efficiency. The challenge for the countrys industry today is to survive and only then to become competitive. Because of past trade barriers, Mexico is likely to have many less industrial sectors than in the past. The process of change along these lines is already obvious in the virtual disappearance of some sectors, as well as in the rapid growth of others. Much of this change, however, will take years to consolidate.

Since Mexico faces a relatively small problem of unemployment (7-8 percent in the worst years of stagnation, including the current period after the December 1994 devaluation), the transformation of industry and agriculture is unlikely to affect employment levels. Mexico's real problem lies in so-called underemployment, which encompasses some 20 percent of the economically active population. Underemployed people typically do not have the minimum skills to work in the modern economy. The critical question for Mexico's long-term stability dwells on the efforts that should be done to step up training and formal education, so that the children of today's underemployed can be effectively incorporated into the labour force. The original assumption at the beginning of the Salinas term was that, by the time the ranks of the children of today grow, the economy would be in a position to absorb them. Or, in other words, that reform would have been completely successful.

A basic tenet of the reform process is liberalization. This implies that anybody can import virtually anything (with the exception of agriculture, where import-permits are still required; and automobiles, which can only be imported by the manufacturers themselves). The natural consequence of this new reality is that some sectors will be successful while others will not. The new environment entails dramatic consequences. First, wages will naturally grow much faster in the most successful sectors than in the less successful ones. Second, many firms will face bankruptcy and layoffs. And third, one implicit bet in the reform process is that, despite some bankruptcies and adjustments, a very large part of the industrial plant will succeed, hence delivering the anticipated results. The evidence strongly favours reform, even despite the recent currency collapse, but mostly at the micro level. The successful exporters, for example, have been increasing real wages every year for the last four years, and many firms have not only recovered the real level of wages of the early 1980s but have significantly gained over such levels. Another point of evidence is that manufactured exports have risen from less than $4 billion in 1985 to $17 billion in 1990 and to over $50 billion in 1994.

Sector by sector, evidence gives positive signs that reform has advanced fast. But an overall increase in the standard of living of Mexicans is yet to be seen. The new issue is one of timing. Will the benefits of reform come about in a timely fashion? Will the reform succeed in numbers, but fail at the political level? Can a program of partial liberalization succeed, or will it fail until every sector of the economy is equally liberalized? These are crucial questions, which have embodied added relevance in the wake of the crisis brought about by the peso devaluation. The point is still valid today as it was at the outset of the Salinas administration: to the extent that the majority of the population perceives that reform does deliver, then it will be successful.

The reform still faces a dilemma that is more political in nature. Given the fact that the transition implicit in reform entails an enormous adjustment for productive activities, only some of which will succeed, the name of the game of reform is perseverance. Thus, the systematic and permanent pursuit of reform is the only viable policy. Yet, that is not necessarily the politically plausible course—especially in light of the anti-market backlash following the currency crisis. The pressures to increase spending are endless; old hard-line politicians often attempt to recover lost territory through "informal" regulations; a few entities sometimes pursue short-term objectives even at the expense of reform as a whole. Sustaining reform in place and giving it permanent vitality becomes the crucial factor for its long-term success. This will be the key element in the policy decision making process during the new Ernesto Zedillo administration, although the advent of NAFTA has already diminished the room for altering the economic course.

This is not the first time that reform has been pursued. Mexico's governments had attempted to reform Mexico's economy since the early 1970s, but all had failed to garner the political will to affect deeply entrenched political and economic interests that benefited from the status quo. It was always easier to give in to pressures—with devastating results, among them $100 billion dollars of public debt. More importantly, the objective in the administration of Luis Echeverría (1970-76) was not to liberalize, but to expand the governments grip of the economy. In the mid-1980s, in the midst of a recession and while confronting increasing demands from all quarters of the political spectrum, the dilemma became very obvious. While it was recognized that affecting vested interests creates short-term instability, it also became obvious that not affecting them made any reform impossible and assured long-term instability. Hence, for the governments spanning the period since 1982, the logic of reform followed a profound political rationale. In other words, economic reform in Mexico is not the product of an ideological commitment, but rather the result of political factors— in particular, a political calculation brought about by a structural economic crisis.

Thus, completing the reform process and restoring economic growth in an open society became a political must for the Salinas administration. Negotiating a free trade agreement with the United States and Canada was a response to an economic interest as well as to a political imperative that only became evident to the government by the second year of the administration. The economic rationale had to do with the natural extension of the process of reform: securing a market for Mexico's goods, eliminating non-tariff barriers to Mexico's exports, reducing the high maximum tariffs that limit access to the United States, and creating a fair trilateral mechanism for dispute resolution. Once Mexico decided to liberalize markets and sought to enhance industrial competitiveness, the single most important obstacle to the success of reform became the lack of certainty of access to Mexico's major (and largest) export market, that is, the United States. Hence, the economic rationale for NAFTA, from Mexico's vantage point, was to make the domestic economic reform process both permanent and viable.

However, economic reform has a profound political underpinning. Thus, NAFTA also embodies major political content. The reform program constituted a dramatic shift in policy. After decades of serving the interests of a small cluster of political and industrial groups, reform represented an unprecedented break with the past and a redefinition of political alliances, as well as of the constituencies sustaining the governing coalition in power. The cement that held that coalition was the expectation of economic recovery and a consequent distribution of the benefits among the coalition partners, which encompassed large sectors of the middle classes and ascendant "popular" classes (such as the working class). For all of these groups, NAFTA constituted a guarantee of permanence of the economic reform process and, consequently, of the viability of the coalition. Furthermore, it was expected that a trade agreement would depoliticize economic reform, as the latter would become "sunk in concrete."

In the case of Mexico, therefore, NAFTA was sought as *political insurance*: a guarantee to all groups in the governing coalition that the private sector would assume the burden of bringing about economic recovery, and that government would have no choice but to pursue the path of reform in order to attain a new stage of development. NAFTA was meant to be, above all, an instrument to depoliticize the economy and thus strengthen the path of change.

The first rationale for a trade agreement with the United States came about soon after Mexico began reforming its economy. Suddenly, a completely new phenomenon came to characterize and dominate Mexico's relation with its northern neighbour: trading conflicts. Every single successful Mexican exporter was slapped with anti-dumping measures whether it was dumping or not. Trade conflicts began to multiply, to the extent that the very process of open reform became threatened. The standard quip was: what is the point of pretending to become globally competitive and integrating into the world economy, if the world's largest market and Mexico's foremost trade partner, was not making its market accessible? Reluctantly, the Mexican government gradually advanced toward recognizing the need to go further than a series of understandings about trade with the United States.

Although highly committed to reform and to a liberal trading regime, the Salinas administration was not oblivious to Mexico's history and to the deep feelings about the United States that pervade Mexican culture. Its first attempt was thus to negotiate more ambitious agreements with the United States, but short of an all out free-trade package. Several sectors were discussed as candidates for liberalization, but no serious talks ever took place. Mexico was changing so fast that the real economic issues between Mexico and the United States soon became not only apparent, but also overwhelming.

By the end of 1989, the Salinas administration had succeeded in persuading the creditor banks to renegotiate all commercial-bank debt, had reduced inflation to a moderate level (19 percent), and had successfully privatized several major industrial concerns. Soon it began privatizing the banking system and the telephone company. Still, despite these successes, long-term investment was not forthcoming. Eventually, the government recognized that investor confidence had been shattered so often in the past, that more than a record good performance was required. Furthermore, investors needed certainty that the ongoing reform as well as the specific policies would remain in place on a permanent basis. The Mexican government thus realized that there was a need for a guarantee that reform would be pursued by future administrations. Such a guarantee, however, could only be provided by the international community. Nothing inside Mexico could provide it. The political component of the free trade agreement thus became evident.

Early in 1990, the government proposed that Mexico and the United States negotiate a free trade agreement with two specific objectives. First, to provide an orderly process for both economies to integrate and exploit comparative advantages, in order to increase overall competitiveness and standards of living. The other objective was to secure the gradual and peaceful transition that Mexico was experiencing, and thus to avert a backlash (and associated potential instability) next to the U.S. border. In other words, a common thread of economic and political interests led to the negotiations. Canada eventually joined the negotiations to avoid being left out. The very concept of a North American Free Trade Area was born.

NAFTA might serve its purpose of guaranteeing the permanence of the economic reform, but it cannot do the same for the old political system. In fact, the economic reform and NAFTA tend to undermine the political system, as they erode or eliminate the traditional structures of political control.

Will reform bring about political stability?

Historically, Mexico experienced rapid economic growth while the political system was tightly controlled, essentially through corporatist structures in labour, the peasantry, professional and middle classes, and business. Limited political participation and subtle quasi-authoritarian controls allowed for economic growth without creating a "pressure cooker" effect that typically characterizes military governments (which generally repress without creating suitable escape valves). The result was a slow process of both economic modernization and political evolution.

The closed nature of Mexico's economy led to severe economic distortions that demanded strict mechanisms of control. For instance, in the absence of foreign competition, wages could have grown significantly had there not been a structure of tight control over labour. Also, productivity tended to lag behind in view that there was no climate of competition to stimulate it. Lack of competition in a relatively small economy required an active government and a very concentrated political structure to maintain control.

Obviously, all societies develop mechanisms of control. The difference between mechanisms in an open *versus* a closed economy is that in the former the mechanisms are created by markets and society, while in the latter they are organized and enforced by the government. In the economy, the presence of foreign competition automatically limits the demands for wage increases beyond productivity growth, or else firms would face bankruptcy: it becomes impossible to break the economic strait jacket imposed from the outside. Hence, the nature of political controls changes qualitatively. The difference lies not in the existence of mechanisms of control, but on how they are enforced and who enforces them. In a closed economy, it is the government and other political structures that enforce political controls, while in an open economy it is the market and other decentralized institutions that accomplish this task. Naturally, governments in closed economies experience a constant political erosion that eventually surpasses their ability to maintain control. Thus, ironically, the more frequent the government resorts to outright controls, the greater the erosion of those control mechanisms.

The common denominator of closed economies (regardless of country-specific differences or histories) is that they are all characterized by a *de facto* repression of political participation. The problem is not limited to sectors, activities, or factors directly linked to the economy (such as wages, savings, consumption, and productivity). Any attempt to control merely a few sectors, activities or groups never works. An attempt to control one area spills over into others, thereby necessitating greater controls. Ultimately everything ends up being controlled.

The relevant question for Mexico as it transforms its economy from a closed to an open regime is: what are the political implications of economic change? In other words, if a closed economy is typically characterized by a more or less authoritarian political system and an open economy tends to be characterized by political processes that are open and participatory, what will be the political consequences of economic liberalization? There are two analytical levels at which this question can be assessed. One would be based on theories that have attempted to understand the relation between economic and political processes. The other would entail speculating about the long-term impacts of economic reform on political life, on the basis of changes that have already become noticeable. At the theoretical level, the theory of modernization has long argued that it is the transition from traditional to modern society that causes instability, and not the so-called traditional society. In other words, theories of modernization stress that what brings about instability is the process of economic and political change. As Mexico moves ahead in the direction of economic liberalization, the question is whether it will face such a challenge. In 1991, the former Soviet Union clearly entered into a stage in its transition where instability became a distinct possibility. In light of the political events of violence that characterized Mexico's political life in 1994 (e.g., the Chiapas uprising, political assassinations, the role of drug-trafficking), the obvious question is whether Mexico will follow the path of the former Soviet Union.

Mexico is clearly abandoning a thrust of economic policy that lasted over 30 years; yet, it is not in a process of transition from traditional society to modern society (which is what modernization theorists speculate about). That kind of transition took place, if anything, from 1940 through the 1960s; and it was successful primarily because of the existence of the PRI. Today, Mexico is involved in a "transition process" (in modernization theory parlance) from one stage of modernity to another. What appears to be at stake is not stability itself, but the political arrangements that characterized the era of a closed and protected economy. This has to do with the whole institutional foundation of Mexico's political system. The relevant question then becomes whether Mexico's political structures can withstand the pressures of change, even while those same structures are in transition themselves. In fact, a crucial issue in Mexico today is the gradual destruction of the institutional framework that gave it political vitality for decades. Thus, Mexico's new imperative is no longer economic: it is political, and has to do with the development of a new social contract for the future. As economic stability is attained, it is political stability that has to be reconceived.

Has liberalization failed?

Shortly after the Salinas administration concluded its term in office, the incoming Zedillo administration found itself before a run against the peso. Its response was to devalue the currency in an attempt to stem the run against the currency, and gain a margin of competitiveness to offset the differentials of inflation that had accumulated since the previous 1987 devaluation. The assumptions on the basis of which the decision to devalue were made ended up being false, and the Mexican economy entered into a process of profound disarray. Most people, including many government officials, have blamed the crisis on the previous administration, on the rapid liberalization of imports, on the management of the exchange rate during the politically difficult months of 1994 (where violence dominated the scene), and so on. The question about liberalization and deregulation is a critical one, for it lies at the core of the process of stabilization in the previous years.

Though space prohibits a more thorough discussion of what went wrong, there are some obvious culprits that led to the crisis of 1995. First of all, though the policy of liberalization and deregulation was clearly the right one, the fact that it was limited to selected parts of the industrial sector only meant that Mexican companies, which had never been subjected to competition before, had to compete against the best in the world without the benefit of a competitive banking system, modern and fairly priced communications networks, competitive electricity and petrochemical inputs, and so on. Mexican companies were, in fact, forced to compete while paying for the extreme inefficiencies of the rest of the economy. Hence, the poorly conceived, and extremely limited, liberalization of the economy is far more important in explaining the difficulties that Mexican businesses were facing, than the fact of liberalization: it was too limited, rather than too much, liberalization that is to blame.

Second, while advocating and promising a fiscal balance, the government ended up running a sizable fiscal deficit in the last two years of the Salinas administration, a fact that had much more bearing on the rapidly growing (and excessive) current account deficit than any other single item. Finally, the political events of 1994 obviously had a major impact on the management of the economy. International reserves declined through the year, while the government issued dollar-denominated instruments (*tesobonos*) to retain foreign investments in the country. The Salinas administration took a major gamble in the decision to postpone a devaluation, for it ended up financing a structural problem (the current account deficit) with short-term instruments (tesobonos). One could argue that they accomplished their main goal, which was to end the presidential term in peace, but they also clearly assumed (in a show of absolute hubris) that there was no problem or challenge that could not be managed successfully.

The Zedillo administration, fresh into a major battlefield, failed to recognize the complexity of the situation it encountered. The new officers in charge of the economy assumed they could devalue the currency without upsetting the markets, and thus failed to plan a new course for the economy, thereby unravelling a major crisis of confidence. One mistake followed another, compounding a problem that may have been manageable, until it became a major item in the international financial agenda. Above all, there were three major mistakes that ended up requiring an extraordinarily stringent economic program to control inflation. First of all, the government mistook investments for debts, and thus, rather that catering to the needs of the capital markets, began to plan for a restructuring of *tesobonos* into long-term debt. By misconceiving the problem, the government created an altogether different situation, one that required external support above $50 billion dollars, in the form of the Clinton bailout package. Second, the government attempted to protect itself and the bureaucracy, rather than proposing a program to attract new investment and take hold of the opportunity to eliminate all remaining hindrances to the development of the economy. Finally, by wishing the crisis away, the government kept on deepening it, thus creating a problem far more serious than needed to be.

The Salinas administration ended up compromising a few critical components of its own successful policies (like liberalization and fiscal balances) and made a bad gamble on the *tesobonos*. Human folly and sheer incompetence by the following administration turned a bad situation into a full-blown crisis. On this basis, it is quite clear that the concept of stabilization pursued before was appropriate and, *if properly followed*, stood a good chance to succeed. It failed not because of what was being pursued, but because of the inability by both administrations to grasp the importance of following the sound principles that the reform itself advocated.

CHAPTER 7

The Mexican Devaluation: Facts and Factors

Luis Pazos[1]

Macroeconomic background

IN MEXICO, THE DISTORTIONS in the exchange rate parity that began in 1990, made the economy highly vulnerable to external shocks and to an unstable growth of the current account deficit, which reached 7 percent of GDP in 1994.

Paradoxically, the higher than expected rates of inflation in 1990, 1991, and 1992 were caused by the excess of U.S. dollars that entered the country in the form of large capital inflows, monetized by the Bank of Mexico. Thus, monetary expansion was provoked by the purchase of foreign currency, which contributed to stable rates of economic growth but also a surge in inflation.

---

1 The author is President of the Instituto de Integración Iberoamericana and the Centro de Investigaciones Sobre la Libre Empresa (CISLE). He is also Professor of Political Economy at the Escuela Libre de Derecho and teaches at the University of Mexico's School of Law. This chapter is drawn from his book, *Devaluación: ?Porqué?, ?Qué Viene? Qué Hacer?* (Pazos 1995).

The goal for 1990 was an inflation rate of 15 percent, which was a reasonable target given the accomplishments of stabilization in previous years. However, in 1990, we find the first of a series of errors in monetary policy. The successful privatizations of the telephone monopoly and the commercial banking system generated an unexpectedly large inflow of dollars in the economy. This provided a temptation for the authorities to expand the money supply without inducing an inflationary impact. Yet inflation in 1990 was 30 percent, double the projected target.

The increase in imports, which signified an increase in aggregate supply, was supposed to absorb the increase in money supply, which signified higher aggregate demand. This, in principle, would lead to greater rates of real economic growth, compatible with a decrease in inflation. This, unfortunately, did not occur.

In 1992, Milton Friedman warned that the solution to the inflationary problem in Mexico was to allow a freely floating exchange rate in order to prevent a rapid monetary appreciation of the peso-dollar parity, based on the expectation of large capital inflows due to structural reforms and trade liberalization. Yet, the government opted to continue the same policy of a semi-fixed exchange rate (a crawling peg), which ultimately caused a gradual overvaluation of the currency.

However, the capital inflows used to finance an increasing trade deficit and an accumulation of international reserves were not the result of direct investment, but of speculative capital that could flee the financial markets at a moment's notice. The high optimism derived from privatization and structural reform, as well as from the advent of three-way trade in North America under NAFTA, was able to sustain an otherwise dangerous course. A paradox that troubled the majority of observers was that, despite the signs of currency overvaluation and the unstable growth of a trade-driven current account deficit, Mexico nevertheless continued to expand the levels of hard-currency reserves. This was due to large levels of foreign investment.

After NAFTA was ratified in November of 1993, the level of capital inflows grew significantly. At the end of 1993, investment in stock market instruments and government paper grew above $80 billion. Unfortunately, this boom turned out to contain the seeds of the currency collapse in 1994. The dollars used to cover the trade gap and to increase reserves, in the period between 1990 and 1993, were not arising from direct and permanent investment, but rather from financial or speculative investment in government securities and the stock market. This kind of investment, so-called hot money, could leave the country in a matter of minutes.

Political violence and investor uncertainty

On January 1, 1994, the very day that the North American Free Trade Agreement came into effect, the Zapatista Army for National Liberation (a guerrilla movement in the southern region of Chiapas) declared war against the government and declared their opposition to what they characterized as "an agreement of death."

In retrospect, one of the aims of the guerilla uprising was to offset the flow of foreign capital. The natural expectation under NAFTA was the arrival of substantial direct investment, in the form of in-bond industry, manufacturing, hotels, etc. This would have lessened the dependence on financial capital. However, from the very outset the Chiapas uprising scared investors into postponing countless new investment projects. The decision of the government was not to alarm the investment community, in order to neutralize negative expectations. Thus, financial speculative capital kept growing, thereby making the economy even more dependant on volatile factors.

The assassination of presidential candidate Luis Donaldo Colosio in March was another factor of political violence that caused a significant drop in stock market activity and a massive bleed on reserves (which fell from $29 billion to $18 billion in the month following the Colosio tragedy). The crime caused a major capital outflow shock and severe problems in maintaining the exchange-rate fluctuation band from breaking. This shows that, despite dubious monetary policy in 1994, there is a kernel of truth behind the account offered by the Bank of Mexico concerning the origins of the peso collapse: political factors of violence and instability eroded the confidence of many foreign investors.[2]

In effect, the August electoral contest was a potential warning sign to foreign investors. The possibilities of a victory by Cuauhtémoc Cárdenas and the left-wing PRD party helped to fuel capital flight, due to the perception that the party was linked to the guerrilla efforts of the Zapatista Army.

The Salinas administration had repudiated its populist predecessors and had made a commitment to place Mexico on first-world status through an ambitious program of structural reforms—reforms that earned the derogatory characterization of "neo-liberal" from the Latin American left. Until 1993, the changes showed signs of obvious success and foreshadowed the permanent disqualification of populist opposition such as the left-wing PRD. If the reform process consolidated, future political struggles in Mexico would be limited to the PRI and the centre-right PAN.

Consequently, in view of this scenario, the populist factions grouped officially under the PRD sought to generate instability before the elections, as an instrument to subtract credibility and electoral potential to the PRI. However, the victory of the PRI in the August elections seemed to offer a guarantee of continuity to foreign investors worried about a radical swing in public policy. Yet, the latent problem in Chiapas and the rise in U.S. interest rates began to generate suspicions on the viability of government programs based on an inexpensive dollar and a high deficit in the balance of trade.

To be sure, the political factors did not originate the exchange-rate problem in Mexico, but they did help accelerate an unavoidable adjustment, albeit in an anarchic and violent fashion. Conspiratorial theories are often used to justify government mistakes, and 1994 is no exception to this questionable tradition in modern Mexican politics. In the 1982 devaluation, López Portillo blamed the commercial banks, and characterized them as intellectual authors of a plot against the peso.

---

2   In chapter 6 of this volume, Luis Rubio details the role of the gradual breakdown in Mexico's political system and the links to economic policy.

This standard argument is part and parcel of a political culture devoid of accountability. However, it is important to point out that there does exist an organized coalition of vested interests that stands opposed to the reform process and that sees those interests as politically threatened by trade and domestic liberalization. According to Dolia Estévez, Washington correspondent of *El Financiero*, the peso devaluation was the culmination of a wide destabilizing plan, involving the influence of powerful drug dealers, some political sectors, and, to a lesser extent, members of the transnational left.

It would be an exaggeration to blame the December 1994 peso crash on a breakdown of the political system in Mexico and on a carefully structured conspiracy. But it is important to recognize that the violence that erupted in 1994 was the originator of the tragedy of errors that led to the new crisis. The best explanation of the crisis suggests that political interests opposed to reform sought to destabilize what seemed destined to succeed. Yet, the influence of political violence in 1994 does not, in any significant fashion, exonerate the mistakes of the central bank and the administration in their refusal to modify an implausible exchange rate regime and their pursuit of dubious monetary policy.

Errors of strategy and accountability

Despite the economic imbalances characterized by a high deficit in the current account, currency overvaluation, political violence, and the ensuing expectation of an impending exchange rate adjustment, the chaotic reactions of financial markets were due primarily to strategic errors and a poor tactical approach to revise the rate of exchange.

The Salinas government had held fast to an unalterable commitment to maintain the exchange rate. In the closing months of the Salinas administration, no effort was taken to increase the fluctuation band and the rate of the crawling peg, due to the belief that future capital flows would remain apace. However, in the last days of 1994, the drop in reserves became systematic. The new government, as Zedillo himself acknowledged, "underestimated the problem."

The chaotic fashion in which the devaluation came about could have been avoided. It was necessary to make an upward adjustment in the band, but the government possessed the instruments to undertake the modification without generating panic.

There are several key players in the blame drama surrounding the devaluation and the resulting economic crisis in Mexico:

1. Pedro Aspe, the former minister of finance, has a partial responsibility in the peso devaluation in light of the excessive optimism he placed on the constant inflow of volatile speculative capital. This inflow worked for four years to sustain a high current account deficit, but left the economy at the mercy of external shocks, international economic contingency, and national political disorder. The negotiations of Aspe stopped the sequels of all the prior devaluations. Paradoxically, the renegotiation of external debt in 1990 and the high level of confidence generated by the privatization programs translated into an investment boom where excess private spending occurred in the form of a massive inflow of dollars, whose sudden departure is largely responsible for the crisis.

2. The ex-president, Carlos Salinas de Gortari, is also responsible for postponing a key decision to accelerate the rate of depreciation in the maximum limit of the band. He assumed, erroneously, that Mexico could sustain long and large trade imbalances. But the Chiapas crisis and the murder of Luis Donaldo Colosio rendered that possibility remote in the extreme, due to the severe capital outflow shock that took place. Although Salinas accelerated the rate of depreciation in the first semester of 1994, by as much as 11 percent, this proved to be insufficient to sustain the parity.

3. Jaime Serra Puche was the architect of NAFTA from the Mexican end. However, as new finance minister, he blundered the decision to increase the fluctuation band by 13 percent and underestimated capital market reactions to an abrupt change in policy. If Serra had announced, simultaneously with the parity adjustment, an increase in interest rates and a new round of privatizations, similar to the one announced days later after the currency collapse, the severity of the crisis could have been substantially diminished.

4. The economic cabinet thought that the isolated announcement of an exchange rate modification in the band would be sufficient to neutralize capital outflows. Instead, a massive bleed ensued. This was a critical error of judgment derived from the hubris of many technocrats who believed they could trick the markets.

5. Ernesto Zedillo, the new president, is both competent and austere. However, he has been completely unable to project a program that restores confidence among investors and savers. His zeal of achieving peace in the Chiapas conflict, through a "wishy-washy" policy of adjustment and relinquishing, has been read as a weakness by the Zapatista Army and its intellectual kin in the PRD.

The devaluation according to the Central Bank

In a document entitled *Exposition of Monetary Policy 1994-1995*, the Bank of Mexico offers its own version of the causes behind the currency crisis. According to the document, the devaluation was generated fundamentally by violent political events and not by mistaken foreign exchange policies or an expansion in the money supply.

Thus, the central bank contends that monetary policy in 1994 was adequate. The economy showed signs of growth and greater productivity. In 1994, the GDP grew 3.1 percent with an inflation of 7 percent. The productivity levels in manufacturing industry increased by 10.1 percent, one of the highest increases of the last decades. A large number of observers claim the problem derived from substantial currency overvaluation and the resulting high expansion in the current account deficit. On this, the report disagrees:

> Manufacturing exports grew in the first eleven months of 1994 at a rate of 22.1 percent, the highest since 1989. With this, manufacturing exports constitute 83 percent of total sales to foreign markets. The dynamism observed in 1994 non-oil exports, and in manufactured goods, reveals the international competitiveness of the Mexican economy, derived from structural change and the vast private investment process that has been carried out in the country in the last years. In fact, the important expansion of

non-oil exports has surpassed the levels observed in the majority of nations around the world [Banco de México 1995: 10-11].

This datum, according to central bank logic, confirms that there was no significant degree of currency overvaluation that would act as a disincentive to exports. And, on the nature of capital outflows, the report claims that the increase of the rate of exchange was exacerbated in March, as a result of serious criminal acts, such as the kidnapping of a prominent banker, and, above all, the tragic murder of the candidate of the Institutional Revolutionary Party to the Presidency of the Republic. During the remainder of the year, the rate of exchange was maintained almost at the ceiling of the band and in certain stages reached it outright. When this occurred, it was necessary for the Bank of Mexico to intervene in the market in order to prevent the parity from surpassing the maximum limits of the fluctuation band [ibid.: 6].

The report concludes that political and criminal occurrences "coincided with the stages where the exchange rate reached the upper limits of the band and, consequently, when reserves were lost." This is particularly noticeable after the Colosio murder, when some $13 billion fled the domestic capital markets.

On the situation near the end of 1994, the report notes that:

New unfavourable events in mid-November and in the second week in December produced a very difficult situation to solve, in view of the following: (a) the space that allowed an adjustment in the exchange rate within the band had been exhausted; (b) international reserves had fallen sharply from $16.2 billion on November 11 to $11.1 billion by December 16; and (c) real interest rates had reached levels that were generating serious difficulties to financial intermediaries and to debtors at large. All these factors, in the context of renewed volatility in the international financial markets, and in the context of the popular perception that the current account anticipated for 1995 would be impossible to finance in those circumstances, as well as the escalation of hostile acts by the Zapatista Army, instigated an assault against the domestic currency, which could no longer be detained through the measures that had previously demonstrated their total effectiveness [ibid.: 7].

This report presents important and convincing arguments. However, I disagree with the main thrust of the argument, on the basis that distortions in the rate of exchange had been occurring since 1990. This gradually made the economy vulnerable to the type of shocks that the report alludes to. No doubt, had the violence that characterized 1994 not taken place, and had the modification of the parity not been done so ineptly, the monetary and financial authorities could have avoided the chaotic devaluation that eventually ensued and, by extension, the high social costs that it has produced in Mexico.

The "December mistake"

According to former President Salinas de Gortari, the fundamental cause of the peso devaluation is a series of errors made at the outset of the new administration. In an interview with local media stations in January 1995, he baptized these errors as the "December mistake." What does he mean by this?

International reserves began to plummet in December, after being $18 billion at the beginning of the month. The drop in reserves coincided with renewed declarations of war on the part of the Zapatista Army on December 12, 1994. It also coincided with an ambiguous stance on the exchange rate by the Zedillo administration. His team began to quietly suggest the idea that the fluctuation band had to be modified by 10 percent. The problem was how to achieve this in the context of a well-defined economic strategy, one that could minimize the negative fallout.

There were sharp differences in perspective between the new members of the Finance Ministry and the orthodox line of the central bank—particularly the thesis that a modification of any sort would endanger hard-won stability. On the other hand, the fall in reserves convinced the administration to undertake a 13 percent adjustment in the maximum limit of the band.

On December 19, government officials and private sector and labour leaders met for an emergency meeting. Reserves had fallen to $11.3 billion. The representatives were told that this cushion had to be protected, and therefore that a floating exchange rate policy would be adopted. The labour and private sector leaders argued for hours, trying to demonstrate the dangers behind the decision. In the midst of argument, the cabinet proposed an adjustment of 13 percent in the band.

This was the first mistake; namely, showing the ace in the hole and not playing it. The government exhibited indecision. When the decision was announced on December 20th, panic spread about the lack of decision. Investors began a massive bleed on reserves, buying dollars and tesobonos. The capital stampede forced the government to switch to a float by December 21, with no emergency plan to back up the decision and neutralize investor panic. This was the second mistake.

No communication with foreign financial intermediaries took place, despite billion dollar investments in Mexico. Similarly, no communication occurred with international authorities and creditor agencies. The investment community construed this failing as an inherent weakness in the new government, and ran for good. These were the December mistakes. However, it would be wrong to claim that these failings of communication were the only causes behind the crisis. An adjustment was unavoidable, although it could have been done in a more coordinated fashion, in the context of an economic emergency plan.

Post-devaluation policy issues

The issues surrounding the December mistakes have been a source of controversy. There are three areas of dispute, namely, the role of monetary policy, the role of trade policy, and the role of fiscal policy. I will address each area in turn.

Today, many citizens ask why a devaluation of less than 10 percent in 1994 has caused more bankruptcies and unemployment than a devaluation close to 500 percent back in 1982-83. For most of the industrial and commercial establishments, times have never been tougher. The fundamental reason for this difference owes to different responses to the inflationary impact of devaluation. In 1983, a plan was adopted to fight inflation gradually. This enabled authorities to temper the recessionary effects of devaluation, but at the expense of record levels of parity depreciation and inflation during the De la Madrid period. In 1987, inflation reached an all time high of 159 percent.

In 1983, national output fell by 4.2 percent, but price increases registered more than 100 percent, and the rate of inflation remained high during the whole presidential tenure of De la Madrid. In 1995, on the other hand, the government chose a "shock" plan in order to prevent the effects of devaluation in the price system to translate into an inflation rate close to 100 percent. This would have signified a devastating price shock, after two years of single-digit inflation. In essence, monetary restrictions on the growth of internal credit and a tight monetary policy are being used to offset so-called cost-push inflation. This entails a sharp contraction in growth, but also the possibility of stabilizing prices in a less prolonged period.

Zedillo and his team opted for the non-populist way out, choosing a squeeze on credit, practically for the first time in Mexico's modern history. The money in circulation has fallen, in both nominal and real terms. Thus, for instance, M1 (bills, coins, and checking accounts) was raised in 1983, by more than 40 percent; meanwhile, in the first six months of 1995, M1 fell in nominal terms by 26.7 percent. The increase in prices during that time was about 29 percent. This is unprecedented for an economy used to the easy, but deadly, way out provided by monetary expansionism.

Chile applied a similar medicine in 1982, after its currency collapse. The initiative caused a fall of GDP close to 20 percent, and the government was forced to rescue several financial institutions. However, despite recession and unemployment, Chile managed to find its way out. Now it has one of the most solid and dynamic economies in the emerging market world. Brazil, on the other hand, opted for a gradual anti-inflation policy. To date, despite a recent recovery, it has yet to overcome the vicious cycle of inflation-devaluation-inflation. This is the cycle which Mexico lived in the 1980s, and which would resurface without the implementation of the current "shock therapy."

Naturally, to mitigate the recessionary effects of the program of austerity, the government has to lower taxes, embark on deregulation, and reduce public sector spending. The grave danger is to abandon the policy of squeezing liquidity, falling prey to the temptations to grow via greater public expenditures. So far, the administration claims that austerity can lead Mexico in the right direction through high growth levels in the export sector and in the correction of the nation's external accounts.

This brings us to the second area of dispute, trade policy. In the first six months of 1994, the trade deficit reached $7.9 billion, whereas in the same period of 1995, the trade deficit registered a surplus of $2.8 billion. Superficially, this suggests that devaluation can be a positive instrument of policy, making the nation more competitive and promoting export growth. Is this so? In a word, no. The level of overvaluation or undervaluation of the currency with respect to international currencies can influence the evolution of the trade balance, but it is not the main factor. In addition, sharp and unexpected movements in the exchange rate cause more harm than good.

In 1994, the inflation rate was 7.1 percent, the lowest in a quarter century. After the peso devaluation, an inflationary process was generated which is estimated to bring inflation to 50 percent in annual terms. This erases the artificial benefits of devaluation. Before the devaluation, the view was that the peso was overvalued, principally due to the inflation differential between Mexico and the United States. On the other hand, exports were growing at over 20 percent, and the trade deficit was concentrated mainly with Europe and Asian countries. Still, Mexico has become an expensive country for foreigners who plan to make direct investments and for domestic products in general. This situation required a carefully planned adjustment in the exchange rate band, consistent with low inflation and with a temporary setback in growth, but not the devastating stagflation that has ensued after the peso collapse.

The economic policy during the Miguel De la Madrid period constituted a clear example of how the vicious circle of devaluation-inflation-devaluation undermines economic progress. The competitive advantages obtained through devaluation were lost in the short run with a greater rate of internal inflation. In the Salinas administration, a heated debate took place concerning the decision to devalue or not to devalue. If the issue was based on inflation differentials between Mexico and the United States (our number one trading partner) and the growth in the trade deficit, then the answer was to increase the rate of the crawling peg. But if the issue is interpreted in terms of capital inflows and the rise in reserves, then the answer is that there was no need to modify the exchange rate (at least up to November 1, 1994, when reserves were $18 billion).

The devaluation was due to a conjunction of economic, political, and strategic factors. Now, the government is pursuing a policy of deflation (squeezing money out of the market). The monetary base is projected to grow by only 0.8 percent in 1995, while it grew by more than 20 percent in 1994. This seems equivalent to putting the gear forward in a car going backwards, as a means to neutralize post-devaluation inflationary inertia. But despite strict anti-inflation monetary policy, the advantages accrued to exporters through the peso devaluation will be gradually absorbed by a much higher inflation level in 1995 (compared to 1994).

The exchange rate should be neutral with respect to exports and imports. A deficit in the trade account, with an overvalued currency, does not necessarily translate into an inefficient productive plant. By the same token, devaluation, cheapened assets, and a surplus in the trade balance does not necessarily reflect greater productivity or a more competitive, productive plant. The principal lesson of the peso devaluation is to avoid the manipulation of exchange-rate policy as an instrument to influence trade. The economy and the industrial and commercial sectors of Mexico will be far more competitive under a stable price system and under a regime which completely divorces exchange-rate policy from trade policy. The only permanent way to increase productivity and commercial competitiveness is to reduce high transaction costs associated with needless red tape, to deregulate, and to stimulate production with initiatives such as lower taxes and a more flexible regulatory framework. Exports will grow more under this policy than under any policy seeking artificial exchange rate boosts.

This brings us to our final issue of dispute, the nature of fiscal policy in a recession and inflation environment. The most serious challenge for the Zedillo administration is to maintain the fiscal balance in the federal budget without raising taxes to punitive levels or to embark on monetary expansionism. In the final stages of De la Madrid administration, the governmental deficit was 17 percent of GDP. In addition, crushing interest rates signified a perpetual source of expenditures. In 1988, for every peso that the government spent, 44 cents were destined to meet interest-rate obligations.

Under the Salinas government, financial expenses (interest payments on public debt) were reduced through the 1990 renegotiation of external debt, as well as through significant amortization of internal debt. The latter was done through allocation of most of the privatization receipts derived from the sale of state entities, such as the banks and the telephone monopoly. By the end of the Salinas term, interest obligations fell to less than 10 percent of total public expenditures. However, programmable or current expenditures never decreased. This was a mistake derived from the belief that the government could sustain the operation of a bloated bureaucracy.

Since the December devaluation, interest rates have shot up to an average of 40 percent, after a dramatic high of 109 percent in March. Thus, financial expenses of the public sector for 1995 will at least double in relation to 1994. The government is bound to refrain from using monetary expansion as an instrument of growth—as part of the conditions imposed by the IMF and the Clinton administration for the bailout package. This means that the only resources left for the Zedillo administration are to increase taxes or reduce expenditures, such as so-called current investment, social subsidies, transfers, and the like.

An increase in taxes is less harmful and less pernicious than monetary expansion, as a means to finance public expenditures. However, the social effect is the same: to impoverish the citizenry. The responsible course is to reduce public expenses to levels that no longer require an increase in taxes or the use of the printing press. Yet, the administration acted against the shortfall in public sector expenses by increasing consumer VAT taxes, from 10 percent to 15 percent, instead of a wholesale reduction in expenses—overlooking that the latter course is the only viable way to resolve budgetary problems.

References

Banco de México (1995) *Exposición Sobre Politica Monetaria, 1994-1995.* Mexico City: Banco de México.

Pazos, L. (1995) *Devaluación: ?Porqué?, ?Qué Viene? Qué Hacer?* Mexico City: Editorial Diana.

CHAPTER 8

From Stability to Stagflation: Lessons from the Mexican Fiasco

Roberto Salinas-León[1]

THE ATTEMPTS TO EXPLAIN THE INTENSITY of the crisis generated by the devaluation of the peso in December 1994 generally fail to note the role of a crucial but unquantifiable variable: confidence. The Zedillo administration inherited a crucial dilemma in exchange-rate policy. The growth of the current account deficit, projected at $31 billion for 1995 (8 percent of GDP) and higher thereafter, was assumed a constant factor for the future in light of two variables: strong private capital flows and trade liberalization under NAFTA. However, political turbulence in 1994 had shifted policy toward an excessive reliance on high interest rates as a mechanism to sustain capital inflows. This generated a decision making problem associated with the following alternatives:

---

1   The author is Executive Director of the Centro de Investigaciones Sobre la Libre Empresa (CISLE) in Mexico City and an Adjunct Professor of Political Economy at the Escuela Libre de Derecho.

- A "big-bang" macrodevaluation to reduce the increasing trade deficit, remove currency overvaluation, and stimulate a gradual decrease of interest rates
- An adjustment or microdevaluation in the maximum limit of the fluctuation band
- An unambiguous commitment with the practice of using high interest rates as the "variable of adjustment," that is, as an important engine to sustain capital inflows
- A strong push for wholesale liberalization of restricted sectors in the economy, such as energy generation and financial services, to stimulate greater direct investment flows

The Zedillo administration opted for the second alternative. The damage wrought by this move was an immediate erosion of confidence. According to the Bank of Mexico, the day after the decision to amplify the fluctuation band, the country experienced the largest amount of capital flight observed in a 24 hour period: almost $5 billion in cash and another $6 billion in dollar-denominated securities (*tesobonos*).[2]

The collapse of market confidence has vitiated the positive results obtained since 1989 in macroeconomic stabilization. In the first six months of the Zedillo administration, instability has run rampant:

- The rate of inflation has increased from 7.05 percent in 1994 to an official estimate of 42 percent in annual terms
- An increase in the peso-dollar parity from 3.44 in mid-December 1994 to 6.55 in mid-1995
- An increase in interest rates from an average of 14 percent in mid-December 1994 to a floor of 40 percent, with a dramatic high of 109 percent in March 1995
- A collapse of hard-currency international reserves from $17 billion in November 1994 to a low of $3.5 billion in January 1995. Reserves are currently $14 billion, due to the large cash inflow derived from the Clinton $52 billion bailout package

---

2   The interventions in the foreign exchange markets during 1994 show a two-day intervention of almost $5 billion between December 20 and December 21 (see *Banco de México* 1995: 58-61).

- A collapse of foreign investment expectations. In 1994, despite political turbulence and electoral uncertainty, new investment inflows registered $12.1 billion, with a 63 percent increase in the share of direct investment. In 1995, the government projects a lower inflow of $7 billion, but private sources estimate much lower projections
- A collapse of output. New projections estimate a negative 4 percent growth rate for 1995, after a mid-year devastating fall of 7 percent
- The rate of unemployment has jumped from 3.2 percent in 1994 to 6.6 percent in the first six months of 1995; this is equivalent to 2.3 million post-devaluation layoffs

In short, the peso devaluation has replaced stability with stagflation.

Three fundamental lessons

There are three fundamental lessons to be derived from the new Mexican fiasco. The premium placed on stability entailed that devaluation was inconsistent with the goals of structural reform and stabilization. Thus, despite the political shocks observed in 1994, the government had defined policy in accordance with the requirements of exchange rate stability. The peso currency collapse can be understood as the by-product of a gradual abandonment of the principles of confidence, fiscal discipline, and market certainty that had led to the highest foreign investment boom in Mexico's modern history.

1. In 1994, fiscal and monetary policy witnessed a departure from the principles of strict discipline and stability observed in earlier years—mostly for political reasons. The fiscal slippage derived from "financial intermediation" of state-run development banks amounted to 4.4 percent of GDP. In addition, the central bank opted for an expansion of internal credit (an estimated increase of 14 percent in real terms) instead of a hike in interest rates to compensate negative capital outflows resulting from falling international reserves. The monetary base grew from 0.6 percent in 1993 to 20.4 percent in 1994. In short, too many pesos were chasing too few dollars.

2. An excessive reliance on short-run debt and volatile short-term capital flows to finance external accounts. In the period 1990-94, it is estimated that over 70 percent of new capital inflows were channelled through securitized financial markets and short-term instruments. This made the large requirements of the capital account highly vulnerable to sudden shifts in investment expectations. The unwillingness to open up sectors of society such as oil, energy generation, and financial services to direct foreign investment played an indirect role in the crisis.[3]

3. There was a poor policy approach to a delicate situation. The absence of a new exchange rate regime to substitute for the band system, coupled with the lack of a global strategy designed to neutralize the negative impact of devaluation (such as financial liberalization, a new set of privatizations, foreign investment deregulation, and other confidence-boosting policies), sent financial markets into a frenzy of panic-driven capital flight. An unstable situation was thereby turned into a full-blown financial crisis.[4]

Self-deception and the lack of credibility

The Zedillo administration has yet to produce a consistent account of the crisis. The gamut of explanations includes the renewed declarations of war in Chiapas, the systematic sixfold rise in U.S. interest rates, the violent political events that plagued a fragile electoral year, an unsus-

---

3   In 1992, I argued that one concern surrounding the problematic "of how to erase current account red ink" was that capital account surpluses were primarily the result of investments in financial instruments of high liquidity. The danger always loomed that increasingly growing current deficits would "be serviced by quicksilver capital flows which can flee elsewhere as a result of unexpected outcomes" (Salinas-León 1992: A13).

4   This is the fundamental kernel of truth in Pedro Aspe's account of the crisis. The exchange-rate adjustment was not undertaken in the context of a "global economic strategy." See Aspe's recent version of the events before the devaluation, in Aspe (1995).

tainable current account deficit, an overvalued currency, the vulnerability of speculative capital, and the like. All these explanations have one salient feature in common: the concerted attempt to escape blame and public accountability.

On the other hand, authorities are now wont to defend the devaluation of the peso as a positive "adjustment" that will help boost exports. This fails to explain why exports were already growing above 20 percent under the previous exchange rate regime. It is gratuitous to claim that the devaluation will "help" exports in a genuine fashion, since short-term gains derived from a cheaper currency will begin to erode as stagflation sets in, together with standard demands for higher wages, exorbitant interest rates, and the unavailability of capital goods required for domestic modernization.

Indeed, the main obstacle to sustainable export growth is the lack of a clear and credible exchange rate regime that is able to neutralize instability and restore order in the price system.[5] Nonetheless, despite stagflation and rampant uncertainty, the administration cites success on the basis of the consistent trade surpluses that the country has obtained since the devaluation. In the first six months of 1995, the surplus escalated to $2.8 billion, owing to a 33.5 percent jump in exports versus a sharp 5 percent decline in imports (year to year). The new trade surplus (the first in seven years) is celebrated as proof that the medicine of devaluation and austerity are working. But, to paraphrase Paul Krugman (1994), this view harbours a dangerous obsession. Seven years ago a trade surplus also coincided with stagflation and capital flight. This coincidence is not accidental: in an undercapitalized economy such as Mexico's, a trade surplus is a symptom that the country is exporting its most valuable resource—private investment. Indeed, the Bank of Mexico estimates that a staggering $7.1 billion has fled the country in the first three months of 1995.

Mexico's surplus is fundamentally a sign of poverty, not progress. The fall in imports includes a 29 percent drop in capital goods like

---

5   The following four paragraphs are edited extensions taken from my "Mexico's Economy Will Remain Weak Until Peso Gets Strong" (Salinas-León 1995).

technology assets, materials, and updated machinery—just the type of equipment that small and medium size concerns need to enhance export performance. In addition, a portion of the trade figures represents the sale of capital assets by desperate, cash-stripped companies selling their fixed assets—like tractors and other heavy machinery—at fire sales. Many local suppliers have been forced to sell goods at giveaway prices to meet crushing debt payments. This is reflected in the balance of payments as an increase in exports, while it is just a reflection of decapitalization, misuse of inventory, and similar distortions brought about by devaluation instability.

The Mexican government's self-deception concerning trade figures helps explain why it remains oblivious to the need for an exchange rate regime that focuses explicitly on guaranteeing the long-term value of the peso. Notwithstanding the central bank's opposition to manipulation of the parity as a vehicle for competitiveness, the recently unveiled "National Development Plan 1995-2000" foreshadows an exchange rate regime that targets a "slightly undervalued" real exchange rate to regulate a "proper evolution" of the balance of payments. This reveals that a nondiscretionary exchange rate policy, in the form of a currency board or a similar rule-bound system, does not figure in Zedillo's efforts to consolidate recovery.

Moreover, such a characteristically bureaucratic policy of a "micro-managed exchange rate" embodies a fundamental dilemma for the prospects of sound monetary policy. The idea of keeping the real exchange rate undervalued to boost export growth will tend to generate sharp inflationary expectations, as agents seek to compensate dollar-valued losses (e.g., in goods with imported materials) with an increase in prices. This leads to both inflationary inertia and cost-push inflation. On the other hand, the central bank has a mandate to procure price stability and guarantee sound monetary policy. Thus, under this exchange rate regime, the central bank would be forced to act against inflationary expectations, keeping credit excessively tight and selling assets, thereby increasing interest rates. The effect would endanger the projected growth rates of 5 percent that the Zedillo administration is seeking once the crisis subsides.

The dilemma is obvious, and of great practical consequence. The Zedillo administration cannot coherently combine the manipulation of the parity to act as roundabout subsidy to export growth and the central bank mandate to maintain price stability. One of these has to go.

In the aftermath of the crisis, Rudiger Dornbusch has been mentioned repeatedly, as one of many who "warned" that a peso devaluation was imminent. Dornbusch and others, however, never predicted a devaluation. On the contrary, they proposed devaluation as a desirable tool to enhance competitiveness and generate more growth. This is the familiar argument that the former policy of maintaining a stable parity paid off at the expense of growth-inhibiting high interest rates. The logic was that economic growth would fail to materialize unless the peso was devalued and interest rates fell to levels that facilitated greater credit availability and a more active economy.[6] This scholastic prescription ignored the danger of a resurgence of inflation following the acute loss of confidence that a sharp devaluation creates in a dollar-dependent economy such as Mexicos. So far, the results overwhelmingly inveigh against devaluation apologists like Dornbusch.

Debasing the currency and cheapening assets in order to strengthen exports is bad policy. To be sure, exporters and producers require competitive institutions and economic conditions. But this will not ensue from the counterproductive magic of "currency undervaluation." The first step in the right direction is to establish a framework where the value of money embodies first and foremost importance. Thus, the challenge for the Zedillo administration is to combine the requirements of high export growth with a sound and stable currency. This challenge will remain idle unless the government abandons the fatal conceit that the economy requires "proper bureaucratic fine-tuning" of the medium of exchange.

---

6 This argument for a "competitive devaluation" was developed in many places, most notably the oft-cited paper by Rudiger Dornbusch and Alejandro Werner (1994), "Mexico: Stabilization, Reform, and No Growth." Two weeks after the peso devaluation, Dornbusch commended the administration and predicted that interest rates would fall to single-digits in one month.

In effect, the element governing policy implementation prior to the Zedillo term was to measure the desirability of an exchange rate modification relative to the goal of strong economic growth compatible with the constitutional mandate of an autonomous central bank to sustain price stability. The recent annual report of the Bank of Mexico argues that the peso devaluation was not an outcome of lax monetary policy, that the mandate for price stability was respected, but that the crisis erupted due to unanticipated reductions in reserves linked to the political events which undermined confidence in 1994.

According to John Crow, the answer to the problem of credibility in the monetary decision making process is to fashion a framework where confidence "in the future value of money is given explicit importance."[7] This involves a guarantee that the institution charged with creation of money "be given the mandate and the tools to limit such money creation to a rhythm consistent with maintaining confidence in moneys future value." This represents the normative basis for the autonomous regime of the central bank. Prior to the devaluation, the goal was to strive for a long-term target of 0-3 percent annual inflation. Yet the peso collapse made manifest that a nondiscretionary approach is the only option to consolidate a return of confidence.

The official versions behind the factors that led to the peso devaluation are based on the dubious premise that the crisis was the outcome of forces beyond the control of fiscal and monetary authorities. Of course, this entails that government cannot be held accountable for undermining the value of currency. In an important paper, Francisco Gil Díaz (currently a vice-governor of the Bank of Mexico) argues that disputes about Mexicos recent collapse has been characterized by a "frantic search for evidence to fit some economists preconceived model" (Gil Díaz 1995: 19). In other words, Gil Díaz claims that the standard monetarist attack on the execution of monetary policy in 1994 begs the question against the central banks claim that the immediate cause of the devaluation was a massive capital outflow shock and the suspension of external capital flows. This point is important, but it can also be effec-

---

7   See John Crow's excellent contribution to this volume, "Central Banks: Independence, Mandates, and Accountability."

tively reversed. Indeed, the central bank story is highly convenient, and can be interpreted as "frantic search for evidence" to free the monetary authorities from responsibility and public accountability. The fact is that there is no intrinsic causal connection between acts of political violence and currency devaluation, *pace* Gil Díaz and the Bank of Mexico.

A sound monetary regime

An explicit focus on accountability and monetary credibility acknowledges the normative dimension of money and the need for policy mechanisms that ensure what Crow claims—namely, that the value of currency will remain stable in the future. This is the basis behind the widely misunderstood idea of a currency board: it functions as a legal framework of stability and accountability. A currency board rules out the three fundamental mistakes which led to the crisis: it precludes fiscal expansion through an institutional rule that prohibits public spending beyond levels that imperil reserves; it encourages attractive direct investment policy as a vehicle of growth; and it is completely nondiscretionary.[8]

This element of nondiscretionary policy is what the central bank report misses in its claim that *monetary policy was not lax during 1994*. The report argues, in effect, that the increase in net domestic credit observed in the period following the August 1994 elections owed to the compensatory effects generated through the decrease in hard-currency reserves. This seems innocuous: more pesos were being injected into the economy to substitute for the drop of liquidity generated via the unexpected retirement of dollars. However, the non-expansionist purpose of the central bank is supposed to be a constitutionally guaranteed condition of policy. The criticism of central bank policy centres on the discretionary basis of deciding against a rise in interest rates to protect falling reserves. This would have endangered growth objectives for 1994,

---

8 For an extensive assessment of the currency board option for Mexico, see my contribution "Problems and Prospects for a Mexican Currency Board," this volume.

which was a turbulent political and electoral year. Thus, the obvious issue is whether autonomy was sacrificed in the interest of party politics.

This is a legitimate concern. The central bank claims that internal credit was increased to satisfy stronger demand for currency. However, the increase in monetary demand could have been quelled with a suitable increase in the price of currency—that is, in interest rates. As Heath points out, this policy may not have been "expansionist," but it was surely accommodating.[9] The correct policy decision was to tighten net internal credit against the fall in reserves. The central bank argues that a mere increase in interest rates would have failed to short-circuit exchange rate nervousness and that this could have imperiled the stability of the banking system. The obvious answer to such questionable exercises in discretionary speculation is twofold. On the one hand, the banking system has fared far worse since the peso collapse. On the other hand, it is not the business of the central bank to protect the banking system; it is to protect the value of the currency.

Moreover, this story contradicts the story articulated since 1993, when the public and the investor community were assured that an increase in domestic interest rates would be sufficient to counteract speculative onslaughts, come what may. However, to borrow from Gil Díaz, there is no question that such a story conveniently "fits the preconceived model" of purity that prevails in the central bank.

Some claim that the main lesson of the Mexican crisis is the need to establish monetary union in North America. The argument, in broad outline, is that monetary union is good for regional trade and growth because it eradicates unanticipated exchange rate adjustments. However, notwithstanding the theoretical benefits of a "one market, one money" model, such a proposal embodies the practical risk of institutionalizing discretionary monetary policy at a supra-federal level. This does not remove the problem involved with the factors that led to the exchange rate collapse. The issue is not union per se, but whether a monetary framework can be fashioned consistent with the permanence of a sound and stable currency.

---

9   See Jonathan Heath's contribution to this volume, "Reflections on Mexico's Devaluation: The Debate over Economic Policy in 1994."

In sum, the fundamental lesson of the peso devaluation is that monetary policy is more than just technical economics and short-term prescriptions based on complex models divorced from human action. It is a normative science fundamentally concerned with purchasing power, with credibility, and with accountability.

References

Aspe, P. (1995) "Mexico's Ex-Finance Minister Sets the Record Straight." *Wall Street Journal* (14 July): A15.

Banco de México (1995) *Reporte Anual 1995*. Mexico City: Banco de México.

Dornbusch, R., and Werner, A. (1994) "Mexico: Stabilization, Reform, and No Growth." *Brookings Papers on Economic Activity* (1): 253-317.

Gil Díaz, F. (1995) "A Comparison of Economic Crises: Chile in 1982, Mexico in 1995." Paper presented at The Forum of Managed Futures and Derivatives, Chicago, 14 July.

Krugman, P. (1994) "Competitiveness: A Dangerous Obsession." *Foreign Affairs* (January-February): 1-32.

Salinas-León, R. (1992) "Don't Cry for Mexico's Current Account Deficit." *Wall Street Journal* (21 February): A13.

Salinas-León, R. (1995) "Mexico's Economy Will Remain Weak until Peso Gets Strong." *Wall Street Journal* (21 July): A13.

CHAPTER 9

Reflections on Mexico's Devaluation: The Debate over Economic Policy in 1994

Jonathan E. Heath[1]

IN MEXICO, IT IS VERY COMMON to look for whom to blame after a devaluation and an economic crisis like the present one. It is also popular to speculate if it could have been avoided and how authorities could have prevented it from happening. This time around is no exception and the controversy has generated a heated debate.

There are at least four issues at the centre of this debate on different aspects of economic policy during 1994, all of which have a common thread: the Bank of Mexico and Hacienda (the Ministry of Finance) have both put forth different interpretations on why the devaluation had to occur; there is room to believe that a large fiscal expansion took place

---

1   The author is President of Jonathan Heath & Associates, an independent economic consulting firm in Mexico City.

last year, with a considerable impact on the trade balance; did the central bank carry out truly independent decisions; and, the nature of monetary policy during the year.

The causes of the devaluation

When Jaime Serra Puche announced the 53 centavo adjustment on the exchange bands on December 20, 1994, he was very careful not to use the word "devaluation." Again, two days later when the peso was allowed to float, he did not use the "D" word. The media strongly criticized him for not calling things by their proper names: a devaluation is a devaluation. In this sense, both President Zedillo and Guillermo Ortiz (the new finance minister who replaced Serra) decided to talk openly and explicitly call the peso adjustment a devaluation.

Then, the whole public sector began to openly use the reasoning that the current account deficit and the overvalued exchange rate had been the main causes of the devaluation. Nevertheless, all during 1994, the previous administration had insisted time and again that the exchange rate was not necessarily overvalued, since the increase in productivity had given greater competitiveness to exports. It was enough to point out that manufactured exports had grown at an annual rate of over 22 percent during the past year, which would have been difficult to do if the exchange rate had been (significantly) overvalued.[2]

Unlike the government, the Bank of Mexico today continues to be faithful to last year's allegations that a current account deficit does not necessarily reflect an overvalued exchange rate. They argue that the deficit was the result of an excess of investment over domestic savings. Large amounts of foreign capital entered the country due to attractive investment opportunities in Mexico created by the structural changes that the Salinas government had been developing since 1989.

The political events of 1994 reverted this process causing heavy capital flight and the eventual devaluation at the end of the year. The Bank of Mexico has insisted that a policy cannot be validly condemned

---

2   See Banco de México (1995). For a summary of the bank's report, see Mancera (1995).

because of not having considered unforeseeable events. Monetary policy was aimed at always keeping foreign exchange reserves above the monetary base, while maintaining an equilibrium in the balance of payments. From the end of April through the middle of November, reserves remained relatively stable, indicating that capital inflows were financing the current account deficit without causing any major imbalance.

For many years, during the past presidential period, then Finance Minister Pedro Aspe insisted on this point. He said that in the past, especially during the López Portillo administration (1976-82), the external deficit was the result of excessive public spending, unlike today when the government had managed to balance its budget. During the Salinas administration, the current account deficit was caused by the arrival of capital, which came as a result of a renewed confidence in Mexico. Structural changes and market-oriented policies aimed at modernizing the country were paying off. Thus, since capital inflow had caused the deficit, if that were to be reverted, the deficit would begin to decrease by itself. If capital continued to flow from abroad, it was hard to argue that the exchange rate was overvalued. The only thing the government had to do was to maintain a consistent macroeconomic policy in order to preserve confidence in the country.

The calculation of the supposed overvaluation of the exchange rate is based on the purchasing power parity (PPP) theory. Starting with some base year, in which the exchange rate was supposedly in equilibrium, inflation rate differentials between Mexico and the rest of the world placed the exchange rate at a 20 percent overvaluation by mid-1994. However, this theory is considered obsolete by the greater part of the academic world. Nowadays, more comprehensive theories are used such as the fundamental equilibrium exchange rate (FEER) and the desired equilibrium exchange rate (DEER). These theories use many more variables than a simple difference in inflation between countries to determine the equilibrium exchange rate, like productivity differentials. In this light, it becomes difficult to sustain that the exchange rate was highly overvalued.

The Bank of Mexico's argument sustains that the deficit in the current account is the result of the gap between investment and domestic savings. Capital inflow is understood as external savings which complements domestic savings in order to satisfy the investment needs of the country. With the existence of investment opportunities in Mexico, along with a low generation of domestic savings, external savings fills the gap. These inflows cause an increase in the aggregate demand which in turn feeds the demand for imports and creates the current account deficit.

The logical conclusion to this line of reasoning is that since the capital inflows diminished in 1994, the current account deficit should also have decreased. However, this did not happen. So, what was it that induced such strong growth in the external deficit during the past year?

The public deficit and the current account

If we accept the explanation of the external deficit through capital inflow as a "propitious" or "benign" deficit, to differentiate it from a "malignant" deficit, which would result from an excessive public deficit, then we must pause and analyze 1994 with more detail. Between 1989 and 1993, capital inflow was very substantial and thus a growing trade deficit resulted. However, there were no similar inflows in 1994, and yet the trade deficit continued to grow. Is there another explanation for what happened?

On analyzing this data we can find that there was an important expansion in aggregate demand during 1994 which contributed in a significant way to economic recovery and an increase in imports. Toward the end of 1993, the government stated on several occasions that it was going to increase public spending during 1994: in the renewal of the "pacto" agreement between labour, business, and government in October; in the State of the Union Address in November; and in the official document *General Criteria for Economic Policy*. This adds credibility to the hypothesis that the 1994 external deficit was not caused by the arrival of large amounts of foreign capital, such as had occurred between 1989 and 1993, but rather by an excess of public spending, causing a "malignant" external deficit similar to that of the seventies, which Pedro Aspe had warned us about. This being the case, the consistency of macroeconomic policy was lost, and the result was an unstable situation.

However, official data indicates that the government's public deficit was actually 0.3 percent of GDP, which is far from being a large deficit and which rather is bordering on a balanced budget. With these facts, it is difficult to argue that there was excessive spending on the part of the government that might have caused an unstable situation.

On deeper examination of the economy during the past year, we find many different possible sources of fiscal expansion sponsored by the authorities that do not necessarily come under the definition of public deficit. As a result of the effort to decentralize, many expenses that before were considered to be within the confines of the federal government are now in the hands of state and municipal governments. For example, educational costs, which used to be considered at a federal level, have been transferred to the state government. Since state-level public finances are unknown to us, we cannot conclude if a large part of the expansion came from greater regional or local spending.

We also find that the development banks increased their net credit in 1994 by approximately 4.4 percent of GDP. In previous years this amount, known as financial intermediation, was considered to be part of the public deficit, through a broad definition known as the "financial deficit." In 1993, the government decided to discontinue the use of this definition and instead started to report a stricter definition, called the "economic deficit," which does not include financial intermediation. The government reported that the economic deficit in 1994 was 0.3 percent of GDP; however, if we include the intermediation, the deficit was 4.7 percent of GDP. This final number turns out to be very high and could be considered as a cause for the expansion of the current account deficit last year. If this turns out to be true, then we are involved in a "malignant" deficit, which definitely could have caused instability.

One side of the debate sustains that it is too much of a coincidence that the government removed this item from the definition of its deficit, especially in 1994 when there was a sudden expansion in aggregate demand. Being the last year of the Salinas administration, as well as an election year, it was natural that the government wanted to stimulate the economy. Nevertheless, it appears as if this factor contributed to an unstable situation, which ended up in a devaluation.

The other side of the debate holds that the elimination of financial intermediation from the public deficit was the correct thing to do, since credit granted does not at any time represent a contingency of the federal government. The financing that the development banks grant is obtained in the same way it is for commercial banks, through the placement of paper on the market, deposits from the general public, government loans, and the central bank. Capital requirements and the constitution of reserves on nonperforming assets are required by all banks, both development and commercial. At the same time, the development banks operate by granting credits through commercial banks. Thus, their risk is not directly with the small and medium-sized companies, but with financial institutions.

If we accept the argument that the development banks have gone through a process of significant stabilization, not only in their financial structure but in their portfolios, then we should not include intermediation within the public deficit. Nevertheless, the profit or loss that the development banks would have as a result of their operations, should be included in the deficit of the public sector just as it is with any other parastatal company.

This means that we should refocus the debate toward how the development banks obtained the financing to be able to increase their net credit so much. Under normal circumstances, part of this credit comes from abroad, from international institutions like the World Bank or Export-Import Bank. Consequently, there is the possibility that the development banks strongly increased their dollar liabilities beyond normal levels, with an eye on the strong expansion of the economy and under the direct auspices of the government. Also, the development banks and trusts under government control usually obtain part of their credits from the Bank of Mexico. In any of these cases the government would still be responsible for the strong expansion that helped cause the increase in the "malignant" current account deficit during 1994.

Central bank autonomy

The natural extension of the debate involves the role played by the central bank during the past year. If there was an expansionist fiscal policy last year, where was the Bank of Mexico? If the expansion was not the responsibility of the federal government, but rather the cause of a strong increase in the net credits of the development banks, should the Bank of Mexico not have counteracted this action? At the same time, considering that the foreign exchange reserves were decreasing, should the Bank of Mexico not have put into effect a more restrictive monetary policy? Many analysts think that the fundamental problem was that the government did not allow the Bank of Mexico to operate independently after it had granted it formal autonomy starting in April of 1994.

This debate is becoming very important, because the arguments used for justifying the autonomy centred around the fact that an independent central bank would not allow fiscal expansion to generate inflationary pressure. In this case, there would not be any possibility of returning to a crisis situation like that of the 1980s. Nevertheless, there are two sides to this question: on the one hand, we must ask if the Bank of Mexico acted autonomously, regardless of whether it was the correct policy; on the other hand, we must examine the decisions of the Bank of Mexico in order to know if they were appropriate or not, given the economic situation of the country, over and above whether such an action was characteristic of an independent and truly autonomous central bank.

The Constitution guarantees the independence of the Bank of Mexico by making it impossible for the government to demand credit from it. It also clearly indicates that the primary objective of the bank is to maintain stability in purchasing power through control of inflation. Nevertheless, this does not mean that the Bank of Mexico is prohibited from granting credit to the government. It can do it as long as it is the decision of the central bank and not that of the government. If the Bank of Mexico decides to increase its domestic credit as part of its monetary policy, we cannot automatically argue that it is not exercising its autonomy. The decision could be a wrong policy and yet not be a question of independence.

Unfortunately, it is practically impossible to determine if the Finance Ministry put pressure on the Bank of Mexico to grant more credit. However, considering the close resemblance in the formal points of view of both institutions, we can infer that the analysis of the economic situation and the majority of policy implications coincided, so that intuitively it is possible to think that there was no pressure placed on the Bank of Mexico, but rather a coincidence as to how to manage the economic policy during the major part of last year.

Monetary policy

In retrospect, it is easy to find fault with monetary, fiscal, and foreign exchange policies of both the Bank of Mexico and the Finance Ministry. The Bank of Mexico admits, in its document *Exposition of Monetary Policy for 1995*, that with a different combination of fiscal and monetary policies the devaluation could have been avoided. But there was no way that the economic authorities could foresee the frequency and the force of the destabilizing factors that rose up in 1994.

In order to judge the role of the Bank of Mexico we would have to take this into account. The crucial issue is: at the time decisions were made and with the available information at that moment, were those decisions well made? Obviously the Bank of Mexico will answer in the positive. Nonetheless, there has been a lot of criticism of the Bank of Mexico's position, to the effect that it would be difficult to call the 1994 monetary policy "restrictive" when net domestic credit at the central bank was increasing consistently throughout the whole year. The institution even admits that domestic credit was increased in order to satisfy a greater demand for currency. It is arguably extreme to call this policy "expansionist," but it was surely accommodating.

It is clear that during part of the year there was a greater demand for currency. The central bank argues that this was the result of more vigorous economic activity, the effect of substituting bills for checks, and a reduction in the use of credit cards. The reasoning behind this substitution was said to be the increase made by the banks in the commission charged for writing a check. The argument for the decrease in the use of credit cards was said to be the increase in the frequency of frauds and assaults. However, this line of reasoning is unconvincing: if somebody was to stop using their credit card for fear of being mugged, it is highly improbable that they would want to hold more cash.

In this case, what monetary authorities claim is that the growth in demand for currency last year was the result of an increase in aggregate demand caused by exogenous factors. The policy followed was simply to respond to a growth in demand with a growth in supply. Also, the Bank of Mexico always took care that the growth in M1 was less than the nominal growth of GDP and that reserves were always greater than the monetary base.

The other side of the debate holds that the main reason for the increase in demand for currency was fundamentally greater economic activity caused by an increase in the net credit of the development banks and perhaps also an increase in spending on the part of the state and local governments. This caused a greater demand for imports, with the resultant growth in the current account deficit. The Bank of Mexico met this demand through an increase in its net domestic credit, assuring itself that the economy could not recede in an election year.

In a book published by the Bank of Mexico, Vice Governor Francisco Gil Díaz (1991: 67) explains the consequences of an increase in internal credit:

> An expansion of the central bank's credit does not mean simply a growth in the amount of money, but also a decrease in the amount of foreign exchange reserves. If the expansion of credit is excessive, reserves can fall to a critical level. At some point, the public will interpret the credit expansion reflected in the behaviour of reserves as unsustainable and will speculatively attack the currency. The result is that the exchange rate will succumb, falling to another parity and causing a higher price level.

This explanation means that the causality is not necessarily that the domestic credit increase was a compensatory movement for the fall in foreign exchange reserves. Rather, credit expansion could have had a role by itself in diminishing reserves. If so, the action that the Bank of Mexico should have taken when it started to observe the decrease in reserves is exactly the opposite of what it did. It should have diminished internal credit.

The Bank of Mexico argues that the notable flight of capital was the consequence of political and criminal events, which is not surprising, since this type of event "tends to abruptly reduce the expected yield, adjusted for risk, of investing in the country. That, augmented by the present increase in the mobility of capital, causes adjustments of great rapidity and magnitude in investment portfolios which are virtually impossible to counteract through increases in interest rates." If the country's liquidity, eroded by the decrease in foreign exchange reserves, had not been replaced, "interest rates would have reached exorbitant levels, which would have affected debtors in a very unfavourable way, including financial intermediaries. This situation could have become a factor for additional capital flight and could have required an ulterior expansion of primary credit (see Mancera 1995).

After all is said and done, the Bank of Mexico is responsible for price stability. In the sense that the monetary policy did not cause an increase in inflation in 1994, it could be argued that it did not follow an expansionist policy. We could say that the Bank of Mexico fulfilled its priority and avoided an increase in inflation. However, since the final consequence of monetary policy during the year was an exchange rate adjustment that caused an increase in prices, the Bank of Mexico did not avoid an increase in inflation after all.

An increase in aggregate demand not only puts pressure on the general price level, but also generates a greater demand for imports. In a very open economy, we could think that the greater part of this demand was satisfied through imports and that even if the exchange rate was not overvalued, this could help us understand why both exports and imports were increasing simultaneously.

Nevertheless, after the Colosio assassination at the end of March, there was a great surge in capital flight which the Bank of Mexico handled through a combination of the use of reserves, an increase in interest rates and the substitution of 28-day treasury certificates (Cetes) for dollar-denominated domestic debt securities (called tesobonos). At the time, there was only praise for how the situation was handled. Capital flight was contained, a devaluation was avoided, and the negative impact of what could have been a very destabilizing situation was minimized. From that moment on, for a period of about six months, the foreign exchange reserves remained very stable, making people think there was a balance between the current account deficit and the capital account surplus. It was not until the month of November that the balance was clearly seen as much more precarious than had been anticipated.

Still, by the middle of November, international institutions, whose main job was to follow financial flux on a global level, were emitting favourable opinions on the possibility of continuing to finance Mexico's external deficit. The main error was to have undervalued the volatility of foreign portfolio investment, its short-term nature and the effects the political events were to have on investor confidence. However, the fiscal expansion and the monetary accommodation was something that nobody knew about at that time.

Conclusion

The debate on these points has not ended. There are valid elements and arguments on both sides that make it difficult to arrive at a unanimous conclusion. As soon as more data is made available on the economic and financial evolution of the country, we will be able to clarify many more points. Nevertheless, we do not believe that an overwhelming final judgment can be valid for just one side. The truth will be found somewhere in the middle, but only time will tell.

References

Banco de Mexico (1995) *Exposicion Sobre Politica Monetaria, 1994-95.* Mexico City: Banco de Mexico.

Mancera, M. (1995) "Don't Blame Monetary Policy." *Wall Street Journal,* 31 January.

Díaz, F.G. (1991) "Don Rodrigo Gómez, Visionario de la Economía." In F.G. Díaz, *Rodrigo Gómez: Vida y Obra,* pp. 62-87. Mexico City: Fondo de Cultura Económica & Banco de México.

CHAPTER 10

A Market-Based Solution to the Mexican Peso Crisis

W. Lee Hoskins and James W. Coons[1]

Self-inflicted wounds

FINANCIAL DIFFICULTIES AND DEVALUATION of the peso have occurred in each of the last four presidential election years in Mexico: 1976, 1982, 1988, and 1994. And each time, the U.S. monetary authorities have responded with a larger loan package.

The seeds of the 1976-77 crisis were sown by the Keynesian-style government spending program launched by President Luis Echeverría Alvarez in 1971. Initiatives aimed at spurring growth and aiding the

---

1   W. Lee Hoskins is Chairman and CEO of The Huntington National Bank in Columbus, Ohio. He served as President of the Federal Reserve Bank of Cleveland from 1987-1991. James W. Coons is Vice President and Chief Economist of The Huntington National Bank. This chapter is a revised version of their Cato Institute Policy Analysis No. 243 (Hoskins and Coons 1995).

lower economic classes were financed by domestic and foreign borrowing (Purcell 1988: 51). External debt increased more than three-fold from 1970 to 1976 (Grosse 1992: 2). As the program faltered, President Echeverría lashed out at foreign investors and domestic businessmen for exploiting the country, and capital began to flee. During the final weeks of his administration, President Echeverría aggravated fears by expropriating a large amount of private land and distributing it among the poor (Purcell 1988: 51). Rushing to the Mexican government's aid, the U.S. Treasury's Exchange Stabilization Fund (ESF) shelled out $300 million in 1976 and 1977 for "currency stabilization loans" in the wake of the devaluation brought on by balance-of-payments problems. The International Monetary fund (IMF) made $963 million in credits available beginning in November 1976 (Holmes and Pardee 1977: 809).

The 1982 crisis was sparked by capital outflows caused by the expectation that the government would devalue the peso in order to deal with the trade imbalance. The administration of José López Portillo did devalue the peso by 40 percent in August 1982 and announced the debt moratorium that set off the Third World debt crisis (Gooptu 1993: 69-70).

A surge in oil revenue allowed President López Portillo to avoid making the necessary free-market reforms and continue the failed policies of President Echeverría. Proven Mexican oil reserves increased from 15 billion to 72 billion barrels, and oil production surged from 1.2 million barrels per day in 1978 to 2.8 million barrels per day in 1982 (Branford and Kucinski 1988: 76). The added revenues permitted early repayment of IMF loans. The economic boom, driven by the oil-related activity, attracted foreign lenders (Gollas 1985: 81). External debt accelerated, growing more than four-fold from 1976 to 1981 (Grosse 1992: 2-3). Despite the surge in government revenues, spending increased faster, raising the public sector share of GNP from 25 percent in 1970 to 50 percent by 1981 and widening the fiscal deficit (Gollas 1985: 80). In 1982, when the economic crisis erupted, the U.S. Treasury and Federal Reserve extended as much as $1.85 billion in short-term financing to keep Mexico financially afloat until the IMF provided longer-term financing in January 1983 (Schwartz 1995a: 10).

In 1988 the Fed and the Treasury arranged a short-term bridge loan for Mexico of up to $3.5 billion, pending a package of two to three loans from the IMF. The Fed and Treasury again combined for a $1.3 billion facility for Mexico in 1990, which was drawn on in the first quarter and repaid within six months (Schwartz 1995a: 10). Once again the catalyst was capital flight sparked by political unrest and devaluation. As an American banker predicted at the time, "Don't think for a minute this is the last chapter. Mexico will be back at the well again, and the United States will once again have to help, if for no other reason than it cannot afford to turn its back" (Rohter 1988: A13).

The peso's present plight

After two failed starts in January 1995, the United States cobbled together an unprecedented financial assistance package for Mexico. From the ESF, the United States extended up to $20 billion in short-term and medium-term loans and long-term loan guarantees. The IMF pledged $17.8 billion, a group of central banks committed $10 billion, Canada pledged $1 billion Canadian, and Latin American countries agreed to pitch in $1 billion for a total financial assistance package of approximately $50 billion (Schwartz 1995a: 4-5).

The reason for the loans was the inability of the Mexican government to redeem maturing *tesobonos*, short-term debt obligations denominated in dollars. Massive capital outflows, driven in part by rising interest rates in the United States and elsewhere and political unrest in Mexico, drained foreign exchange reserves and forced the abandonment of the peso peg. But these factors merely fired the gun that was loaded by the pattern of past economic policy transgressions and cocked by recent policy errors. The fundamental cause of the 1994-95 peso crisis was an inflationary monetary policy.

The real causes of recurring crises

While the circumstances that led up to the financial strains and subsequent devaluation in each election year differed, the principal cause was the same—bad monetary policy largely driven by electoral politics. The central bank expanded the money supply in an attempt to keep interest rates from rising sharply or to limit the increase during each election year while at the same time attempting to support a fixed or pegged exchange rate. As foreign and domestic investors, wary of inflation and devaluation, began to reduce their exposures, they exchanged pesos for dollars and rapidly depleted the central bank's foreign exchange reserves. The only way to maintain the fixed exchange rate would have been to permit a matching decline in the monetary base (Barro 1995: A14). In each case, however, the central bank refused to shrink the monetary base as reserves ran low and was ultimately forced to devalue the peso.

Attention has been incorrectly focused on the size and mobility of capital inflows as the cause of the current peso crisis (Feldstein 1995: 72-3). In fact, governments that implement sound economic policies have nothing to fear and much to gain from large inflows of capital. The massive capital outflow in 1994-in combination with the practice of pegging the peso-was the proximate cause of the devaluation in December, but monetary policymakers failed to take appropriate actions in light of capital movements in 1994 and prior years. The pattern of behaviour in financial markets across countries during the latest crisis demonstrates that investors can and do distinguish among economic policies in host countries. Good policies are rewarded and bad policies are punished. Financial markets in Argentina fell more than in Chile or Peru, but less than those in Mexico. Other developing country markets fared much better (Meltzer 1995b: 2). Countries, such as Mexico, that run inflationary monetary policies and at the same time attempt to fix exchange rates, are punished quickly and severely for such policies with capital outflows. It is the underlying instability of monetary policies, not capital outflows, that is the primary cause of the current crisis.

Mexico is not alone in learning this lesson. The major central banks of Europe, attempting to support fixed exchange rates inconsistent with underlying economic policies, are believed to have lost up to $6 billion to capital market players in a matter of weeks in the autumn of 1992 (Sesit 1992: C1).[2]

---

2   For a discussion of the difficulties of sustaining the European Exchange Rate Mechanism, see Dowd (1993).

Misguided measures

The response by U.S. officials to the current turmoil in Mexico is the same as in the past: more loans and more onerous conditions on Mexico. There are at least three reasons why this is a wrong-headed approach. First, loans or loan guarantees by the United States create a moral hazard that brews trouble in the future. Second, use of the Treasury by the administration to fund foreign adventure without congressional appropriation raises constitutional issues regarding separation of powers. The administration's use of the Federal Reserve to fund such loans, violates the principle of central bank independence. Third, the loans help special interests and do nothing to raise living standards for most Mexican citizens.

Moral hazard

The regular practice by the U.S. government of extending guarantees to certain countries experiencing financial difficulties underwrites policies in these countries that otherwise would be untenable. It sends a message to investors, both foreign and domestic, that they can invest with little fear of a total loss. This weakens the integrity of financial contracts and the scrutiny that contracting parties would otherwise apply to each other. This situation is analogous to the moral hazard created by Federal deposit insurance. Depositors do not scrutinize which banks are financially strong or weak, because they have no risk of loss. This frees bank officials to take larger risks than they could if there were no deposit insurance.

The Federal guarantee encourages excessive risk taking and threatens large losses to U.S. taxpayers who already paid $150 billion for the thrift bailout. The combination of variable and rising inflation with the common practice among savings and loans of borrowing on a short-term basis while lending on a long-term basis erased the net worth of a large number of institutions in the early 1980s. Increases in inflation pushed interest rates paid for short-term deposits above fixed yields on existing long-term loans, turning net interest income negative for many institutions. By the middle of the decade, the busts in the agriculture, oil, and real estate industries worsened the losses. Lax supervisors failed to close institutions and Federal deposit insurance allowed them to continue to attract deposits. Because of the guarantee provided by deposit insurance, depositors were free to ignore the increasing risks being taken by S&Ls in attempts to earn back their capital.

This example is directly relevant to the Mexican loan agreement since it de facto extends deposit insurance from the U.S. Treasury to investors in Mexican bonds and depositors in Mexican banks. By establishing a practice of guaranteeing investments in developing countries with a third party's money, the U.S. government, IMF, World Bank, and other institutions have created a moral hazard. Government officials in developing countries can behave incompetently or criminally and still expect foreign capital inflows. Foreign investors can target high-return investments, with little regard for the associated risk. The result is a growing potential claim on taxpayers' money.

In the process, there is the potential for creating a two-tier market, whereby sovereign credits are distinguished by whether they are likely to be backed by the United States. The result would be diminished liquidity in some developing countries, investment losses, and fewer willing lenders in non-guarantee markets (Ackerman and Dorn 1995: 21).

Separation of powers

The administration's original proposal of a $40 billion rescue package for Mexico had one redeeming feature. It sought congressional authorization, in keeping with the separation of powers between the Executive Branch and Congress established by the Constitution. Dropping this plan in favour of the smaller program agreed to on February 20 amounted to an end run around the congressional appropriation process. It should be noted that—pleased with the opportunity to side-step a vexing choice—Congress implicitly endorsed this abuse.

The ESF: History, Abuse, and Partial Reform

The ESF is a relic of the 1934 Gold Reserve Act, sought by President Roosevelt as a means of countering perceived advantages in terms of trade secured by Britain through foreign exchange interventions in the early 1930s (Todd 1992: 121). By establishing the ESF, Section 20 of the

Gold Reserve Act gave the secretary of the Treasury, in consultation with the president, the ability to intervene in foreign exchange markets and make loans aimed at "stabilizing the foreign exchange value of the dollar." The temporary authority for the ESF provided by the Gold Reserve Act was repeatedly renewed until it was made permanent in 1945 (Wilson 1995: 22).

After the fixed exchange rate regime of Bretton Woods dissolved in 1973, the purpose of the ESF was changed to "being consistent with U.S. obligations in the IMF regarding orderly exchange arrangements and a stable system of exchange rates" (Wilson 1995: 2). In addition to fuelling intervention in foreign exchange markets, the ESF has been tapped to finance short-term loans to both developed and developing countries.

The fund was capitalized with $2 billion from the revaluation of U.S. gold holdings and was used actively to intervene in foreign exchange markets during the 1930s. In 1947, $1.8 billion of ESF resources were used to make partial payment of the U.S. quota in the IMF, reducing the balance to $200 million (Schwartz 1995a: 11-2). Congress has made no other appropriations to the ESF, but the interest on U.S. and foreign securities, interest and fees on loans, and net gains from foreign currency transactions have raised the balance to approximately $25 billion (Wilson 1995: 1,4).

The lure of the vast, discretionary funds proved too much to resist. As one journalist put it: "The only limitation [on ESF spending] has been the sitting Treasury Secretary's imagination" (Corwin 1995: 22). A series of secretaries tapped the ESF to pay the salaries of CIA and Treasury staffers and diplomats, underwrite luncheons and receptions, and cover lodging, hotel bills, and travel expenses. Apparently, spending for any purpose remotely related to the foreign exchange value of the dollar was considered legitimate. Congress discovered and put an end to these abuses in the late 1970s by requiring that funds could be expended only with an assured source of repayment (Corwin 1995: 23).

Because the ESF is not financed with regular appropriations from Congress, it must "borrow" from the Fed when it seeks additional funds. That practice is known as "warehousing" because the Treasury stores or "warehouses" its foreign currencies at the Fed in exchange for dollars that must be paid back later. The Federal Open Market Committee regularly approves "warehouse" lines for Treasury borrowings. The Treasury borrowed heavily against those lines in the late 1980s and as a result congressional hearings were held in 1990 on the ESF and the Fed's warehousing activities. Loans to the Treasury by the Fed were subsequently discontinued, although the warehousing lines remained in place for future use.

The ESF and Mexico in 1995

After failing to secure congressional approval of a $40 billion loan guarantee for Mexico in mid-January, President Clinton announced an executive order on January 31 giving Mexico access to one-year and five-year loans and ten-year securities guarantees amounting to $20 billion from the ESF. On February 21, the U.S. Treasury signed an agreement with Mexico regarding the exact terms and conditions. The United States made available $3 billion on March 14 (Schafer 1995: 5). In the following three months, an additional $7 billion was disbursed and $2.5 billion was lent on July 5 (Bradsher 1995: 1,18). The remaining $7.5 billion is still available under the terms of the Agreement.

The assistance package is 20 times greater than the largest of the 40 ESF Financing Agreements extended between January 1980 and June 1994 (Wilson 1995: 6). The president declared the existence of "unique and emergency conditions," as required under 1978 legislation to commit resources of the ESF for more than six months in any 12 month period. The largest previously established line of $1 billion was extended to Mexico in August 1982. The longest duration ESF loan was in the amount of $600 million from September 1982 to August 1983 (Wilson 1995: 6).

Additional money is being provided in an equally extraordinary package by the IMF. Under IMF rules, Mexico was able to borrow no more than an additional $3 billion. Under pressure from U.S. officials, the IMF approved a $7.8 billion credit anyway and pledged a further $10 billion after February 1995, provided Mexico abided by terms of a separate agreement. The loan is greater than total IMF lending in 1993 and 1994 combined, twice the amount ever loaned to another country, and seven times its allocation (Meltzer 1995a: 6; Hauge 1995: 49). European governments were understandably irked by the way the United

States pushed the IMF into extending additional aid without seeking approval from them.

The fundamental objection to the involvement of the ESF is that it undermines the separation of powers. A case can be made that circumventing the congressional appropriations process violates Article I of the Constitution. In fact, the Gold Reserve Act itself is of questionable constitutionality, because it gives to the Executive Branch unreviewable authority to engage in covert actions in international finance-a sphere explicitly reserved for Congress by Article I, Section 8, clause 3 (the commerce clause) (Todd 1995b: 7). In effect, the Executive Branch is financing the restructuring of Mexico's entire short-term, dollar-denominated debt without a congressional appropriation (Todd 1995c: 8).

Foreign aid has rarely drawn much support in the United States. As a consequence, administrations have attempted to avoid approaching Congress for appropriations for such ventures-the Iran-Contra scheme being a recent extreme example. The ESF has been a source of discretionary spending for the Executive Branch, the likes of which Congress sought to prevent. The Constitution limits spending by the Treasury to appropriations approved by Congress. Moreover, the statutory authority for ESF activities pertains only to foreign exchange intervention to support the dollar (Todd 1992: 155).

The "obligations" of the United States under the Articles of Agreement of the IMF, as amended in 1978, include maintenance of the "stability of foreign exchange arrangements." The agreement, however, is to avoid taking steps that destabilize markets, not to use financial resources of the United States to defend arbitrary exchange rates. The intent is to ensure the stability of the auction market mechanism, not of a particular set of prices that might arise from that auction (Schwartz 1995b: 5).

A related objection is the destabilizing effect of such financing arrangements on the foreign exchange value of the dollar. Though perhaps small, such disruptions are real and justified. A short-lived surge of enthusiasm boosted the dollar leading up to and following the announcement of the U.S. assistance package on January 31, 1995. In April 1994, the United States entered into an agreement under which it will lend U.S. dollars to Canada that Canada in turn could lend to

Mexico (Todd 1995d: 193-4). The perception that the United States had underwritten Mexico's external and domestic debt and bank deposits, however, may have contributed to the sharp dive in the foreign exchange value of the dollar in February and March.

Central Bank Independence

The use of the Federal Reserve to fund Treasury activities not only raises questions about separation of power between the executive branch and Congress but also does damage to the principle of an independent central bank. Much effort has gone into keeping the Treasury and Fed at arm's length from each other to reinforce both the perception and the reality of central bank independence. The Comptroller of the Currency and the Secretary of the Treasury originally served as ex officio members of the Board of Governors of the Federal Reserve System, but the Banking Act of 1935 ended this arrangement. In addition, the Fed does not purchase securities directly from the Treasury, the governors serve staggered terms, and the Fed does not depend on Congress for appropriations. Executive branch influence on the Fed through ESF transactions unwisely raises questions about the independence of monetary policymakers to pursue price stability.

Relief for special interests

The extension of loans from the U.S. government to the Mexican government favours special interests at the expense of all citizens in the Mexico and the United States. The bailout rescues foreign investors who bought Mexican stocks and bonds in search of fat financial returns, Mexican financiers whose close links to government officials keep them in the right places at the right times, and officials of the long-governing Institutional Revolutionary Party (PRI) who have much at stake. On the other end of the bargain are Mexican citizens who face yet another severe economic recession. American taxpayers bear a significant risk by financing the bailout, but have little to gain for their trouble (Torres 1995b: A10).

At the end of May, Mexico is estimated to have borrowed more than $20 billion in total from the U.S. Treasury, the Federal Reserve, the ESF, the IMF and the World Bank. It is not clear where all of the money has gone, but as of March 31, $14.7 billion of the $17.1 billion that had been borrowed at that point had been spent to redeem public debt, pay off dollar deposits withdrawn from the Mexican banking system, and redeem the foreign debts of privately held Mexican companies (Todd 1995a: 52).[3] U.S. taxpayer money appears to have zipped from Washington to Mexico and through the hands of investors and speculators back out of the country.

The *tesobonos* transactions expose the complex amalgamation of public-private relationships that link the financial and political elite. The mismanagement of economic policy in Mexico in the 1970s carried over into the 1980s, driving domestic interest rates above 100 percent from 1983 to 1985 and above 70 percent from 1986 to 1987. Wealthy investors earned enormous returns until the government could no longer afford to service the debt. In 1989, the Salinas administration implemented debt-for-equity swaps, transferring ownership of many state enterprises into private hands on favourable terms (Marichal 1995a: 4-5).

As political instability chased capital abroad in 1993 and 1994, the government issued dollar-denominated bonds to stem the capital outflow. Mexican taxpayers were exposed to substantial foreign exchange risk in the process. When pressures intensified, officials telegraphed the coming devaluation and the Banco de México bought back $4 billion in *tesobonos* from privileged investors during the first two weeks of December 1994. Large financial companies followed their lead, cashing in close to $15 billion in government debt. This spree wiped out most of Mexico's dollar reserves, removing the wherewithal to defend the peso via foreign exchange intervention (Marichal 1995b: 5-6; Zuniga and Amador 1995a, 1995b).

Other beneficiaries of central bank intervention include U.S. banks, with total outstanding loans to Mexico equalling approximately $18 billion (Todd 1995d: 193). The U.S.-led bailout is a reincarnation of the 1985 Baker Plan, which prolonged the illusion that Mexican bank debt remained current by funnelling new loans from the IMF and World Bank through Mexico (and other Third World debtors) to foreign com-

---

3   According to the Mexican government, as of September 1, 1995, $23.9 billion of the bailout package had been spent (see Zedillo 1995: 8).

mercial banks in the form of debt service payments. In exchange, Mexico agreed to undertake harsh austerity measures. The idea was that the economic reforms would permit Mexico to grow its way out of debt (Tammen 1990: 248; Fauntroy 1988: A24).

The most unfortunate consequence of these developments is the added burden on Mexican citizens, who suffer fewer job opportunities, lower wages, higher prices and taxes, and grim prospects. Unemployment increased by more than 1 million from the end of 1994 through mid-1995. The unemployment rate rose to 6.6 percent, more than double its level a year ago and the highest mark since the statistics started to be collected in 1983 (Solis 1995: A8; DePalma 1995: 11). Real wages now stand approximately 60 percent below 1980 levels in inflation-adjusted peso terms (Todd 1995d: 193). The consumer price level was 35 percent higher than a year earlier in June (Grupo Financiero Bancomer 1995: 71). The price of gasoline will be raised by 48.5 percent by the end of 1995. And, the government hiked the national value-added tax from 10 percent to 15 percent, effective April 1 (DePalma 1995: 11). Real GDP contracted at an annual rate of 10.5 percent in the second quarter and is expected to shrink by at least 3 percent for the year, erasing almost all of the 1994 gain (Grupo Financiero Bancomer 1995: 68).

Market solutions

Four times in the last 20 years, the United States and International agencies have extended loans to Mexico. Each time the loans have been larger and the terms and conditions more intrusive. The calls for bigger safety nets for emerging economies now being proposed by leaders of international agencies demonstrate that these institutions have failed in their efforts to promote development and stability. The opposite, progressively less sizable and visible interventions, would be hallmarks of lasting success. The only permanent solution lies in institutional reform that embraces market forces. Reliance on financial assistance from third parties will at best ease pressures temporarily.

Set a stable price level and credible monetary policy

The first step toward a market solution is to curb inflation by reducing money supply growth. Attempts to peg the exchange rate by any means other than sound policies are deceitful in the short run and ultimately destined for failure. In the end, the change in the price level will be identical under fixed and floating regimes, because monetary policy determines the price level. The deceleration in monetary base growth in 1995 to below 10 percent from 28 percent in November 1994 is a move in the right direction. The second step is to make monetary policy credible. Recent steps toward more timely and comprehensive financial reporting are prudent. Yet a country like Mexico, with a long history of political unrest, monetary mismanagement, and currency devaluation, requires strong statutory measures to establish credibility. Pegging the exchange rate to the dollar does not make monetary policy credible, as the resounding disaster in Mexico makes clear. Discretionary policy aimed at any objective other than price level stability will eventually create inflation or deflation. In the case of Mexico, monetary policy was too loose in 1994 and was inconsistent with the peso peg at 3.5 to the dollar. Foreign reserves left the country until the peg had to be abandoned.

To be credible, the central bank must have a charter that gives it true independence from the political process and directs it to achieve the single objective of price stability.[4] But words are not enough. The new Bank of Mexico Act, which went into effect in April 1994, was supposed to give the central bank greater independence (Banco de Mexico 1995: 4). Obviously it did not. Central bank officials also must be held accountable for achieving price stability, but that is not enough. A properly structured central bank can deliver a stable price level on average, regardless of other economic policies, but monetary policy will be credible only if other economic policies are consistent with the objective

---

4   See Hoskins (1993a: 171-90) and Hoskins (1993b) for the benefits that arise from a statutory requirement for an independent and accountable central bank to maintain a stable general price level.

of price stability. In addition, credibility depends on time-consistency, or the ability of policymakers to keep their promise in the future. No magic pill exists for instantly delivering a credible monetary policy (Gould 1995: 9-10). But a strong statutory objective of price stability, constitutional independence to pursue that objective, and accountability for achieving it can combine over time with successful implementation to build credibility.

The Reserve Bank of New Zealand is an example of a rule-based, accountable central bank that is building credibility. The Reserve Bank of New Zealand Act of 1989 gave the central bank the single objective of maintaining price level stability, which has been defined as a year-over-year change in the Consumer Price Index between 0 percent and 2 percent. The Reserve Bank brought inflation down from above 2 percent at the time the law was enacted and kept it there until recently (Spiegel 1995: 1; Judd 1995: 3). How New Zealand's central bank responds to the challenge posed by the recent rise in inflation will strengthen or undermine its credibility. A single, statutory objective of price stability, the independence to pursue that objective even at the cost of other short-term economic policy goals, and the accountability for doing so are important ingredients to credibility. But performance also matters. The low inflation rates achieved over decades in Japan and Germany have made the Bank of Japan and the Bundesbank among the most credible of central banks (Judd 1995: 3).

Let the peso float

The third step toward a market solution is to allow markets to determine the price of the peso. Fixed exchange rates are rarely and only accidentally consistent with prevailing economic policies and underlying fundamentals. Most of the time, an arbitrary fixed exchange rate masks and over time amplifies imbalances that eventually surface as major crises. Without the veil of a peso peg at 3.5 to the dollar in 1994, the policy errors by the Mexican central bank, which included monetary base growth in the neighbourhood of 25 percent, would have been evident well before the crisis broke. Investors would have been warned and officials forced to take actions that would have averted the crisis.

Moreover, intervention in foreign currency markets is futile. transactions intended to change the market's evaluation of a currency do not address the underlying economic conditions that ultimately determine the foreign exchange value of that currency. Coordinated intervention has appeared to be successful in the past only in instances when it has supported the direction in which the market was already headed (Schwartz 1995b: 3).

The performance of Mexico's central bank in 1994 is the latest spectacular example of failed currency intervention. Mexican monetary authorities attempted to hold the peso within a narrow range against the dollar. They intervened regularly in other financial markets to maintain that band, amassing upwards of $30 billion in foreign exchange reserves early in the year (Schwartz 1995b: 3). Even this massive stake was insufficient to withstand the selling pressures created by the capital flight that ensued when trouble erupted. By the end of the year, reserves were all but depleted. The only true currency protection comes from sound economic and monetary policies.

Allow private debt negotiations

As the fourth step toward a market solution, Mexican debtors should negotiate directly with private creditors (not governments or international agencies) to arrange conditions and terms of repayment. Giant international agencies may once have been useful in orchestrating the financial and economic interactions among the nations of a compartmentalized world economy. Today they get in the way. Government officials must learn to ride the wave of technology and integrated global markets, because it is too large, complicated, and dynamic for an institution of any size and scope to manage. According to one observer, "The new international financial system is a truly private market that is difficult if not impossible for governments to control" (Millman 1995: A20).

A significant difference between the current Mexican debt crisis and the 1988 and 1982 episodes is that Mexico's external debt is owed to a much larger number of creditors, many of whom made investments through mutual funds. This does not in any way, however, preclude a market-based solution. Prior to 1930 all long-term loans consisted of bond issues held by a broad circle of individuals (Marcihal 1989: 236). In the sovereign debt crises of the 1930s, debtors and creditors effectively negotiated significant debt restructurings without the assistance (or interference) of international agencies, usually through bondholder committees (Tammen 1990: 241; Todd 1991: 223-36; Macmillan 1995: 11).

It is likewise not true that the 1982 debt crisis "when only a few big investment banks were involved" could not have been resolved by the market. In fact, the measures imposed by governments and inter-governmental agencies magnified the solvency problem and delayed its resolution by treating it as a temporary liquidity problem. In addition to not being needed, Treasury and IMF involvement often stood in the way of viable market solutions. In mid-1987, U.S. Treasury Secretary Baker thwarted a plan by Brazilian Finance Minister Bresser Pereira to swap new securities for outstanding debt, valued using secondary market prices (Sachs 1988: 20). The Brady Plan later led Brazil, Argentina, the Philippines, and Ecuador to scuttle debt-equity programs (Tammen 1990: 260). The IMF contributed to the contraction in the supply of credit by holding $3.6 billion hostage to banks' participation in the Brady Plan rescue. The forced write-offs speeded exits by important lenders, contributing to systemic instability. Mexico's debt burden dipped slightly, but the longer term effect was to reduce the number of willing lenders (Oliveri 1992: 116).

Bold new government financing programs have not provided solutions in the past and are not likely to do so in the future. Rather, governments need only establish a regulatory and legal environment that encourages and facilitates the adjustment of terms, maturities, and principal of debts by creditors and debtors, themselves.

The effort by senior G-7 officials to establish a new "emergency financing mechanism" at the IMF to tackle future Mexico-like crises is misguided. That is particularly so since the collapse of the peso did not pose a systemic risk to the international financial community; indeed, by August 1995 even the IMF recognized that the peso crisis represented only a modest threat to the world financial system (Chandler 1995).[5]

---

5   In the IMF report, International Capital Markets: Developments, Prospects, and Policy Issues (International Monetary Fund 1995), the IMF's analysis

At issue is a proposed doubling of the $28 billion General Arrangements to Borrow (GAB) facility.[6] Assistance from the GAB has been unsuccessful at achieving reforms, in all too many cases sustaining rather than shuttering inefficient state enterprises. Short-term "adjustment" loans have financed wasteful intervention in foreign exchange markets in support of the peso, redemption of maturing government securities and recapitalization of insolvent banks (Torres 1995a: A10). As Allan Meltzer observed, "The result is that Mexico has a larger debt while foreign and Mexican holders of bonds have been spared some losses." (Meltzer 1995a: 6). This record does not justify the status quo, let alone any increase in authority.

Furthermore, proposals to turn the IMF into a bankruptcy judge for countries are unworkable and unnecessary.[7] The lesson of more than a century of sovereign debt crises is that private solutions work when not impeded by government actions. Unlike a domestic bankruptcy court, moreover, the IMF would have no enforcement authority in practice. In the international context, sovereign nations would not be compelled to comply with the fund's rulings. Developing countries' common disregard of IMF conditionality, and the fund's consistent willingness to overlook such breaches, raises significant doubts that the fund could effectively fulfil the role of international bankruptcy judge. Creating such a mission for the IMF would only institutionalize the problems that the latest bailout of Mexico has heightened: moral hazard, special-inter-

---

runs counter to that of Alan Greenspan, chairman of the Fed; Robert Rubin, Treasury secretary; and even Michel Camdessus, IMF managing director, all of whom warned at the outset of the peso collapse that the crisis seriously threatened the international financial system.

6   The GAB is an IMF reserve that provides financial assistance to governments in distress. It is essentially a line of credit extended to the IMF by 11 large industrialized countries and Saudi Arabia. The GAB was established in 1962 as a means to ensure that the IMF could meet the potential emergency borrowing needs of the United States. In 1982, the GAB revised its rules to allow lending to non-GAB-member countries.

7   Such proposals have been made by economist Jeffrey Sachs and Rep. Jim Leach (R-Iowa), chairman of the House Banking and Financial Services Committee (see Sachs 1994: A14 and Leach 1995: A20).

est protection, increased debt burden, and postponement of market reforms.

Withdraw from the IMF and World Bank

After 50 years it is time for the United States to withdraw its support for the IMF and the World Bank. If these institutions were ever needed, they no longer are. Calls for increased responsibilities and more capital are signs of ongoing failure, not a growing role. The activities of the Fund and the Bank are largely unnecessary, often counterproductive and expose taxpayers in industrialized countries to huge potential financial losses. Senate staffers have prepared draft legislation to end U.S. participation in and funding for the IMF and the World Bank, legislation that should be introduced into Congress and enacted swiftly.

The breakdown of the fixed exchange rate system some 20 years ago made the IMF a lender without a cause. The institution survived anyway, lending heavily during the oil price shocks in the 1970s, the Latin American debt crises of the 1980s, and the collapse of the Soviet Bloc in the 1990s. The emergence of international capital markets weakens the justification for the World Bank. Developing countries attracted $56 billion in foreign direct investment on their own in 1993, dwarfing disbursements by the Bank. And, privatizations of state-owned enterprises further reduces destinations for development aid (Carrington 1994: A1).

Even though currencies now fluctuate independently or in blocs, the IMF money still fuels foreign exchange intervention "a pointless and costly exercise." At least a portion of the financial assistance provided to Mexico this year has gone to peg the dollar exchange rate of the peso (Marichal 1995a: 6; Meltzer 1995a: 6; Schwartz 1995a: 3). This game wastes money, because intervention has no lasting effects and delays necessary economic policy adjustments. The regular IMF practice of extending new loans to prevent defaults by debt-ridden countries creates a moral hazard. It underwrites irresponsible and destructive economic policies by removing the normal incentive for investors to police governments. Loans from the IMF to countries in transition are intended to encourage the development of market economies. Experience, however, is that money is often used to maintain subsidies to inefficient state enterprises instead of eliminating them. The outstanding $18 billion IMF pledge to Mexico is effectively propping up inefficient businesses and inhibiting liberalization of the banking system (Torres 1995a: A10).

The record of the World Bank is no better. Perverse incentives have compromised loan quality, exposing taxpayers in industrialized countries "the ultimate guarantors" to a possible bailout with a price tag comparable to that of the U.S. S&L bailout. The World Bank routinely extends new loans to governments unable to service existing debts to keep loans current. This "round tripping" has benefited many foreign private sector creditors at the expense of debtor-country citizens and impaired the Bank's financial position. Approximately one-fifth of the Bank's loan portfolio is comprised of round-trip credits. And, an internal report leaked in 1992 disclosed that one-third of the Bank's $140 billion in projects were failing. Deterioration of the portfolio was deemed "steady and pervasive" (Adams 1994: 5,7). Even though the bank is now being paid back more than it lends, its meagre reserve for bad loans is troubling. U.S. taxpayers are on the hook for over $30 billion and the commitment will surely grow, as the World Bank plans to lend another $200 billion in the coming decade (Adams 1994: 16,22).

Fifty years is long enough. It is time for the United States to shift its support away from overgrown inter-governmental agencies conceived to address the challenges of a different age and toward today's powerful and nimble market place.

Embrace the market

The last step toward an enduring market solution in Mexico is a full embrace of free-market principles. Wealth losses that have occurred must be recognized. If Mexican enterprises and banks are insolvent, they should be closed, and their creditors should make appropriate compromises on the debts owed. Private property rights should be strengthened and all government-owned commercial operations should be privatized. President Ernesto Zedillo should go beyond his intention to privatize "everything allowed by the constitution" and privatize everything possible, including PEMEX, the state-owned oil complex (*Financial Times* 1995: 12). That would require amending the

Mexican Constitution, but that has been done before, when President Carlos Salinas de Gortari introduced land reforms.

Markets should be opened further to competition by eliminating all remaining protectionist barriers and subsidies to industry, including lifting all remaining limits on ownership of banks and other commercial entities by foreign investors. Under the North American Free Trade Agreement, participation of foreign commercial banks was limited to 30 percent ownership. Since the outbreak of the crisis, the Mexican government has allowed an increase in foreign ownership, in some cases up to 100 percent. However, foreign investment in the largest banks "those that represent the bulk of the industry" is still severely restricted. Mexican officials should liberalize the rules so that private commercial capital, rather than public debt, is used to rescue solvent but troubled banks.

Conclusion

These are the steps necessary to finally and completely resolve the ongoing peso crisis. If they had been taken in 1982, Mexico would not still be in financial distress. The prescription will be the same in 2000, 2006, and 2060. Mexican officials should take the plunge now, eschew the old, failed government model and embrace the market. This is the best way to safeguard the rich heritage of their great country and raise living standards to their potential.

U.S. officials should have resisted the temptation to tap the quick fix. Although the United States forfeited considerable leverage by signing the agreement on February 21, 1995, it can still pressure Mexico to adopt institutional reforms "particularly in the realm of monetary policy" that will all but prevent a relapse of the peso crisis.

The threat of serious contagion from the current situation in Mexico to countries that have followed prudent policies is small. Countries that have pursued unsound policies are at risk, and will suffer the consequences of investor wrath. Superficial solutions involving government guarantees fail to permanently correct destabilizing policies. Such guarantees create moral hazard and increase systemic risk.

Finally, the United States should withdraw its membership in international financial organizations that once may have promoted development and stability, but now encourage irresponsible policies and imprudent risk-taking that disrupt markets.

References

Ackerman, P., and Dorn, J. A. (1995) "Dose of Financial Morphine for Mexico." *Financial Times* (15 February): 21.

Adams, P. (1994) "The World Bank's Finances: An International S&L Crisis." Policy Analysis Paper No. 215. Washington, D.C.: Cato Institute, 3 October.

Banco de México (1995) "Mexican Memorandum of Economic Policies." Mexico City: Banco de México, 30 January.

Barro, R. (1995) "Latin Lessons in Monetary Policy." *Wall Street Journal* (1 May): A14.

Bradsher, K. (1995) "Mexican Bailout Defended Amid G.O.P. Criticism." *New York Times* (15 July): 1,18.

Branford, S., and Kucinski, B. (1988) *The Debt Squads.* London: Zed Books.

Carrington, T. (1994) "It's Time to Redefine World Bank and IMF." *Wall Street Journal* (25 July): A1.

Chandler, C. (1995) "IMF Ties Peso Crisis to Mexican Investors." *Washington Post* (21 August): A1.

Corwin, J. (1995) "The Slush Fund." *The International Economy* (March-April): 22-3.

DePalma, A. (1995) "After the Fall: 2 Faces of Mexico's Economy." *New York Times* (16 July): 1,11.

Diaz-Alejandro, C. F. (1984) "Latin American Debt: I Don't Think We Are in Kansas Anymore." Brookings Papers on Economic Activity (2): 335-89.

Dornbusch, R., and Werner, A. (1994) "Mexico: Stabilization, Reform, and No Growth." Brookings Papers on Economic Activity (1): 253-97.

Dowd, K. (1993) "European Monetary Reform: The Pitfalls of Central Planning." Cato Institute Foreign Policy Briefing No. 28, 27 December.

Fauntroy, W. E. (1988) "Multilateral Lending and the Dead-End Debtors: The Baker Plan Is Bankrupt." *Wall Street Journal* (18 October): A24.

Federal Reserve System (1988) Transcript of Federal Open Market Committee Conference Call. Washington, D.C., 17 October.

Feldstein, M. (1995) "Global Capital Flows: Too Little, Not Too Much." *The Economist* (24 June): 72-3.

Financial Times Editorial (1995) "Mexico's Vigil of Woe." *Financial Times* (2 June): 12.

Gollas, M. (1985) "The Mexican Economy at the Crossroads." In A. Jorge, J. Salazar-Carrillo, and F. Diaz-Pou (eds.) *External Debt and Development Strategy in Latin America*, 79-86. New York: Pergamon Press.

Gooptu, S. (1993) *Debt Reduction and Development: The Case of Mexico.* Westport, Conn.: Praeger.

Gould, D. M. (1995) "Mexico's Crisis: Looking Back to Assess The Future." *Federal Reserve Bank of Dallas Economic Review* (Second Quarter): 2-12.

Grosse, R. (1992) "Introduction." In R. Grosse (ed.) *Private Sector Solutions to the Latin American Debt Problem.* New Brunswick, N.J.: Transaction Publishers.

Grupo F. B. (1995) *Informe Economico GFB: Evaluacion Mensual y Pronosticos de la Economia Mexicana.* Mexico City: Grupo Financiero Bancomer.

Hauge, J. R. (1995) "Second-Guessing the Rubin Treasury." *The International Economy* (May-June): 48-9.

Holmes, A. R., and Pardee, S. E. (1977) "Treasury and Federal Reserve Foreign Exchange Operations." *Federal Reserve Bulletin* 63 (September): 793-810.

Hoskins, W. L. (1993a) "Rethinking the Framework for Monetary Policy." *Cato Journal* 13 (Fall): 171-90.

Hoskins, W. L. (1993b) "Federal Reserve Independence and Accountability." Paper presented at the semi-annual meeting of the Shadow Open Market Committee, Washington, D.C., 22 February.

Hoskins, L. W., Coons, J. W. (1995) "Mexico: Policy Failure, Moral Hazard, and Market Solutions." *Cato Institute Policy Analysis* No. 243, 10 October.

International Monetary Fund (1995) *International Capital Markets: Developments, Prospects, and Policy Issues.* Washington, D.C.: International Monetary Fund.

Judd, J. P. (1995) "Inflation Goals and Credibility." *Federal Reserve Bank of San Francisco Weekly Letter*, 12 May.

Leach, J. (1995) "Country Going Bankrupt? Call the IMF." *Wall Street Journal* (10 April): A20.

Marichal, C. (1995a) "The Mexican Debt Crisis of 1995: Public Debt as Private Business." Paper presented at the annual meeting of the Western Economic Association. San Diego, 8 July.

Marichal, C. (1995b) *A Century of Debt Crises in Latin America.* Princeton, N.J.: Princeton University Press.

Macmillan, R. (1995) "New Lease of Life for Bondholder Councils." *Financial Times* (15 August): 11.

Meltzer, A. H. (1995a) "End the IMF." Paper presented at the Cato Institute's 13th Annual Monetary Conference, Washington, D.C., 25 May.

Meltzer, A. H. (1995b) "Market Meltdown?" *On the Issues.* Washington, D.C.: American Enterprise Institute, 1995b.

Millman, G. J. (1995) "Barings Collapses; Financial System Bears Up Well." *Wall Street Journal* (28 February): A20.

Oliveri, E. J. (1992) *Latin American Debt and the Politics of International Finance.* West Port, Conn.: Praeger.

Purcell, S. K. (1988) "Mexico: Pressures For Restructuring." In R. Wesson (ed.) *Coping With The Latin American Debt*, 49-71. New York: Praeger.

Rohter, L. (1988) "A U.S. Prop For Mexico." *New York Times* (19 October): A1, A13.

Sachs, J. D. (1988) "The Debt Crisis at a Turning Point." *Challenge* (May-June): 17-26.

Sachs, J. D. (1994) "IMF, Reform Thyself." *Wall Street Journal* (21 July): A14.

Schwartz, A. J. (1995a) "Trial and Error in Devising the Mexican Rescue Plan." Paper presented at the semi-annual meeting of the Shadow Open Market Committee, Washington, D.C., 5 March.

Schwartz, A. J. (1995b) "Declaration." In *Schulz v. New York* 95-CV-0133 CGC DNH.

Sesit, M. R. (1992) "Europe Central Banks Said to Have Lost Up to $6 Billion Trying to Help Currencies." *Wall Street Journal* (1 October): C1.

Shafer, J. R. (1995) "Declaration." In *Schulz v. New York* 95-CV-0133 CGC DNH.

Solis, D. (1995) "Number of Mexicans Stopped at Border with U.S. Rises as the Economy Sinks." *Wall Street Journal* (8 August): A8.

Spiegel, M. (1995) "Rules vs. Discretion in New Zealand Monetary Policy." *Federal Reserve Bank of San Francisco Weekly Letter*, 3 March.

Tammen, M. S. (1990) "The Precarious Nature of Sovereign Lending." *Cato Journal* 10 (Spring-Summer): 239-63.

Todd, W. F. (1991) "A History of International Lending." In G. Kaufman (ed.) *Research in Financial Services: Private and Public Policy*, 201-89. Greenwich, Conn.: JAI Press.

Todd, W. F. (1992) "Disorderly Markets: The Law, History, and Economics of the Exchange Stabilization Fund and U.S. Foreign Exchange Market Intervention." In G. Kaufman (ed.) *Research in Financial Services: Private and Public Policy*, 111-79. Greenwich, Conn.: JAI Press.

Todd, W. F. (1995a) "Dollar Drain." *The Nation* (10 July): 52.

Todd, W. F. (1995b) "Overview of the Fourth (Federal) Claim." In *Schulz v. New York* 95-CV-0133 CGC DNH.

Todd, W. F. (1995c) Letter to the Honorable Marcy Kaptur, U.S. House of Representatives, 12 May.

Todd, W. F. (1995d) "Bailing Out the Creditor Class." *The Nation* (13 February): 193-4.

Torres, C. (1995a) "Mexico Overhauls Banks Amid Turmoil." *Wall Street Journal* (6 March): A10.

Torres, C. (1995b) "Mexico, Banks in U.S. Hit Snag Over Credit Line." *Wall Street Journal* (23 March): A10.

U.S. Treasury (1995) "U.S.-Mexico Framework Agreement For Mexican Economic Stabilization." Washington, D.C.: U.S. Department of the Treasury, February 21.

Welch, J. H., and Gruben, W. C. (1993) "A Brief Modern History of the Mexican Financial System." *Federal Reserve Bank of Dallas Financial Industry Studies* (October): 1-10.

Wilson, A. (1995) "The Exchange Stabilization Fund." *CRS Report for Congress* No. 95-262 E. Washington, D.C.: Congressional Research Service, 9 February.

Zuniga, J. A., and Amador, R. G. (1995a) "En diciembre, gran negocio con Tesobonos." *La Jornda* (Mexico), 7 February.

Zuniga, J. A., and Amador, R. G. (1995b) "Llego la deuda publica a 147 mil 300 mdd." *La Jornda* (Mexico), 27 June.

Zedillo, E. (1995) "Message to the Honorable Congress of the Union from the President of Mexico, Ernesto Zedillo Ponce de León, at the Presentation of His First State of the Nation Report," 1 September.

Part III:
Proposals for
Monetary Reform

CHAPTER 11

Central Banks: Independence, Mandates, and Accountability

John W. Crow[1]

W E ALL OPERATE IN ECONOMIES where money and monetary exchange is a vital component. So how money is managed is everywhere a lively and important subject. And very appropriately, the subject gathers interest and concern well beyond the cares of central banks—even though they have of course very relevant experience to bring to bear.

In recent years, such interest and concern has been apparent in many parts of the world. In particular, exactly what the role of the central bank, which is by definition the statutory creator of national money, should be in regard to how the nation's money is actually managed has been a subject of debate and reappraisal.

---

1 The author is a former Governor of the Bank of Canada and former Chairman of the Central Bank Governors of the Group of Ten.

Change is very evident in Europe, as economic structures to help the process of European union are developed. There, on the monetary front, the strong record of the Bundesbank has been the central point of reference. But the process has been far from limited to Europe and the particular institutional concerns of European union. It is evident in the Antipodes and of course in the Americas. Clear central banking change has taken place in a number of countries in Latin America. North of Mexico there has been a fair amount of discussion, but no significant shift. That is, of course, not the same as saying that everyone has been satisfied that the structures of monetary management in Canada or the United States are not also capable of improvement.

Now admittedly, the political environment and immediate motivation for reexamination and change may vary quite a bit across regions and across countries. However, the underlying economic argument for change, or at least for reappraisal in this area of central bank independence, mandate, and accountability, is essentially everywhere the same. And indeed, I plan to be quite general. I will focus mainly on the economics of the matter, without, I trust, having to forget that the territory is one that belongs squarely in the camp of political economy.

In reviewing the issues, I shall begin by suggesting how the various concepts tossed around in this area are most sensibly ordered. A number of ideas are important, but some ideas definitely come first. After that broad exercise, I shall look particularly at the relationship between what central banks should do and how they should be set up to do it from the viewpoint of the open economy.

This is only being realistic. All our economies are open and are becoming increasingly exposed internationally. And while the general question of exchange rates and exchange rate regimes can well be a subject all in itself, this matter has such intimate links to what central banks might do in the real world that I cannot afford to ignore it.

The meaning of independence

From the title of my chapter, one would readily infer that the main issue was the matter of central bank independence. Indeed, if there is one term that has become associated with this general territory of central bank polity, it is "independence"—the wisdom of it for the central bank, or how the central bank should be given it.

Certainly, "central bank independence" has through custom and repetition become a useful way of identifying the kind of terrain to be covered. But if not put carefully in its context, the term can prove an obstacle to understanding what is really involved for monetary policy, and in particular for the central bank.

As the rest of my title—"mandates and accountability"—is meant to suggest, it is important to move behind the essentially political concept of independence. In particular, it is important to address what it is that would constitute an appropriate mandate, or purpose, for a central bank. To put it another way, I want to approach these matters by first posing the question: Independence (or "autonomy" if one finds that term less jarring) for what? The answer is to be found not in politics but in economics.

In the first place, it is now more widely accepted that inflation, rather than being part of the package for a good economic outcome, as used to be commonly believed, actually is a hindrance. It does not create jobs, not in the end. And by eroding the monetary underpinnings of economic exchange it can actually inhibit job creation. Both economic theory and economic experience have shown why and how this is so. Essentially, this demonstration involved the discrediting and demise of the view that there is a permanent tradeoff between inflation and unemployment—that is, that more inflation lowers unemployment and generates more jobs.

An additional development that reinforces the case for improving confidence in the future value of a nation's money has been the shift in so many countries to a more decentralized, market-based, economy. Such a shift means that the role of market finance and of investors' and savers' expectations become progressively more significant. There is less reliance on command, more reliance on price signals and incentives. Expectations and price signals obviously work better in a climate of monetary stability. So does the tax system, by the way, if it is broad economic welfare we are concerned with as opposed to exploiting the inflation tax.

Now, considerations of this nature certainly suggest why national governments will, in the national interest, likely wish to follow less inflationary policies than used to seem acceptable. But this is only part of the answer to my question. It does not in itself show why a particular policy role in safeguarding the national currency should be entrusted to the central bank. As I already noted, the central bank is by definition the institution through which national money is ultimately created, but it does not directly follow that this institution should also decide how much money should be created. In fact, it does not even follow that there should be a separate central bank at all—as opposed, for example, to a government department for primary liquidity creation. The other part of the answer also stems from economic experience. It derives from the fact that while governments may wish in principle to engage in sufficient monetary restraint to deliver a noninflationary outcome, in practice they tend to compromise that principle under the pressure of other objectives that are likely shorter run in nature.

However, the problem with inflationary surprises, whatever their short-run attractions—a good case in point is the political business cycle, or taxation through inflation—is that people are bound to learn, or fear, that they are coming. The result then, to be very practical about it, is a trend of higher interest rates than the country need experience—higher in real terms (accounting for risk premia) as well as in nominal terms. This of course is damaging to growth. So something needs to be done about the monetary policy decision making process also.

The answer to this consistency, or credibility, problem is to establish a policy framework where the need to generate confidence in the future value of money is given explicit importance. That framework, to be robust, involves political precommitment. It involves ensuring that the institution statutorily charged with the creation of the nation's money be given the mandate and the tools to limit such money creation to a rhythm consistent with maintaining confidence in money's future value.

This is the essence of what is meant in institutional terms by monetary or price stability. And that is what I think must be behind the idea of an "independent" central bank.

I might add, and contrary to what often seems to be assumed, that such a mandate does not rule out monetary actions that help stabilize economic activity in the near term. What such a mandate does do is help ensure that such actions respect the longer term objective of maintaining trust in money. And this also is fundamentally stabilizing. Nor, and for similar reasons, does it stand in the way of the contributions the central bank can make to the stability of the domestic financial system through its lending of last resort.

Let me also add very briefly, in case it does not go without saying, that central bank independence does presuppose sound domestic fiscal management. To be very direct, the central bank cannot be viewed as creator of finance for government. To be sure, the bank will acquire government debt. But it will only buy such debt as required to fulfil its basic monetary responsibilities for the economy as a whole. Now let me turn to the matter of the central bank's accountability.

The question of accountability

A clear mandate is a vital requirement for proper accountability—whether generally at the bar of public opinion, or specifically before the political authorities. From my experience, a lot of the discussion on central bank accountability that takes place gives inadequate attention to this point—the need for a mandate for the central bank that is clear, and which it can achieve. Rather, the discussion often tends to focus one rung down—on the specific accountability mechanisms that might be used. These would be, for example, how and to which bodies central banks should report for monetary policy actions, and in which way the executive or the legislature might intervene in the monetary policy process. Such mechanisms need careful examination of course. But even more important—indeed the essential starting point for proper accountability—is the need to think hard about and to set out what it is that the central bank is supposed to be answerable for. What is needed is a monetary policy mandate that is clear and rooted in what monetary policy can achieve with the tools at its disposal. Without this, with the best will in the world it is difficult to see how the accountability mechanism can be truly effective.

In Canada, the central bank and the Government are required to consult regularly on monetary policy. This means at least no surprises. And in the event of serious disagreement over the policy, the legislation provides that a directive on monetary policy can given to the Bank of Canada by the Government. Such a directive has never been issued. Still, this provision has been seen, quite understandably, as helping to clarify the accountability structure for the Bank. Furthermore, since the directive has to be made public, it adds valuable transparency that in a sense secures the Government's accountability in this particular regard as well as the Bank of Canada's.

All the same, in Canada the central bank's monetary policy mandate, contained in the preamble to its statutes, is demonstrably less than clear. Therefore, in the absence of a clear mandate, this directive provision might be seen more as giving the government the power of override rather than as being an instrument of accountability in the fuller, and better, sense of the term.

One potential area of economic override, perhaps in all countries, would be in relation to major shocks hitting the economy. I am thinking in particular of major shocks to supply and to prices through drastic economic changes—in the supply of energy, or through natural disasters, for example. One would trust, however, that a better formula could be found for dealing with such rare events than dropping the monetary stability framework itself.

It is of course possible, as in New Zealand, to create formal mechanisms for dealing with contingencies of this nature. But what needs to be stressed here is that a path back to monetary stability really must be seen as integral to the adjustment. Indeed, it is worth underlining that in the case of the Reserve Bank of New Zealand, and, I might add, in the case of the Bank of Mexico under the recent legislation providing it with autonomy, the law itself spells out that achieving price stability is indeed the institution's primary monetary policy objective. In other words, this objective, or monetary stability contribution, does not change unless the basic law governing the central bank is changed.

Thus far, I have sketched out some important features for a robust and constructive monetary policy role for a central bank. This sketch has highlighted the desirability of a central bank with a clear responsibility, and therefore powers, for safeguarding the purchasing value of the national currency—thereby making a monetary contribution to good national economic performance overall.

I could now perhaps contend that there is little to add at this broad level and possibly embark on some more detailed examination of particular instances. If, for example, the discussion were being limited to the situation for the United States, there would be a lot of sense in going in this direction. For instance, one could discuss the adequacy of the Federal Reserve's mandate in terms of what monetary policy can really be expected to achieve and the extent to which it provides a basis for accountability. One could also review the particular accountability mechanisms that apply to the Federal Reserve, especially via the U.S. Congress, for example. Attention could also be given to the role played by the regional reserve banks in the whole constellation of policy independence, accountability, and political legitimacy.

However, for virtually all other countries, certainly all other countries in the Americas, this would leave out a broad consideration that logically precedes any review of particular central banking institutional arrangements. That consideration is the matter of the exchange rate regime.

Central bank independence and the exchange rate regime

The United States is a true exception in the matter of regime choices for exchange rates. It is an exception because of its economic size and the correspondingly dominant international role of the U.S. dollar. This means that aside from really exceptional situations (such as those in 1971 surrounding the collapse of the gold exchange standard and the subsequent, and short-lived, Smithsonian Agreement on exchange rates; and again, perhaps, those surrounding the Plaza Agreement of 1985), the United States does not have the same kinds of possibilities as are in principle available to others in deciding on an exchange rate relationship. In particular, the United States never really faces the classic polar choice of whether to peg or to float. One simple reason is that there is no other currency (or basket of currencies even) it could realistically fix to.

But for other countries of course, the question of the exchange rate relationship is a real-world decision point with real-world implications for monetary arrangements. It is therefore also a very important matter in regard to what the relevant central bank should be expected to do.

While I have thought quite a bit about exchange rate regimes, particularly in the context of Canadian choices, I will focus here on the immediate matter at hand—the particular role of central banks in relation to the exchange rate regime.

Clearly, arrangements such as common currencies, monetary unions, currency boards even, rule out a lot of what I have been discussing—except, perhaps, as filtered through U.S. monetary policy choices. And no doubt such arrangements, centring on the U.S. dollar and therefore on U.S. monetary policy, might have a lot to commend them if the realistic alternative for the national partner concerned is a poor performance for its money when managed domestically.

Let me be clear, however, that I do not take it at all for granted that the common currency, or monetary union, route is the one that is in the cards. I would tend to agree with anyone who argues that merely deciding to fix the exchange rate without proceeding to a stronger form of link is likely not to be enough—or even, to use Sir Alan Walters' famous phrase, that such a decision will be "half-baked." But I believe there are persuasive reasons why the fixed exchange rate loaf does not need to be put in the oven in the first place.

The reason I suggest that this route cannot at all be taken for granted is precisely because of the role that well-conceived national monetary policies, that is, with independent central banks along the lines I have sketched earlier, can play. They not only help sustain good domestic economic performance through the monetary route. They also help to promote a solid financial and economic relationship across trading partners—themselves in distinctive real economic circumstances.

The basic economic point in this regard is a non-monetary one. It is that the differences among many economies are large in regard to structure, and therefore in regard to how their economies are behaving at any given time. Therefore, variation in real exchange rates provides a valuable margin of adjustment and stabilization. Clearly, if this is accepted as a valid approach then, realistically, nominal exchange rates can be expected to move around. And this movement will be part of the mechanism through which real exchange rates adjust in an economically appropriate manner.

What this means for domestic monetary policy is that the reality of the open economy reinforces the arguments made earlier from a purely domestic viewpoint. The independent central bank provides the domestic nominal anchor—domestic monetary stability. In so doing it generates a stable monetary platform for nominal and real exchange rate movements that can be broadly supportive of coherent economic adjustments. Conversely, of course, if monetary policy does not provide a solid domestic anchor, the adverse effects from domestic financial uncertainty are more likely to make the exchange rate an additional source of instability. National monetary policy, and the exchange rate that goes with it, will then hardly do anything that is useful for the national economy as a whole.

This point should be taken further still. Such a central bank, acting in the way suggested, and in a way that is beginning to be realized around the world, would be promoting a profoundly consistent basis for international economic adjustment. Furthermore, its actions would promote stability of the more lasting kind in exchange rates. This is because these actions would be based on national monetary policies rooted in sound principles that are the same for each currency.

Conclusion

By way of conclusion, let me reemphasize that any discussion about central bank independence should be viewed as a discussion about what it takes to generate a good monetary policy—one that is purposeful and accountable. Such a policy is public good. Moreover, it not only pays off within national borders. It also provides a robust framework for good monetary linkages across such borders.

CHAPTER 12

Real versus Pseudo Free Trade in Banking: A Critique of NAFTA's Financial Services Provisions

George Selgin[1]

THE NORTH AMERICAN FREE TRADE AGREEMENT (NAFTA) has been heralded as a breakthrough for free trade generally and for free trade in financial services in particular. It succeeds in substantially reducing barriers to inter-American trade in banking, especially by allowing U.S. and Canadian banks to enter Mexico for the first time in

1   The author is Associate Professor of Economics at the University of Georgia.
    My thanks to George Benston, Don Boudreaux, William Gruben, Ed Kane,
    George Kaufman, Jim Michaels, Gerald P. O'Driscoll, Jr., and Joe Sinkey,
    who were kind enough to help me but who bear no responsibility at all for
    much of what I have ended up writing.

more than half a century and by exempting American and Mexican investors from limits on foreign ownership of Canadian banks.[2]

Nevertheless, NAFTA stops well short of introducing real free trade in banking. Contrary to what some (e.g., Gunther and Moore 1992: 2; Gruben and Welch 1993: 5-8) have claimed, this is not just because U.S. and Canadian firms will continue to face capital-based barriers to entry into the Mexican market until and to some extent even beyond the year 2000.[3] The real shortcomings of NAFTA as a basis for free trade in banking have to do, not so much with such capital-based barriers to trade in banking, but with other barriers left entirely untouched by NAFTA. These barriers consist of (1) the requirement that U.S. banks enter the Mexican and Canadian markets by establishing subsidiaries, instead of branches; and (2) the principle of "national treatment," which seeks to impose the same activity, geographic, and prudential restrictions on Mexican and Canadian bank operations in the U.S. as are presently imposed on operations of U.S. banks at home.

International trade in banking services limiting foreign entry to subsidiaries or subjecting foreign banks to "national treatment" is pseudo, not real, free trade in banking. As such, it denies North American consumers some of the most important potential benefits to be achieved from real free trade. The policy of national treatment in particular precludes competition among national regulatory authorities, allowing inefficient and burdensome regulations to persist. Real free trade in banking, unlike NAFTA's pseudo free trade regime, would promote a more rapid erosion of inefficient and burdensome regula-

---

2   Although U.S. banks have been prevented from entering Mexico for many decades, Citibank has long had a Mexican branch, established there in 1929 and grandfathered when foreign entry barriers were erected during the 1940s.

3   Prior to the year 2000, NAFTA allows U.S. investors to own no more than 8 percent of total Mexican bank capital. The limit increases to 15 percent between 2000 and 2015, and to 25 percent thereafter. Gruben, Welch, and Gunther (1993: 17-18) discuss other minimum and maximum capital requirements applicable to *individual* foreign banks wishing to enter Mexico. These requirements, unlike limitations on aggregate foreign bank capital, were unaffected by NAFTA and remain in effect indefinitely.

tions, by threatening obstructive national regulators with a likely loss of market share to their relatively less heavy-handed foreign counterparts.

Investor choice

A bank may offer its services to a foreign market in several ways. It may invite foreigners to partake of its "cross-border" services, without actually establishing any physical presence in the foreign market; or it may seek to physically enter the foreign market, either by establishing an independent foreign subsidiary or by setting-up a foreign branch office (Key and Scott 1992: 37).[4] Article 1404 of NAFTA eases restrictions on North American cross-border trade in financial services, while Articles 1403 and 1405 remove barriers to the establishment of foreign-bank subsidiaries. However, NAFTA leaves in place barriers to the establishment of foreign bank branches, by allowing U.S. banks to enter the Canadian and Mexican markets through subsidiaries only. NAFTA does this despite its stated endorsement of "investor choice"—the principle that any North American investor "should be permitted to establish a financial institution [anywhere in North America] in the juridical form chosen by such investor" (NAFTA 14-2).

By failing to secure acceptance by Mexico and Canada of the principle of investor choice, NAFTA leaves in place substantial barriers to U.S. financial firm entry into the Mexican and Canadian financial markets: it is generally much more costly for a firm to operate in a foreign country through an independent subsidiary than through a branch. A branch can do without the extra administrative, legal, and agency costs involved in operating an independent subsidiary; and by drawing on the consolidated capital and credit standing of its parent firm, a branch can acquire funds in wholesale and interbank markets on better terms and in larger amounts than any subsidiary owned by the same parent (Key and Scott 1992: 49). Branches can also obtain liquid funds at

---

4   Foreign banks may offer cross-border services through representative offices or agencies, which do give them some physical presence in a foreign country but which do not take deposits. (Agencies, unlike representative offices, may make loans and offer other services apart from accepting deposits.)

minimal cost directly from their parent firms. Such considerations account for banks' marked historical preference for having branches rather than subsidiaries in foreign markets: as of June 1992, branches accounted for 64 percent of the foreign assets of U.S. banks, and branches or agencies accounted for 82 percent of the U.S. assets of foreign banks (Schwab and Tucker 1993: 7). By allowing U.S. banks to enter Mexico and Canada through independent subsidiaries only, NAFTA forces them to pay the equivalent of a tariff to export their services to those countries. Some bankers fear that this tariff will altogether preclude U.S. bank participation in Mexico's retail banking market (Sczudlo 1993: 32).

National treatment

It would be wrong, however, to view Mexican and Canadian policies as posing the main barriers to genuine North American free trade in banking. Although U.S. authorities have resisted political pressure to follow Mexico and Canada by disallowing foreign bank branches altogether,[5] NAFTA nonetheless retains substantial barriers in the way of Mexican and Canadian entry into the U.S. financial services market. It does this by subjecting Mexican and Canadian bank branches and subsidiaries alike to "national treatment."

In theory, "national treatment" requires each North American nation to accord financial institutions from other North American nations "treatment no less favourable than that it accords to its own financial institutions" (NAFTA 14-3). In practice, however, government authorities interpret "national treatment" to mean that they should accord foreign institutions treatment that is also no *more* favourable than that accorded to domestic institutions. Thus, since the passage of the International Banking Act in 1978, U.S. branches of foreign banks have been

---

5 A few years ago the Treasury proposed that all foreign banking in the United States be conducted through subsidiaries rather than branches. A joint Treasury-Federal Reserve study undertaken as part of the 1991 Foreign Bank Supervision Enhancement Act and completed at the end of 1993 fortunately rejected the idea in favour of the established U.S. policy allowing investor choice.

subject to most of the same regulatory restrictions applied to U.S. banks: new foreign entrants were required by the act to select a single "home state"—usually New York or (for Japanese banks) California—as the headquarters of their main branch or subsidiary, and were prohibited from branching outside that state.[6] The act also imposed domestic reserve requirements on branches of foreign banks having worldwide assets in excess of $1 billion while prohibiting all foreign banks from owning security-trading affiliates in the U.S.[7] These restrictions were further strengthened in December 1991, when the Foreign Bank Supervision Enhancement Act came into effect, requiring Federal Reserve approval for any foreign bank branch in addition to approval by some (state or national) chartering authority. The same legislation also prohibits foreign bank branches (but not subsidiaries) established since December 1991 from maintaining retail deposits under $100,000, under the pretence of limiting foreign-bank participation in the U.S. deposit insurance scheme (Misback 1993: 4). The overall effect of these laws is to subject foreign banks to the full force of regulatory restrictions imposed on domestic operations of U.S. banks, notwithstanding the ability of foreign banks to operate in the United States through branches rather than subsidiaries.

NAFTA does not substantially alter these established conditions for foreign bank entry into the United States. (The prior U.S.-Canada trade agreement did, however, allow both Canadian and U.S. banks operating

---

6 This requirement amounted to an extension of the McFadden and Bank Holding Company Acts to state-chartered foreign bank branches. Before passage of the International Banking Act, there was no legal barrier to a foreign bank's setting-up branch offices in several states—something nationally chartered U.S. banks could not do. The International Banking Act's grandfathering of existing multistate branches of foreign banks accounts for several foreign bank's having a multistate presence today. As of December 1993 "grandfathered" facilities accounted for more than half of all foreign bank branches and subsidiaries operating in the U.S.

7 As of December 1993, 75 out of 362 U.S. branches of foreign banks were exempt from Federal Reserve requirements. So-called International Banking Facilities, whether U.S. or foreign-owned, are also exempt from reserve requirements but are not allowed to have demand deposits.

Table 1: North American Banking Regulations			
Regulation	**United States**	**Canada**	**Mexico**
Reserve requirements	Yes	No	No
Capital requirements	Yes[1]	Yes[1]	Yes[1]
Branching restrictions	Yes	No	No
Deposit insurance	Yes	Yes[3]	No
Restrictions on securities underwriting and brokerage	No[4]	No[4]	No

[1]The United States and Canada have both adopted the BIS capital adequacy standards. Mexico plans to enforce minimum capital standards equal to or exceeding the Basel recommendations.
[2]Branching restrictions vary by state.
[3]United States: 100% of transactions deposits $\leq$ US$100,000; Canada: 60% of transactions deposits $\leq$ CA$60,000.
[4]Wholly owned subsidiaries of Canadian and U.S. banks are allowed to deal in non-government securities.

in the United States to underwrite Canadian government securities to the same extent as previous laws allowed them to underwrite U.S. government securities.[8]) Moreover, despite any appearance of symmetry, NAFTA's "national treatment" policy imposes a much greater burden on Mexican and Canadian banks seeking to enter the U.S. market than it imposes on U.S. banks seeking entry into Mexico or Canada. The reason has to do with the less restrictive nature of banking regulations in Mexico and (to a lesser extent) in Canada compared to U.S. regulations: While U.S. banks must hold non-interest-bearing re-

---

8   NAFTA also promises to include Canadian banks in any future relaxation of the Glass-Steagall Act, instead of continuing to make them subject to separate securities-underwriting restrictions contained in the International Banking Act.

serves equal to at least 10 percent of their transactions deposits, and while they continue to face legislative restrictions on branching and product diversification, both Mexican and Canadian banks are now completely unhindered by reserve requirements or barriers to nation-wide branching. Mexican banks enjoy as well freedom to offer a broad range of financial services to their clients, including direct underwriting and brokerage services and insurance (table 1).

Under NAFTA's national-treatment regime, U.S. banks entering the Mexican or Canadian markets through subsidiaries enjoy all of the regulatory advantages presently enjoyed by Mexican and Canadian banks in their home markets, but not available to U.S. banks at home. Indeed, *a U.S. bank might be better able to compete in either Mexico or Canada through a host-regulated subsidiary than it could through a host- or home-regulated branch* (Harrington 1992: 142).[9] In contrast, Mexican and Canadian banks attempting to enter the U.S. market must confront a host of burdensome and unfamiliar legal restrictions, part of whose aim has been precisely to protect the market shares of established U.S. financial firms. There is no reason to think, for example, that regulations that for decades have protected small Texas banks from competition from, say, New York will be any less effective in protecting the same banks from competition from Mexico.[10]

The refusal of Mexico and Canada to allow U.S. banks to branch into their markets can, in fact, be viewed as a largely symbolic protest against U.S. entry barriers implicit in NAFTA's "national treatment" policy. As long as domestic U.S. banking regulations continue to be substantially more restrictive than Mexican or Canadian regulations, the Mexican and Canadian governments can legitimately argue that

---

9   In practice, foreign bank branches may be subject to either host- or home-country regulations, whereas foreign-bank subsidiaries, being independent firms, are practically always subject to host-country regulations.

10   Contrary to one reader's suggestion, the fact that the United States has so many banks is not so much a reflection of freedom of entry as one of regulations on branching. These regulations actually restrict entry into, and hence limit the contestability of, particular U.S. banking markets.

their banks gain less by being permitted to branch into the U.S. market than U.S. banks gain by being allowed to establish subsidiaries in Mexico and Canada. Such a protest seems implicit in section 3 of NAFTA's Article 1403, which states that Mexico and Canada will reconsider allowing U.S. banks "to choose the juridical form" of their Mexican and Canadian operations (i.e., to enter those markets through branches instead of subsidiaries) "at such time as the United States permits [Mexican and Canadian banks] located in its territory to expand...into substantially all of the United States Market."[11]

The logical alternative to NAFTA's concept of "national treatment" is a policy subjecting foreign bank branches to home- rather than host-country regulations. Although bypassed by NAFTA, this alternative is not merely hypothetical: it has recently been embraced by New Zealand and also by the European Community through the latter's Second Banking Co-Ordination Directive of 1989, which came into force at the start of 1993.[12] The Directive's "single banking license" requires every EC nation to grant free entry to branches of banks headquartered in any EC nation, while its "mutual recognition" policy in turn makes foreign bank branches subject to home- rather than host-country regulation and supervision (Bank of England 1993; Swary and Topf 1992: 430-45).

The EC's "mutual recognition" approach is admittedly far from being absolute. For one thing, the European law contains a serious loophole, allowing national regulatory authorities to deny entry to particular foreign banks on ill-defined grounds of management "unsuitability." The mutual recognition policy is also supplemented by a set of

---

11 The article in question also makes reconsideration of the branching question contingent upon relaxation of U.S. laws separating banking and insurance.

The circumstances leading to the refusal of Mexico and Canada to allow entry to U.S. bank branches point to the futility and hypocrisy of the so-called "Fair Trade in Financial Services" bill (HR 3248; S 1527), which would allow the Treasury to "retaliate" against countries, including Mexico and Canada, that prohibit foreign bank branches by preventing their banks from expanding in the U.S.

12 Non-EC members of the European Free Trade Association, with the exception of Switzerland, became parties to the Directive as of May 1992.

"minimal regulatory requirements" imposed on all participants. These include the requirement (based upon the Basel Capital Accord of 1987) that participating financial institutions have capital equal to at least 8 percent of their risk-weighted assets or ECU5 million—whichever is greater. A proposal presently being debated would also require all participating nations to provide no less than 90 percent insurance for deposits of ECU20,000 and under. Finally (and reasonably) the "mutual recognition" approach leaves host-country authorities responsible for matters having to do with "the conduct of a firm's business with customers" (Bank of England 1993: 93), including the prosecution of fraud, money laundering, and other violations of national laws not strictly related to financial-market policy. Loopholes and regulations notwithstanding, the EC approach embodies a radically different understanding of the meaning of "free trade in banking" than that implicit in NAFTA.

Of wine, bottles, and banks

Real, as opposed to pseudo, free trade in banking requires something like the EC policy of mutual recognition and not the North American alternative of national treatment. It requires, in other words, that foreign firms be allowed to establish home-regulated branches as well as or instead of host-regulated branches or subsidiaries in domestic markets. The failure of many commentators to appreciate this fact seems to be due in part to difficulties encountered in applying the concept of "free trade" to services, including banking services, as opposed to physical goods.

An analogy may help us to get around this conceptual road-block. Suppose that, instead of talking about free trade in banking services, we switch to the more appetizing subject of free trade in wine. Consider three alternative ways in which the United States might allow its citizens to have access to French wine. One option would be to let U.S. citizens enjoy French wine in France only: French wine in French bottles abroad. A second would be to allow French wineries to establish subsidiaries in the U.S., which would be required to produce wine in strict accordance with U.S. winemaking practices, including government regulations imposed on domestic winemakers: U.S.-type wine in French bottles. A third option would be to allow French winemakers to market real French wine, produced according to French winemaking practices and regulations, within the United States: French wine in French bottles at home.

You do not have to be a wine connoisseur to realize that the third option—French wine in French bottles at home—must be part of any genuine "free trade in wine" policy: merely permitting U.S. citizens to enjoy French wine in France is better than preventing them from having it at all, but it is not free trade in wine, because French wine available in France only is not the same product (in the eyes of U.S. consumers) as French wine available at home. Likewise, allowing French firms to produce wine in the United States according to U.S. rules and regulations is not free trade in wine, because wine made by Frenchmen (or by Americans employed by a French-owned company) according to U.S. rules and regulations may be quite different from real French wine. Indeed, it is likely to bear a closer resemblance to wine produced in the United States by U.S.-owned firms.

Whether U.S. consumers suffer much from a policy allowing French winemakers to enter the U.S. market only through host-regulated subsidiaries will depend, of course, on just how inferior U.S. winemaking conditions—including regulations—are to winemaking conditions in France. If U.S. winemaking conditions are already favourable, e.g., if the climate and soil are appropriate and domestic winemakers are not hindered by wrongheaded regulations, then consumers presumably will not suffer much in having to go abroad to enjoy genuine French wine. On the other hand, if U.S. winemaking conditions are poor, either for natural reasons or because of wrongheaded regulations ("all wine must be made from white grapes and must have an alcohol content not exceeding 5 percent"), U.S. consumers could suffer a great deal.

In fact, (though the French will disagree) the standing of U.S. winemaking is not obviously beneath that of winemaking in France, thanks at least in part to the U.S. government's benign neglect of the U.S. winemaking industry. U.S. consumers might not, therefore, suffer a great deal were the import of genuine French wines (as opposed to the manufacture of U.S.-style wine by Frenchmen) prohibited. Nevertheless, no one would propose such a policy. Nor would anyone be fooled by official references to the policy as one embodying the principle of "free trade in wine."

Now back to banking. If foreign-banks are unable to establish a physical presence in some banking system, or if they are subject to national treatment in that system either by being required to operate as subsidiaries or by having even their branches subject to host-country regulations, domestic consumers may be denied access to higher-quality banking services available from foreign banks in the banks' home countries. In particular, consumers unwilling or unable to rely on "cross-border" banking services—retail bank customers especially—are forced to "consume" bank services adulterated by domestic bank regulations, regardless of the merits of those regulations. In contrast, if foreign banks can establish branch offices subject only to home-country regulations, consumers will enjoy a genuine choice between foreign- and domestic-style bank services and regulations.[13]

Because it subjects foreign banks to host-country regulations, NAFTA does not achieve real free trade in banking. At best it achieves a form of pseudo free trade, repackaging old domestic bank services and regulations in new foreign-bank bottles.

Such pseudo free trade in banking cannot be expected to produce gains from inter-American trade equal to what real free trade could achieve. If, instead of imposing domestic regulations on foreign banks, NAFTA allowed North American banks to branch across national boundaries while being subject to home-regulations only, U.S. banks might find entry into the Mexican and Canadian markets less costly. More likely, Canadian and Mexican banks could capture a much more substantial share of the market for U.S. loans and deposits, including loans and deposits made both to U.S. residents and to Canadian and Mexican businessmen engaged in U.S. trade. The extent of U.S.-Canada bilateral trade and the impressive size and credit standing of many Canadian banks make the U.S. market a natural target for Canadian bank expansion (Harrington 1992: 139).[14] Were genuine free trade in

---

13 Compare Neven (1990), who equates free movement of capital, i.e., freedom of cross-border trade in banking services, with "classical" free trade in banking.

14 Foreign banking is by-and-large an undertaking of large banks only. In 1990,

banking allowed, Canadian banks would be better able to "follow their customers" into various regions of the United States because they could do so without having to purchase existing U.S. banks at high prices and without being constrained by nationwide branching restrictions and statutory reserve requirements imposed by the International Banking Act (ibid.: 149; see also Gordon 1994; Saumier 1988: 328-9; and Douglas and Drake 1988: 335-6).[15] Mexican banks might also make inroads into the U.S. market, given their lack of reserve requirements and unlimited freedom to branch as well as to sell brokerage and insurance services, which could give them important advantages over U.S. banks (Gunther and Moore 1992: 3).[16] The gains from trade realized by both Canadian and Mexican banks would be gains to their U.S. customers as well, because customers who switch banks do so only in order to enjoy

---

four large holding companies owned half of all overseas assets of U.S. banks, and ten holding companies owned 80 percent of all U.S. overseas banking assets (Kaufman forthcoming, p. 18).

15 Canada recently eliminated reserve requirements on Canadian-resident demand deposits. Previous Canadian law did not require Canadian banks to hold any fixed percentage of reserves on deposits of non-Canadian residents (Swary and Topf 1992: 247). Because all Canadian banks presently having U.S. operations have assets in excess of US$1 billion, none of them is exempt from U.S. reserve requirements.

16 At present Canadian banks operate several dozen U.S. subsidiaries and branches, many of which were grandfathered upon passage of the International Banking Act. Although this number might seem substantial, given the small number of Canadian banks, it actually reflects very limited involvement in the U.S. retail market, as is seen by considering the extensive branch networks maintained by most Canadian banks in Canada. Mexican participation in U.S. banking is limited to a single bank subsidiary: the Grossmont Bank in San Diego, owned by Bancomer.

It is of course true that freedom from U.S. regulations might not offer any substantial competitive advantage to Canadian and Mexican banks operating in the U.S. Some argue, for example, that universal banking as practised by Mexican banks is no longer as efficient as specialized banking of the sort regulations have promoted in the United States. But this is no argument against real free trade in banking. On the contrary: only a policy of real free trade in banking can reveal which banking arrangements are truly efficient.

superior products. Present NAFTA arrangements, however, may prevent U.S. citizens from enjoying some potential gains from trade. In so doing they also inadvertently limit U.S. bank participation in the European Community, by precluding such reciprocal (home-country) treatment of European banks as is required by European Community authorities as a condition for involvement in their scheme.

Recent assessments of NAFTA's financial services provisions (e.g. Gunther and Moore 1992; Gruben and Welch 1993; Sczudlo 1993) appear to overlook the agreement's failure to realize potential gains to U.S. consumers from trade in banking, as if the only gains from trade that mattered were potential gains to U.S. banking firms, measured by opportunities for such firms' foreign expansion. Not surprisingly, given the mercantilist bent of U.S. trade policy, NAFTA is in fact more geared toward aiding U.S. banks by opening foreign markets to them than toward aiding U.S. consumers by opening the U.S. market to foreign banks. Assessments of NAFTA that focus on the goal of expanding the foreign presence of U.S. banks therefore tend to overstate NAFTA's accomplishments while overlooking its most serious shortcomings.

Long-run gains

My discussion so far has considered only short-run potential gains from real free trade in banking services—gains from greater consumer access to foreign-style banking services, assuming unchanging national regulatory regimes. But this is only a small part of the story. There are also likely to be long-run gains from real free trade in banking—gains associated with changes in national regulatory regimes that real free trade in banking tends to sponsor.

Real free trade in banking, unlike the psuedo free trade allowed by NAFTA, gives consumers the right to choose, not only between domestic and foreign bank owners, but between domestic and foreign bank regulatory regimes. In doing so free trade in banking in effect places national regulatory authorities in direct competition with one another for shares of the international (in the present instance, North American) financial services market. As Edward Kane (1987, 1988) has argued at length, regulators imposing overly burdensome regulations on firms falling under their jurisdiction will invite greater penetration of their domestic banking-services markets by foreign bank branches subject to home regulations. On the other hand, regulators offering relatively favourable conditions to firms falling under their jurisdiction will improve the odds of firms they regulate expanding into foreign markets, while encouraging foreign banks to enter through host-regulated subsidiaries (or, if possible, branches) rather than home-regulated branches.

These insights, plus the assumption that a national regulator's own well-being depends on the extent of the banking industry falling under its jurisdiction, lead to the conclusion that relatively heavy-handed regulators operating in a free-trade-in-banking zone will suffer some loss of their regulatory "market share" unless they take steps to make their regulations no more burdensome than those of other national regulators within the zone. In consequence, national regulations throughout the zone will eventually come to resemble the particular national regulations embodying the least "net regulatory burden" when free trade in banking was first implemented. Applied to the European free trade zone, for example, this view suggests that bank regulatory regimes throughout Europe will come to resemble more-and-more the relatively low-burden regimes present at the onset of 1993 in Germany, Luxembourg, the United Kingdom, and the Netherlands (Swary and Topf 1992: 445-6), with Italian, Spanish, and Greek regulatory authorities having to undertake the most extensive deregulations to preserve their regulatory market shares.[17]

---

17 Luxembourg already functions as a kind of safe haven from banking regulations, with foreign banks accounting for 87 percent of all bank assets there. This is only slightly less true of the U.K., 83 percent of the banking assets of which are foreign owned (Kaufman, forthcoming: 20). Our prediction is that these percentages will continue to grow in consequence of the single banking license, unless regulations in other European countries are reduced. By way of contrast with Luxembourg and Britain, only 25 percent of U.S. bank assets are foreign owned, despite New York City's preeminence among world financial centres (Ibid.).

On the other hand, it is rather puzzling that foreign banks have accounted for only a small fraction (4 percent in 1987) of bank assets in Germany, despite that country's relative lack of burdensome regulations and restrictions on foreign entry (Neven 1990: 158-59).

Applied to North America, Kane's model of competition among national regulators suggests that real free trade would eventually lead to a North American regulatory regime more like the present Mexican regime than like the one presently in place in the U.S.—without statutory reserve requirements on banks and without barriers to either product or geographic diversification. Under real free trade, U.S. regulatory authorities would face a continued threat of invasion of the U.S. market by Mexican and also by Canadian banks if they failed to take steps to reduce the regulatory burdens imposed on U.S. banks to levels consistent with burdens implied by Mexican and Canadian regulations. Mexico in particular might then come to play a role for North American banks similar to that played by Delaware for U.S. corporations, by Hartford, Connecticut for insurance companies, and by Liberia for trans-oceanic shipping.[18]

What Kane calls "competitive reregulation" is likely to be the most important consequence of real free trade in banking—a consequence far outweighing in importance the consequences stemming from mere changes in domestic- versus foreign-bank market shares under given national regulatory regimes. Under the right circumstances, competitive reregulation can be relied on to promote an optimal regulatory structure, consisting of private (and perhaps also) government-based regulations, by weeding-out those regulations that fail to enhance the overall efficiency of banking services. NAFTA, however, precludes competitive reregulation and its potential benefits to consumers of banking services by preserving national regulators' territorial monopolies. Its "national treatment" policy amounts to a form of national regulatory protectionism (cf. Kane 1987: 123, 127).

---

18 At present many U.S. banks avoid domestic regulatory restrictions by establishing branches in the less-regulated systems of the United Kingdom, Hong Kong, the Bahamas, and the Cayman Islands (Kaufman, forthcoming: 17). The branches can then offer their "cross-border" services, including some retail services, to U.S. customers. But like French wine available in France only, these services are unlikely to be enjoyed by the mass of U.S. consumers. Under the proposed home-regulation scheme, a U.S. bank could establish a Mexican subsidiary, which could then offer its services directly and conveniently to U.S. consumers through U.S. branches.

Whether NAFTA deserves criticism for this depends, of course, on whether the "right conditions" are in fact present for real free trade to give rise to an optimal North American regulatory regime, or at least to one superior to the regimes left in place under pseudo free trade. The necessary conditions are (1) the absence of substantial regulatory subsidies to domestic or foreign banks and (2) the absence of any significant externalities within the market for banking services.

Subsidies

The net regulatory burden borne by any bank is equal to the gross burden of restrictive regulations minus the value of any regulatory subsidies financed by other banks or by non-bank taxpayers. By offering subsidies to regulated firms under their jurisdiction, regulators can preserve or extend their regulatory market share while preserving inefficient and harmful regulations. Regulatory subsidies thus undermine the tendency of interregulatory competition to eliminate burdensome and inefficient regulatory restrictions (Kane 1987: 112, 132). When resorted to in a free-trade context, such subsidies can be viewed as an instance of what is often termed "unfair" international competition, with domestic regulators expanding their shares in foreign banking markets by using taxpayer- as well as bank-funded subsidies to "dump" inefficient domestic regulations abroad. This tendency is compounded if foreign-country depositors respond rationally by favouring banks subsidized at foreign taxpayers' expense to ones subsidized by means of their own tax payments.[19]

Regulatory subsidies in banking typically take one of three forms: subsidized central bank lending, subsidized deposit guarantees, or

---

19 George Benston (1992: 206) argues in favour of free trade in banking "even when foreign banks are subsidized by their taxpayers, and hence have an advantage over domestic banks. Domestic consumers benefit from these subsidies, much as they benefit from any subsidies paid for by others." The "others" might, however, end up being *us* (meaning U.S. taxpayers), since the subsidies might well be ones going from U.S. taxpayers to U.S. banks abroad. Benston's argument also seems to overlook the harm subsidies in any direction might do in the long-run by short-circuiting the process of competitive reregulation.

subsidized settlement facilities. All three kinds of subsidies might be used to promote the foreign operations of domestic banks and to encourage foreign banks to join domestic regulatory arrangements by entering through host-regulated subsidiaries rather than through home-regulated branches. In Mexico, for example, U.S. bank branches offering deposits insured by the FDIC while also having access to the Federal Reserve's discount window might, other things being equal, have a competitive advantage over rival Mexican banks, which do not have access to any similar discount facilities[20] and whose deposits are uninsured. Under the circumstances, U.S. banks operating in Mexico might attempt to outcompete their Mexican rivals for depositors by holding higher proportions of more lucrative as well as riskier assets, extending their (and their regulators') market shares, despite and in part because of their greater regulatory overhead. The same subsidies, plus access to subsidies that may (despite recent reforms) still be implicit in Fedwire, could be used to encourage Mexican banks to enter the U.S. through host-regulated branches rather than home-regulated subsidiaries.

The most straightforward solution to the problem of regulatory subsidies is simply to eliminate the subsidies altogether, or at least deny them to foreign banks' domestic subsidiaries and to domestic banks' home-regulated foreign branches. For example, U.S. subsidiaries of Mexican and Canadian banks could be prevented from offering and advertising FDIC insurance on any of their deposits, though they might nonetheless be allowed to keep uninsured deposits under $100,000 for anyone willing to have such deposits.[21] (In fairness of course uninsured

---

20 At three times the market rate of interest on short-term Mexican Treasury notes ("cetes"), the rate charged by the Bank of Mexico for overnight loans to banks that have overdrawn their clearing accounts embodies no subsidy at all (Garber and Weisbrod 1992: 37n15).

21 In contrast to this, the International Banking Act requires foreign bank *subsidiaries* to participate in the federal deposit insurance plan, while the Foreign Bank Supervision Enhancement Act of 1991 prohibits new foreign bank *branches* from having any retail deposits of under $100,000. The latter policy is contrary to both the national-treatment and the home-country treatment (free trade) principles. Under real free trade, foreign branches

subsidiaries and foreign bank branches should also not be required to pay any deposit insurance premiums.) Mexican and Canadian bank subsidiaries could also be denied access to Fedwire or to the Federal Reserve's discount window, or could be given discounts only at genuine penalty rates.[22] In turn, restrictions could be placed on transfers of funds to Mexican and Canadian branches of any domestic banks indebted to the Federal Reserve, in the same way that restrictions are presently placed on transfers of funds from banks to their holding companies.[23]

Fortunately, many of these desirable restrictions on regulatory subsidies are already in place in North America. For example, deposits at foreign branches of U.S. banks and Canadian banks are not insured, and Mexico does not have deposit insurance. Mexican banks as a whole also do not benefit from any low-interest central bank loans or discounts. Furthermore, U.S. and Canadian deposit insurance schemes do not involve any overall subsidy to the U.S. or Canadian banking industries, and therefore cannot be said to give U.S. or Canadian banks considered as a whole any advantage over their foreign counterparts. Banks seeking to cross North American borders are therefore unlikely to be enticed by regulatory subsidies into choosing an operating form—host-regulated subsidiary or home-regulated branch—different from what they would have chosen in the absence of any such subsidies. In short, the problem of regulatory subsidies, viewed as something that might pervert the outcome of free trade in banking, is something of a red herring: although in theory subsidies could undermine the process of regulatory competition, in practice they are unlikely to do so.

---

would be excluded from any host-country deposit insurance scheme, but would nonetheless be allowed to accept deposits, including small retail deposits, on the same terms as are applicable in their home countries. The depositors themselves would, of course, bear any risk associated with holding uninsured deposits, as holders of offshore deposits of U.S. banks must do at present.

22 France, for instance, does not let foreign banks participate directly in Sagittaire, its net-settlement system for cross-border payments.

23 Cf. sections 23A and 23B of the Federal Reserve Act, as amended by the Banking Act of 1987.

Externalities

If financial-market transactions involve externalities—that is, if the transactions impose costs on or reward benefits to persons apart from those directly involved in them—then free trade in banking cannot be relied on to preserve desirable financial-market regulations. More specifically, if some of the costs stemming from decisions made by bankers and their clients are being borne by persons other than the bankers and clients themselves, unfettered competitive reregulation is likely to result in inadequate regulations that maximize net *private* benefits from bank-related activities (gross private benefits minus internal costs only) instead of maximizing net *social* benefits (gross private benefits minus internal as well as external costs).

Critics of free trade in banking insist that banking transactions can in fact involve important external costs. Such costs can arise whenever an individual bank is suspected of insolvency or whenever an individual bank fails to meet its net interbank settlement obligations. Either event can lead to so-called contagion effects. The perceived insolvency at one bank that causes its depositors to stage a run on it may cause depositors at other banks to run on them as well, on account of the fear that those banks may also be insolvent. Also, the failure of any one bank to meet its settlement obligations may cause other banks to default on their obligations, because they had depended on the first bank to supply the means needed to pay their own interbank dues. Either way, a "chain reaction" of bank failures can result, placing the banking and payments system as a whole at risk (Baltensperger and Dermine 1990; Key and Scott 1992: 36; Benston 1992: 202; Laub 1991: 22).

This perceived risk of system wide or "systemic" failure has led many theorists and policy makers to reject a policy of real free trade in banking along with its requirement that foreign banks be subject to home-country regulations only. According to these experts, instead of leading to the emergence of an optimal regulatory regime, free trade would support regimes lacking prudential controls needed to check and contain systemic risk. Failures of foreign banks subject to inadequate controls and constraints by their home-country regulators could then pose a threat to the entire host-country banking system even if host-country regulations were themselves adequate. Worse still, international regulatory competition would tend to punish those national regulators who maintained adequate prudential controls while rewarding those who failed to do so (Pyle 1987; Neven 1990: 160). Competitive reregulation would, in the words of former Fed chairman Arthur Burns, end up being mere "competition in laxity."

The desire to avoid competition in laxity is supposed to justify impediments to genuine free trade in banking. These may involve (1) supplementing the principle of home-country regulation with a list of certain "minimal" prudential regulations to be enforced throughout the trade zone, as the European Community has done; or (2) rejecting home-country regulation in favour of host-country regulation, as is done by NAFTA. The latter approach becomes essential if countries within the trade zone are unable to agree on "minimal" necessary prudential regulations. Countries convinced of the need for more strict regulations than ones involved in the banking systems of their trade partners must then insist on national treatment as a way to limit their banking systems' exposure to systemic risks inherent in the less-regulated banking systems of their trading partners (Key and Scott 1992: 51-2; Laub 1991: 27).

"Essential" prudential regulations are supposed to include such things as portfolio (activity) restrictions, minimum reserve, liquidity, and capital requirements, government deposit insurance, and central-bank lender-of-last resort guarantees. If the arguments against real free trade in banking are valid, some or all of these regulations ought to be capable of rendering banking systems subject to them less exposed to systemic risk than other, less regulated systems. Experience suggests, however, that the truth is more nearly the opposite: that many so-called prudential regulations expose banking systems to more rather than less risk of systemic failure.

Systemic risk: fact versus myth

In examining claims about systemic risk and regulations needed to deal with it, the first inquiry that needs to be undertaken is one concerning the actual historical record of system-wide banking crises. Conventional thinking about systemic risk in banking would have us believe that contagion effects posing a threat of systemic failure have been a common phenomenon in fractional-reserve banking systems, and especially in systems characterized by low-levels of "prudential" government regulation.

Experience deals a crushing blow to this popular conjecture, by showing contagion effects to be quite rare, with the most notable instances of contagions occurring in the heavily regulated U.S. banking system. In a recent survey of U.S. experience, George Kaufman (1994) concludes that bank-run contagion effects occurred only on three or four occasions prior to the founding of the Federal Reserve System in 1913, and that these contagions were regional ones only, posing no systemic threat. The only genuine system wide bank runs in the United States occurred on the Federal Reserve's watch, during the first months of 1933; and these were due more to fears that Roosevelt intended to devalue the dollar than to any actual loss of confidence in the banking system (Wigmore 1987). As for contagions linked to default in interbank settlements, these remain a purely hypothetical notion, though one whose real occurrence has become more rather than less likely thanks to government intervention involving implicit guarantees of payment finality (Kane 1992).

Other countries' experience of systemic banking crises has been even more limited than that of the United States, despite failures of and runs upon many individual banks (Selgin 1994, Saunders 1987). All told, the evidence strongly suggests that bank customers are after all capable of distinguishing banks that are really in danger of becoming insolvent from ones that are not: actual bank runs have for the most part been neither irrational nor particularly ill-informed.

Common sense would suggest, furthermore, that panic is if anything particularly unlikely to spread contagion-like from a troubled foreign bank to its domestically owned and regulated rivals, because the assets of foreign banks are likely to be more diverse than and otherwise different from assets held by most domestically based banks, and because banks with foreign operations tend to be relatively large and well capitalized (Baer 1990), and therefore less prone to failure. Thus if U.S. depositors can detect a difference between Continental Illinois and other U.S. banks (including other banks with substantial uninsured offshore deposits), as they appear to have done in April 1984 (Saunders

1987: 218), then they should be even more capable of detecting a difference between a U.S. branch of, say, Banamex and its U.S.-based counterparts. The experience following the Mexican banking and debt crisis in 1982 supports this view. Even though U.S. banks tried not to reveal their sovereign exposure, investors had no difficulty telling which banks were actually involved in the crisis, causing the equity values of those banks alone to fall without altering equity values of unexposed banks (ibid,; 225). Presumably depositors would have made the same sort of distinction between actual Mexican bank branches operating in the United States (had any existed at the time) and offices of U.S. banks.

The international evidence also suggests something else that is quite contrary to conventional thinking about systemic risk: this risk appears greatest in more heavily rather than less heavily regulated banking systems. Although it was more heavily regulated than many other banking systems, the 19th century U.S banking system seems to have been exceptionally crisis-prone, while some practically unregulated systems of the same era, like those of Canada, Scotland, and Sweden, were more-or-less crisis-free (Selgin 1994). Today much the same pattern remains apparent, notwithstanding the increase in regulations worldwide. The still-heavily regulated U.S. system, now supposedly "strengthened" by a central bank, the Glass-Steagall Act, and deposit insurance, continues to be wracked by crises, and home to many of the most fragile banks in the world, while less-regulated systems with less extensive "safety nets," including the network of Eurodollar banks and the banking systems of Germany and Canada, support some of the world's safest and strongest banks. Those fearing "competition in laxity" as a by-product of free trade in banking seem blind to this obvious fact, as well as to the reason underlying it, namely, that banking systems are on balance weakened instead of strengthened by government regulations, including so-called prudential regulations (Selgin 1989, Benston 1991, Kane 1992). Reserve requirements and branching restrictions hamper banks' ability to diversify their assets and liabilities while reducing their flexibility in meeting crises, while deposit insurance and central bank lending facilities invite excessive risk taking. Barriers to genuine free trade in banking themselves are an important cause of fragility in the world banking system, because such barriers limit stronger banks' ability to diversify on a worldwide basis while protecting the home markets of relatively weak, inefficient, and underdiversified banks. As Kane has observed (1992: 258), regulatory authorities and other opponents of real free trade in banking simply "fail to see that globalization is strengthening the financial system's immune systems in important ways."

The upshot of all this is that real free trade in banking will enhance, not reduce, the safety of banking arrangements exposed to it. Real competition from foreign banks will promote safer banking all around, by weeding-out weak banks as well as harmful regulations, "prudential" or otherwise, while allowing stronger and safer banks to offer their services to a larger set of consumers.

Conclusion

NAFTA reduces some important barriers to North American free trade in banking, but stops well short of establishing real free trade, especially by insisting on the national treatment of foreign banks. A far better approach, and one much more consistent with genuine free trade, would subject foreign banks to home-country regulation only, thereby hastening the process of deregulation. Although some writers claim otherwise, such deregulation would represent unmitigated progress, resulting in a North American banking system both safer and more efficient than any of the three systems in place today. For this reason real free trade in banking—whether unilateral, North American, or worldwide—remains a policy ideal worth striving for.

References

American Bankers Association. (1990) *International Banking Competitive-ness...Why It Matters*. A report of the ABA Economic Advisory Committee, Washington, D.C.

Baer, H. L. (1990) "Foreign Competition in U.S. Banking Markets." Federal Reserve Bank of Chicago, *Economic Perspectives* (May/June): 22-29.

Baltensperger, E., and Dermine, J. (1990) "European Banking: Pruden-tial and Regulatory Issues." In J. Dermine (ed.) *European Banking in the 1990s*, 17-36. London: Basil Blackwell.

Bank of England. (1993) "The EC Single Market in Financial Services." Bank of England *Quarterly Review* 33 (1) (February): 92-97.

Benston, G. J. (1991) "Does Bank Regulation Produce Stability? Lessons from the United States." In F. Capie and G. E. Wood (eds.) *Unregulated Banking: Chaos or Order?*, 207-232. London: Macmil-lan.

Benston, G. J. (1992) "International Regulatory Coordination of Bank-ing." In J. Fingleton and D. Schoenmaker (eds.) *The Intermediation of Capital Markets and the Regulatory Response*, 197-209. London: Graham and Trotman.

Garber, P. M., and Weisbrod, S. R. (1992) "Opening the Financial Ser-vices Market in Mexico." Paper presented at the Brown Univer-sity Conference on the Mexico-US Free Trade Agreement, Providence, RI, 2 October 1991.

Gordon, S. (1994) "Banking on U.S. Customers." *Canadian Banker* (Janu-ary/February): 24-26.

Gruben, W. C., and Welch, J. H. (1993) "North American Free Trade in Financial Services." Research Department, Federal Reserve Bank of Dallas.

Gruben, W. C.; Welch, J. H.; and Gunther, J. W. (1993) "U.S. Banks, Competition, and the Mexican Banking System: How Much Will NAFTA Matter?" Federal Reserve Bank of Dallas *Financial Indus-try Studies* (October): 11-25.

Gunther, J. W., and Moore, R.R. (1992) "Mexico Offers Banking Opportunities." *Financial Industry Issues* (Fourth Quarter). Dallas: Federal Reserve Bank of Dallas.

Harrington, J. W., Jr. (1992) "Determinants of Bilateral Operations of Canadian and US Commercial Banks." *Environment and Planning A* 24 (1) (January): 137-151.

Kane, E. J. (1987) "Competitive Financial Reregulation: An International Perspective." In R. Portes and A. K. Swoboda (eds.) *Threats to International Financial Stability*, 111-145. Cambridge: Cambridge University Press.

Kane, E. J. (1988) "How Market Forces Influence the Structure of Financial Regulation." In W. S. Haraf and R. M. Kushmeider (eds.) *Restructuring Banking and Financial Services in America*, 343-382. Washington, D.C.: American Enterprise Institute.

Kane, E. J. (1992) "Government Officials as a Source of Systemic Risk in International Financial Markets." In F.R. Edwards and H. T. Patrick (eds.) *Regulating International Financial Markets: Issues and Policies*, 257-65. Boston: Kluwer.

Kaufman, G. (1994) "Bank Contagion: A Review of Theory and Evidence." *Journal of Financial Services Research* 8 (2) (April): 123-150.

Kaufman, G. (Forthcoming) Manuscript for *The United States' Financial System*, 6th ed., chapter on international banking. Englewood Cliffs, N.J.: Prentice Hall.

Key, S. J., and Scott, H.S. (1992) "International Trade in Banking Services: A Conceptual Framework." In J. Fingleton and D. Schoenmaker (eds.) *The Intermediation of Capital Markets and the Regulatory Response*, 35-67. London: Graham and Trotman.

Laub, P. M. (1991) "International Regulation: How Much Cooperation is Needed?" In C. England (ed.) *Governing Banking's Future: Markets vs. Regulation*, 21-31. Washington, D.C.: Cato Institute.

Misback, A. E. (1993) "The Foreign Bank Supervision Enhancement Act of 1991." *Federal Reserve Bulletin* 79 (1) (January): 1-10.

Neven, D. J. (1990) "Structural Adjustments in European Retail Banking: Some Views from Industrial Organization." In J. Dermine (ed.) *European Banking in the 1990s*, 153-82. London: Basil Blackwell.

Peters, D. D., and Drake, P.L.. (1988) "Implications for Financial Services of the Canada-United States Free Trade Agreement." In M. Gold and D. Leyton-Brown (eds.) *Trade-Offs on Free Trade: The Canada-U.S. Free Trade Agreement*, 332-39. Toronto: Carswell.

Pyle, D. H. (1987) Discussion of Kane (1987). In R. Portes and A. K. Swoboda (eds.) *Threats to International Financial Stability*, 145-49. Cambridge, U.K.: Cambridge University Press.

Saumier, A. (1988) "The Canada-U.S. Free Trade Agreement and the Services Sector." In M. Gold and D. Leyton-Brown (eds.) *Trade-Offs on Free Trade: The Canada-U.S. Free Trade Agreement*, 323-31. Toronto: Carswell.

Saunders, A. (1987) "The Inter-bank Market, Contagion Effects and International Financial Crises." In R. Portes and A.K. Swoboda (eds.) *Threats to International Financial Stability*, 196-232. Cambridge: Cambridge University Press.

Schwab, T. W., and Tucker, E. A. (1993) "FBSEA Study Favouring Foreign Bank Branches will be Good for U.S." *Banking Policy Report* 12 (3) (February): 7-10.

Sczudlo, R. S. (1993) "NAFTA: Opportunities Abound for US and Canadian Financial Institutions." *The Bankers Magazine* (July/August): 28-33.

Selgin, G. (1989) "Legal Restrictions, Financial Weakening, and the Lender of Last Resort." *Cato Journal* 9 (2) (Fall): 429-59.

Selgin, G. (1994) "Are Banking Crises Free-Market Phenomena?" *Critical Review* 8 (4) (Fall): 591-608.

Swary, I., and Topf, B. (1992) *Global Financial Deregulation: Commercial Banking at the Crossroads*. Cambridge, Mass.: Blackwell.

Wigmore, B. A. (1987) "Was the Bank Holiday of 1933 Caused by a Run on the Dollar?" *Journal of Economic History* 47 (3) (September): 739-55.

CHAPTER 13

Applying Monetarism: What Have We Learned?

Juan Andrés Fontaine[1]

THE MONETARIST SEA HAS BECOME DEEP ENOUGH to include many different currents. I will concentrate my analysis on what I see are the crucial tenets of monetarism for the design and implementation of monetary policy. These are the beliefs that (1) price stability is the main goal of macroeconomic policy, (2) inflation is "always and everywhere a monetary phenomenon," whose cure depends on appropriate mone-

---

1   The author is Chief Executive and Partner at Fontaine y Paúl Consultores Asociados and a Professor of Economics at the Instituto de Economía at the Universidad Católica de Chile. He served as Director of Research at the Central Bank of Chile, participating on Chile's Monetary Policy Committee and helped draft the new central bank law.

    This article is adapted from a speech given at the Cato conference, "Monetary Arrangements in the Americas After NAFTA," held in Mexico City on May 25-26, 1994.

    I am very grateful to Francisco Rosende for his very helpful comments. As usual, the views expressed here (and any remaining errors) are my responsibility.

tary treatment, and (3) price stability is best served by a rules-based monetary policy.

This chapter reviews the current standing of these three basic propositions in light of the recent Latin American experience, as well as their implications for future monetary policy. No attempt is made to discuss the very rich theoretical foundations of monetarism. I was trained in the monetarist tradition. I learned to admire the depth of the theoretical analysis of the monetarist school. I am convinced that the monetarist doctrine provides an enlightening guide to monetary policy in the real world. But I also think its precepts cannot take into account all the complexities of actual policy making. The standard monetarist prescriptions have become an unavoidable ingredient of the policy making cocktail, but surely not the only one.

Price stability as the goal

Monetarists are known in Latin America and elsewhere for their aversion to inflation. The term "monetarism" in Latin America is often used to characterise such a policy stance, perhaps because it has typically been incarnated by the International Monetary Fund in its feared "adjustment programs." There were times, not long ago, in which inflation aversion was highly controversial, and the monetarist preachers formed a combative minority. But times have changed, and nowadays this chapter of the monetarist gospel has achieved widespread respect and support.

In the old days price stability was thought to be inconsistent with economic growth. Rigid economic "structures" were seen as the cause of inflation in a growing economy.[2] Inflation had the advantage of facilitating relative price changes and helping achieve full employment. The attempt to stop inflation through monetary means was linked to a "social cost" that outweighed any "social benefits" it might produce. Typically income redistribution and the reduction of unemployment had to take precedence as policy goals over disinflation. The latter could only be attained very gradually over time. Of course, this view was

---

2   On "structuralism" see Little (1982).

instrumental for politicians interested either in the proceeds of the "inflation tax" or in the electoral rewards of the "populist" business cycle.[3]

Over the last 10 or 15 years these views have changed dramatically. Experience showed in country after country that the monetarist warnings against a benevolent view of inflation were right. Inflation served as a useful lubricant of economic growth only as long as it came as a surprise. But as expectations of future price level changes begun to be adjusted, as people become to expect populist behaviour on the part of governments, inflation had to climb to ever increasing heights to perform its role. Chile got to the verge of hyperinflation in 1973-75 and had to turn back through a painful, but ultimately successful, stabilization program. Later on, in the mid-1980s Bolivia underwent a similar experience, only that this time hyperinflation was already there, and its cure was also harsh and quick. In the late eighties Mexico joined the club, to be followed by Argentina, El Salvador, Peru, and others in the early nineties. Of the largest countries, Brazil and Venezuela have both experienced the duress of high inflation without them being yet capable of tackling it, while Colombia has followed a less spectacular gradual disinflation from moderately high levels.

These experiences have taught Latin American policy makers—the hard way—that there is something worse than the social costs of stabilization, namely, the social costs of populism. Economic thinkers, politicians, technocrats and, more importantly, "public opinion," have embraced the monetarist aversion to inflation. Preserving "macroeconomic equilibrium" has become a border condition of all economic policy proposals. Achieving some sort of price stability has become the centrepiece of macroeconomic programs. One would listen, for example, to a Bolivian presidential candidate stressing the need to get annual inflation below 10 percent in a country whose per capita income is still 18 percent below its 1980 level. Similar statements are heard from (successful) politicians all over the region, including Argentina, Chile, and Peru. Suddenly combating inflation has become popular: the mon-

---

3   See Dornbusch and Edwards (1990).

etarist goal is being endorsed enthusiastically by politicians and policy makers throughout Latin America.

Before turning to the discussion of the policies applied to tackle inflation, let me add a few words about the causes of this change of mood. I see three causes. The first has already been mentioned: the traumatic experience of high inflation and its painful cure. And for this purpose not only one's own experiences are most valuable, but also those of one's neighbours. For example, for the Chilean economic team starting in 1990, after the 1989 election that put an end to the Pinochet era, opposed as they were to that government's policies, the failure of the populist attempts by President Alfonsin in Argentina and President García in Peru seem to have been extremely instructive.

The second reason is that stabilization policies in Latin American economies have been implemented together with deep structural reforms that have opened and liberalized those economies. In an open and free economy populism is punished much faster than in the closed and controlled economies of the old days. Exchange and interest rates reveal inflationary expectations almost instantly. Elsewhere I have told how, in my view, in Chile the "rebellion of the money desks" was able to derail a dangerous turn to populism during the "debt crises" (Fontaine 1993). To this purpose the elimination of price controls has also been useful, as well as—and surprisingly so—the introduction of widespread indexation. In Chile most long-term bank loans are indexed to the price level so every CPI increase is directly felt in their pockets by mortgage and other debtors with the corresponding political outcry: financial indexation has eradicated money illusion.

The third and final cause of the current popularity of stabilization policies may be a weaker and less permanent one. Current stabilization episodes have been fortunate to count with large capital inflows and the corresponding appreciation of domestic currencies. This feature of recent Latin American stabilizations has created an initial boom in consumption that has no doubt helped to enhance their popularity. Recent events in Mexico and Argentina cast some doubts about the durability of the support to stabilization policies as the consumption boom starts to recede.

The current anti-inflationary stance in Latin America and elsewhere is a clear triumph of the monetarist school. Price stability is nowadays the main goal of macroeconomic policies in many countries. The definition of price stability, of course, varies. In the most advanced industrial countries, the achievement of zero inflation—that is, true price stability—timidly starts to show up in policy discussions. In "emerging economies" the discussion is about the speed of the convergence to industrial countries inflationary levels—that is, ultimately, to zero inflation as well. In this respect, at least, I see a future monetarists will enjoy and justly feel proud of.

Money, deficits, and inflation

Three decades after the debate over the monetary origin of business cycles was revived by Milton Friedman and the Chicago School, the issue seems fairly settled. Inflation is indeed the consequence of excessive monetary growth; no stabilization program can succeed without controlling and reducing the rate of growth of the supply of money. The theoretical foundation for this assertion stems from the ancient and revered quantity equation, MV=PQ. The empirical support, in turn, was drawn from numerous "monetary histories" that followed the seminal Friedman and Schwartz (1963) work. The evidence comes also from stabilization experiences in LDCs. This finding though, important as it is, does not tell the whole story.

The direct cause of inflation is excessive monetary growth, but, from the perspective of economic policy, to learn and control the causes of monetary growth is crucial. Experience in Latin America suggests excessive monetary growth, and thus inflation, are typically a symptom of the inability of the political system to check a tendency toward excessive spending—or, what is the same, of insufficient savings.

The problem has traditionally been located in the public sector. Monetarists in Latin America came fairly soon to the conclusion that the typical source of monetary expansion was the financing by central banks of high and persistent fiscal deficits.[4] The closing of the window

---

4   See, for example, Harberger (1963).

for central bank financing to the public sector became a top priority in stabilization programs. In Chile a reform of the statutes of the central bank that prohibited it to grant loans to the public sector or buy public debt was one of the initial measures of the stabilization program of the mid-1970s. This precept was subsequently incorporated to the Constitution of 1980 and to the new Central Bank law of 1989. Stabilization experiences in Argentina, Bolivia, Mexico, and elsewhere have also introduced some limitations to deficit financing by the printing press.

The mere closing of the central bank window, though, does not conclude the work. The experience of Argentina in the early 1980s, for example, illustrates well the point. A high fiscal deficit, when financed in the capital market, can also cause inflation. In an open economy, the government can typically finance its deficit in the international capital market. Governments have obvious advantages over the private sector in tapping official and private sources of external financing. If the initial level of foreign debt is considered low and the country is seen as reasonably stable and well managed, this expedient can be used repeatedly for a relatively long period of time. At some point, however, international markets will become worried about the accumulation of excessive debt and start charging higher interest rates or rationing additional financing. Beyond this point the government in deficit has two alternatives: either eliminate the deficit or resort to the domestic capital market. The latter option sounds less costly, but has the disadvantage of inducing an increase of real interest rates and the usual "crowding-out" of private spending. A weak central bank can then easily succumb to political pressures and fight the increase in interest rates through monetary expansion. The attempt would of course in the end be futile, resulting only in inflation and currency devaluation.

The moral of the above story is that to control the money supply and inflation it not only is necessary to cut the financial link between a central bank and the rest of the public sector, but to eliminate the fiscal deficit as well. All stabilization programs are now directly aimed at that objective. However, the elimination of the fiscal deficit again does not do the full job. To me, that is the most important lesson the Chilean experience of 1979-81; namely, that excessive spending on the part of the private sector can also be very dangerous and in the end lead to inflation.

The Chilean case is interesting because at the time Chile had already applied a successful stabilization program that had brought inflation down to about 30 percent per year from nearly 400 percent in 1975. This result had been achieved through a severe fiscal adjustment that had not only eliminated the high deficits of the early 1970s (equivalent to 24 percent of GDP in 1973 and 8 percent in 1974), but had managed to create a surplus of 3.5 percent of GDP in 1979-81. Despite this auspicious development, a severe macroeconomic imbalance showed up in a rapid deterioration of the current account deficit, which in 1981 reached the equivalent of 14 percent of GDP. Adverse external shocks did play an important role in the process, but there is no doubt that it also was the consequence of an excessive expansion of private expenditure in consumption and investment.

The point is that once the economy moved into a situation of excess aggregate spending, real interest rates went up and external debt started to increase very rapidly. As in the Argentine case, beyond some point overindebtedness led to the debt crisis. Then, only a prompt elimination of excess spending would have avoided an upsurge of inflation. This action would have required either very high interest rates—to restrain private expenditure—or a counterbalancing additional fiscal adjustment. In practice both policies were attempted with different degrees of intensity between 1981 and 1984. But those efforts were not severe enough because of the weak state of the economy in general and of the financial system in particular. The central bank had to reluctantly tolerate some increase of inflation and provide the necessary monetary expansion to this end.

The conclusion is that inflation, although being the direct consequence of monetary expansion, has as its ultimate cause an excess of aggregate expenditure over the sum of income plus "sustainable" net external financing. The source of the excess quite often can be found in fiscal policies, but the problem can also originate in the private sector. Excess spending can be temporarily "parked" (as Arnold Harberger is fond of saying) abroad in the form of a high and unsustainable current account deficit, or in the domestic market by accumulating a high level of public domestic debt and putting upward pressure on real interest rates. But ultimately it will find its way toward higher inflation, with the diligent help of a weak central bank.[5]

This conclusion has important implications for stabilization policies. First, the elimination of fiscal deficits may be a necessary condition for stability, but not a sufficient one. At times an excessive private spending expansion may call for a fiscal surplus. I have been asked many times why Chile still has inflation rates of around 10 percent per year despite having solved the fiscal deficit problem long ago. The answer is, I think, that private consumption and investment have been persistently very strong, fostered by good expectations and a moderate fiscal impulse. The central bank, on the one hand, has been unwilling to "park" abroad too large a fraction of such excess spending out of the fear of a rerun of the 1979-81 imbalance. Therefore, it has in general fought the resulting appreciation of the peso, with the enthusiastic support from export lobbies. On the other hand, it has also been unwilling to let interest rates rise all the way to choke off the excess spending and risk a recession, although on occasions it has acted pretty tough in that direction. Thus, the central bank has chosen a "middle-of-the-road" approach that has implied the monetary validation of some (hopefully declining) inflation.[6]

The second implication of this view of the inflation process is that the only true and definitive solution to inflation is to correct its ultimate roots, that is, to adjust expenditure (both private and public) to potential income plus sustainable foreign financing. In the meantime the parking abroad of the excess spending can create a misleading, temporary

---

5   This view is close to the inflation-tax approach that sees inflation as determined mainly by the fiscal deficit (Sargent 1990, for example), but instead of focusing only on the intertemporal fiscal budget constraint, it extends the analysis to the whole economy's intertemporal budget constraint.

6   Therefore, in Chile moderate inflation plays the role of curbing aggregate demand so as to eliminate, *ex-post*, any excess of spending over income plus the current account deficit consistent with the prevailing real exchange rate. The contractionary effect of inflation over aggregate demand is due to imperfect wage-indexation and good indexation of the tax base.

situation of price stability. The counterpart of this situation is a danger-ously wide current account deficit and an overvalued real exchange rate. But such stability is not stable. In the end the excess spending will have to be carried home and become an inflationary pressure. This seems to characterize the factors behind the recent exchange-rate col-lapse of the peso in Mexico. Stability is only stable when it is the consequence of the termination of excess spending in the sense defined above.

Finally, this termination is very much related to the speed that one can reasonably bring down inflation and the nature of the correspond-ing policy measures. If the problem is one of excessive growth in consumption or investment, one cannot expect to see results too soon. Of course, the stabilization process will depend very much on the nature of the inflation problem. Hyperinflations, being typically driven by expectations, can be stopped fairly quickly. But protracted, chronic inflations, either high (as the Brazilian ones) or moderate (as the Chilean or Colombian one) seem to need a long treatment. Time has to be allowed not only to control spending, but to create new and enduring habits of savings among individuals, firms, and the public sector. Given all this, I think one has to be sceptical about the stability of rapid stabilizations.

Regarding the measures needed to be included in a successful stabilization package, the key in my opinion is that they all have to be consistent with the ultimate objective of reducing the excess spending. Often the only safe way to achieve this goal is at the same time to create the conditions for a higher rate of economic growth. Excess spending is then reduced by both controlling spending and expanding income. In most "emerging economies" this approach means starting or furthering structural reforms aimed at economic liberalization. Once that opening is realized, the scope of contractionary measures is severely limited. For example, the use of high reserve requirements for reducing the rate of monetary growth or for improving the "quasi-fiscal" deficit has the serious drawback of limiting the development of the financial market, a key growth-fostering structural reform. Likewise, solving a fiscal deficit by raising import tariffs or raising income taxes may end up causing more harm than good, because such measures may have an adverse, long-term impact on exports and savings. Other measures may have a short-term adverse effect—widening the fiscal deficit— and yet have a long-term positive effect on stability by generating economic growth and narrowing the gap between expenditures and income.

To recapitulate, it is indisputable that the "structuralists" who imagined all kinds of nonmonetary causes of inflation were wrong. The monetarists won the debate: inflation is always a monetary phenomenon. Yet, behind such monetary phenomenon one typically finds excess spending fostered or at least unchecked by weak governments. To achieve price stability a solution has to be found to this problem. And, alas, such a solution may very well be "structural," but not in the sense envisaged by the old structuralists. The structural reforms needed are those capable of generating the right climate for economic growth.

The search for a good monetary rule

From the monetarist emphasis on price stability and stabilization as the main goal for macroeconomic policy and on monetary overexpansion as its main threat, it follows that monetary institutions have to be built in such away to prevent this risk. The crudest institution one can think is one that ties the central bank to behave according to a fixed rule. Monetarists, following the lead of Henry Simons (1936) and Milton Friedman (1968), have come to support fixed rules for the conduct of monetary policy against discretion.

The case against discretion is very strong. Friedman was right to point out that long and variable lags make it almost impossible to apply good "fine tuning" monetary measures. The experience of almost every central bank is that the attempt to stimulate a depressed economy— given long and exasperating lags—typically ends with an overdose and the ensuing inflationary upsurge. Conversely, monetary authorities tend also to overdo it when applying contractionary measures to slow aggregate demand and inflation. The public choice literature introduced an even more radical argument against discretion: political incentives are seldom consistent with stabilization objectives, and thus central banks may end up creating "political business cycles"—an argument that is reinforced by the recent literature on the "time inconsistency problem" and the political economy models of central bank behaviour.[7]

On the other hand, the case for rules received a strong endorsement from the so-called rational expectations revolution. In particular, Lucas (1976, 1981) demolished the intellectual foundations of discretionary fine tuning, arguing that only the reactions of economic agents to different policy rules can be predicted using the economic way of thinking, that is, assuming rational behaviour. Therefore, pure discretion yields unpredictable results and cannot be employed for stabilization purposes. To evaluate alternative macro policies, we would have to think in terms of alternative policy rules.

The basic monetary rules favoured by monetarists are a fixed quantitative target for the money supply (the "k-rule") and a fixed exchange rate. These are fixed rules in the sense that they eliminate or minimize central bank discretion. As will become apparent, the search for "rigid rules" for the conduct of monetary policy has been the least successful element of the monetarist credo. Still, such rules can serve as guiding principles or criteria for the conduct of monetary policy.

Quantitative monetary rules

The first fixed-rule option—the k-rule—has not been seriously tried in Latin America. IMF-supported adjustment programs, though, do include a rule that can be thought of as a close relative of the k-rule. The IMF typically requires from central banks a commitment not to increase the net domestic assets of the central bank above a certain limit. Under certain conditions (limited international capital mobility), this restriction is similar to a k-rule applied to the rate of increase of the monetary base. IMF programs typically set quarterly limits to net domestic assets in absolute terms, and derive those limits from the projected increase in the nominal quantity of money using the MV=PQ framework.

---

7   On time inconsistency, Kydland and Prescott (1977) is the standard source. Political economy models are studied, for example, in Cukierman (1992).

The k-rule idea, although theoretically appealing, has failed in practice.[8] I see three sets of problems associated with the implementation of a k-rule.[9] One is the familiar one of finding a monetary aggregate with a stable demand to subject to the k-rule. It is well known that to use a k-rule for an aggregate whose demand is unstable would be directly counterproductive in terms of price stability. Financial innovation has made it increasingly difficult to find such a stable-demanded monetary aggregate. This is particularly true of Latin American countries undergoing drastic stabilization programs (that, if successful, lower the expected cost of holding money and thus raise its demand in a fashion very difficult to predict) and, at the same time, liberalizing their capital markets. In Chile, for example, M2 has increased from 11 percent of GDP in 1970 to 30 percent of GDP in 1993. This increase has been the result of the lifting of interest and credit controls, the reduction of reserve requirements, and the accumulation of financial savings—including time deposits—by the new private pension funds that replaced the old pay-as-you go social security system.[10]

The second set of problems is associated with the degree of control the monetary authority has over the chosen monetary aggregate. Although macro models may have the central bank as controlling monetary aggregates, the truth of the matter is, as a former Chilean central banker used to say, that they just do the monetary statistics. All "wide" monetary aggregates are market determined with commercial banks playing a key role. Central banks can influence their behaviour, for example, via reserve requirements, but only very indirectly. Also, central bank control of a monetary aggregate may be undermined by substitution away from it. For example, nonbank liabilities may play a monetary role in a free capital market environment. To some extent this

---

8   For a discussion of these issues in the context of OECD countries, see Bernanke and Mishkin (1992) and Goodhart (1989).

9   Poole's classical model shows this to be prerequisite for a k-rule to be optimal (Poole 1970).

10 Financial deregulation also led to the abandoning of M3 targeting in England (see Bernanke and Mishkin 1992).

argument applies also to narrower monetary aggregates such as M1 and MU or currency.

This leaves only the monetary base as the monetary aggregate to be monitored. In many Latin American countries, though, changes in the monetary base are influenced strongly by changes in government deposits with the central bank. This is typically the case of countries receiving large foreign official grants (e.g., El Salvador and Nicaragua) or that in general have large-sized public sectors. Control over the monetary base in such cases depends very much on the central bank being able to anticipate and offset movements in these deposits.

Even more important than the fiscal source of shocks on the monetary base are abrupt changes in international reserves. Unless central banks are willing to tolerate an absolutely clean float of the exchange rate, such shocks will affect the monetary base through net purchases of foreign exchange by the central banks. In the particular case of IMF programs mentioned above, the limit on the change of the net domestic assets would yield an unstable monetary base, if international reserves shocks are important and the central bank intervenes to stabilize the exchange rate. In the more general case of a monetary base k-rule, the central bank will have to stand ready to sterilize any monetary impact of its foreign exchange operations, so as to keep the monetary base on its pre-determined path. This is not an easy thing to do from an operational point of view.

The final set of problems associated to a k-rule are those related to the correction of any deviation from the rule. After a given positive deviation, for example, how should the central bank react? Should it stick to the pre-established level or aim at the stated rate of growth, thus allowing some "base drift"? How rapid or gradual should a correction be? All these are tough questions to answer, and they constitute the "bread and butter" of the workings of an operating monetary committee. The k-rule approach cannot answer them and unavoidably leaves the central bank some discretion.

Fixed exchange rate rules

Aware of the drawbacks of the k-rule, Latin American monetarists have turned to fixed exchange rules. Of course, to be credible they have to be implemented within a currency board set of rules for monetary policy that replicate the workings of the gold standard. Accordingly, central banks would be allowed to increase the monetary base only to purchase foreign exchange at a fixed rate against other currency (or basket of them), and forced to sustain that rate through foreign exchange operations. The best known current fixed exchange rate (FER) regime is the Argentine since April 1991.[11]

The beauties of a FER rule are many. The rule is clear, understandable, and publicly announced. It serves as a public commitment to price stability on the part of both the monetary and the fiscal authorities. Any deviation from it is politically and economically very costly: it creates a crisis of confidence that typically forces out from their offices central bank presidents, ministers of finance, and even presidents. It effectively eliminates discretion, and thus achieves the monetarist objective of removing that source of price instability. It actually amounts to the substitution of a sort of computer for central banks and their expensive bureaucracies. It is also operationally very simple: none of the definitional and practical problems of k-rules is present with a FER rule. Nominal exchange rate stability acts directly on inflationary expectations and on the price of traded goods. It also serves to foster international trade and finance as proved during the classical gold standard.

Despite their appeal, evidence on the many recent experiments with FER rules has not been good. The failure does not lie so much in the theory of fixed exchange rates, but in the difficulties of establishing the required, real-world institutions. In my view FER rules are subject to the following problems.

First, the precondition of a currency board framework for monetary policy is not easy to meet. In the Chilean experience of 1979-82, there was no public commitment in that sense. Predictably, when in late 1981 several banks ran into trouble as a consequence of the high real interest

---

11 In Argentina the central bank is legally responsible for keeping the exchange rate fixed to the U. S. dollar. It is also legally prohibited from holding domestic assets except certain foreign-denominated government bonds (BONEX) and short-term liquidity loans to commercial banks, both of which are subject to strict limits.

rates dictated by the "automatic adjustment" typical of such regimes when facing capital outflows, the monetary authorities could not refrain from intervening as lenders of last resort. From then on, markets were alerted that politically the FER automatic adjustment was not tolerable, and thus the days of the FER rule were numbered (Fontaine 1989, 1993). The Argentines have been more careful and enacted a law stipulating the commitment of the central bank with a fixed rate and the full backing of the monetary base with international reserves. Thus in principle, no lender of last resort role is allowed to the central bank. This led the Argentine government to tolerate an abnormal rise in interest rates, tough fiscal measures and a sharp drop in output in order to keep the regime afloat in the face of the financial crisis originated by capital outflow shocks following the Mexican currency collapse—the so-called tequila effect.

The second problem is that, in all cases I know, the introduction of the FER has been initially unable to stop inflationary pressures in the non-tradeable sectors. In other words, this difficulty stems from the short-term rigidity of certain prices and wages. In the Chilean case this rigidity has been connected with the prevailing practice of backwards wage indexation. In Argentina the precaution was taken to forbid such a practice. Nevertheless, in the three years of FER, Argentina's CPI inflation accumulated to around 50 percent, well above international levels. The consequence has been a strong appreciation of the real exchange rate, the widening of trade and current account deficits, and the loss of competitiveness in export sectors. For small, open economies this may mean a long stagnation, after an initial consumption boom.

The third problem is connected with the previous one. A gradually appreciating real exchange rate provides a strong incentive for capital inflows. External loans become cheap in real terms as compared to domestic sources. Real asset prices and shares look cheap to international investors. If at the same time the likely success of the stabilization program or other policies (as happened both in Chile in the early eighties and Argentina in the early nineties) lowers country risk perceptions, capital inflows can become very large. The problem is that this causes an equilibrium appreciation of the real exchange rate that can be accomplished only through further inflation (of non-tradeables). This appreciation creates additional incentives for capital inflows, thereby giving rise to a spiral of inflation-real appreciation-capital inflows-inflation that only ends when the continuity of the FER starts to lose credibility. The FER acts then as sort of subsidy to capital inflows.[12]

It may be argued that it would be irrational for international arbitragers to continue pouring capital into a country that promises only nominal exchange rate stability, instead of real exchange rate stability. The point is that real exchange rate adjustments under a FER rule are always gradual. They are achieved through inflation differentials, and thus allow plenty of time for investors to readjust their portfolios if they come to expect a real devaluation. The dynamics of real devaluations under a floating exchange rate regime is very different: devaluations take place overnight and catch investors by surprise. The existence of such risk provides an automatic control valve for capital inflows that is absent from FER regimes.[13]

The fourth problem is not, as the previous two, linked to the initial stages of a FER regime. It points rather toward a more structural problem. In the presence of some price or wage rigidities, real exchange rate adjustments are extremely slow under a FER rule: real appreciation takes time and cause inflation; real depreciation requires deflation and usually this is preceded by recession and high (often politically unbearable) unemployment. Then FER rules are an inefficient way of achieving price stability and a flexible system of relative prices. The problem is more serious the larger the fraction of non-traded goods in GDP and the higher the volatility of the equilibrium relative price of tradeable goods. In turn, such volatility depends on the variance of terms of trade, autonomous shifts in investment and consumption, country risk-adjusted international interest rates, and the supply of foreign financing.

The four aforementioned problems of a FER rule regime have to weighed against its advantages. In the end, the choice of an exchange rate regime should be a matter of cost-benefit analysis, and the evalua-

---

12 On the effect of FER on capital inflows, see Fontaine (1994) and De la Cuadra-Valdes Prieto (1990).

13 Of course, the counterpart of this advantage of floating rates is their higher volatility which presumably harms exports and investment.

tion of such costs and benefits are very much determined by the specific characteristics and circumstances of the country under analysis. For example, it is perfectly justifiable that a country with a long and painful experience of monetary mismanagement may choose a FER rule despite its drawbacks. A country also may choose a FER rule if the proximity with its trading partners and degree of openness significantly reduce the share of non-traded goods in GDP, or if a country expects sufficient access to foreign financing to accommodate terms of trade and other shocks.

A case of bounded discretion: Chilean monetary policy

The above analysis of the practical application of fixed rules seems to lead to a defense of flexible, feedback rules. Some authors have come out in favour of less rigid rules, by which the use of central bank policy instruments would be linked to the observed level of certain variables in a precise formula. The purpose of these feedback rules would be to preserve some of the stabilization properties of good monetary policy, while at the same time avoiding the dangers of discretion. For economic model builders, of course, this is the only activist macropolicy that survive Lucas's critique.

Several recent contributions have stressed the advantages of rules such as tying the money supply to the achievement of price stability, the achieving of certain targets for nominal income growth or final sales, or the adjusting of interest rates according to some function of deviations of these variables from projected levels.[14] Although these rules are presented as an alternative to discretion, in my view, they can only be interpreted as criteria orientating rational discretion. For model building purposes they may be written as fixed feedback formulas. But in a complex reality (in which many shocks are simultaneously occurring, expectations changing, and lags are long and unpredictable), one cannot think of them as useful rules. In other words, once one has admitted the costs of tying the hands of the monetary authorities with fixed rules, it

---

14   See McCallum (1990), Stockman (1992), and Taylor (1993).

would be irrational to follow oversimplistic, backward-looking feed-back rules.[15]

On the other hand, such rules can be reinterpreted as useful criteria for guiding policy decisions. This is what may be called "bounded discretion," that is, an institution for monetary policy that allows its authorities to exert judgment and discretion within a well-defined set of criteria.

A precondition for bounded discretion to work is having a central bank that really cares about price stability. The best way yet known to achieve this is by granting the central bank independence from the political authorities. Of course, this arrangement is not free of its own shortcomings, but there is no better alternative available. In the next and final section, I will return to the issue of central bank independence.

In Chile, the 1980 Constitution gave the central bank a status of independence.[16] This status was further specified in the Central Bank Law of 1989. This law follows the model of the Bundesbank, in the sense that it frees the monetary authorities from any subordination to the political authorities and, at the same time, gives them a very precise mandate. In particular, both the German and the Chilean law state as their only objectives the safeguarding of the stability of the value of the currency (or price stability) and the normal operation of the payments system. This latter objective is associated with the prevention or cure of financial or foreign exchange crises.

Monetary policy in Chile is thus legally constrained to fight inflation and prevent major balance of payments imbalances. In principle, no consideration should be given to other objectives (e.g., economic growth and full employment), except as they indirectly affect inflation or the balance of payments. The mandate to achieve price stability has been interpreted by the central bank authorities as the gradual reduction of annual inflation from the 25 percent range of the mid-1980s to "single digit figures" in the near term. By and large, the strategy has succeeded. During 1993 inflation was about 12 percent and fell to less than 9 percent

---

15 The point is stressed, for example, by McCallum (1993).

16 On the Chilean Central Bank Law, see Fontaine (1989) and Rosende (1993).

in 1994, a remarkable achievement for a country whose historic inflation averaged 30 percent per year. The mandate to avoid balance-of-payments crises has been executed through the monitoring of the current account deficit, so as to take appropriate measures to keep it within a 2-4 percent range as a proportion of GDP. Since 1990 current account deficits have averaged about 2 percent of GDP.

Monetary policy is thus conducted with clear objectives in mind. The Central Bank Law mandates the monetary authorities to state once a year before the Senate their precise goals for inflation and the balance of payments accounts for the following year. They also are required to provide their macro assumptions (such as the rate of economic growth) and indicate how they plan to achieve them.[17] The timing of this discussion is defined to be coincident with the parliamentary debate of the fiscal budget. No formal approval of the central bank plans is required from the Senate. Rather, the idea is to provide an opportunity for an informal, but public, evaluation of the conduct of monetary policy. In practice, however, the Senate has not showed much interest in actually doing such evaluation, and monetary authorities are totally free to choose their specific goals and instruments.

How does monetary policy pursue its twin goals of price stability and balance-of-payments equilibrium?[18] The central bank holds the view that these two goals are at risk when real aggregate spending increases above the potential output plus sustainable foreign financing. A high real rate of growth of aggregate spending (consumption plus investment, both private and public) serves as an early warning of future problems in one or both fronts. Thus, the real rate of growth of aggregate spending serves as the key indicator that triggers monetary adjustments as could be modelled by a feedback rule. Of course, actual measurements of real spending come with some delay, so what really enters the feedback rule is the expected growth of real spending. These expectations are formed from a wide range of coincidental and leading

---

17 In this sense, the Central Bank announcement stresses more *goals* than *targets*, something that Bernanke and Miskkin (1992) find advantageous also of the German and Swiss experience.

18 For a detailed exposition, see Fontaine (1991).

indicators (including monetary aggregates, trade figures, output figures, prices, the stock market, and even anecdotal evidence collected from newspapers and at cocktail parties by open-eyed central bank officials. Also, the estimates of potential output growth and sustainable current account deficits are debatable, subject to a significant margin of error, and inherently unstable because of continuous domestic and external real shocks. The implied rule then is far from rigid and requires a significant amount of (hopefully intelligent) discretion.

The intermediate target used to influence real aggregate spending is real interest rates.[19] Specifically, the central bank conducts its credit operations in such a way to achieve a given targeted real interest rate on its 90-day paper. Operationally, this objective is reached by opening a window at the bank to offer unlimited amounts of such paper at the targeted price. In times of excess liquidity (due, for example to large foreign exchange purchases or large amortizations of central bank paper), this window acts automatically to contract the monetary base. In times of a liquidity crisis, either an automatic reduction of net sales of paper by the central bank (gross sales through the window less amortizations) solves the problem or some liquidity injection is needed through open market operations or other means.

In most economies, real interest rates are not observable, so the first thing one must clarify is how does the Chilean central bank estimate them? In Chile this is possible due to the widespread use of CPI-indexed financial assets. Virtually all bank deposits and bonds (including those issued by the central bank) of maturities above 90 days (a regulatory restriction) are CPI-indexed. The precise indexation formula is probably the closest real world counterpart to the Fisherian "tabular system."[20] Indexed securities are denominated in a unit of account called the UF (which stands for Unidad de Fomento). The peso value of the UF increases

---

19 The terminology of goals, intermediate targets, and instruments can be found in Bernanke and Miskkin (1992) and McCallum (1990).

20 The literature on financial indexation is surprisingly scarce. An exception is Hetzel (1992) and corresponding references.

daily according to the average daily inflation of the previous month.[21] The value is computed and published by the central bank using the official CPI. The UF has been widely used since the mid-1970s and has survived unharmed serious financial crises and strong political pressures.

Because it is widely trusted, UF-denominated assets are seen as fully protected from inflation, and their yields are taken to indicate market determined *real* interest rates. Of course, this is only an approximation to the "true" real interest rate, because it is distorted by a (short) lag, and different people probably have different reference price levels to measure relevant real values. But this approximation is an extremely good one. In fact, the Chilean capital market seems to use the UF as *the numeraire*, and this explains why despite relatively high and variable inflation rates Chile has been able to develop the strongest and deepest long-term capital market in Latin America.[22]

The use of the real interest rate as a target for monetary policy was introduced in Chile in early 1985 after experiencing with many other policy rules, and was chosen despite the many suspicions it initially raised among monetarist-leaning economists as myself. But in the end we came to the conclusion that it was a practical policy tool, and evidence since then proves it has worked well. The arguments made in the previous section against the use of fixed monetary rules were, of

---

21 Specifically, the peso value of the UF increases by exactly the previous month's rate of inflation between the 10th day of every month and the 9th day of the next month. These values are published by the Central Bank as soon as the official CPI of the previous month is released. I know of no other indexation scheme that follows so closely the current price level. Other experiences in Argentina and Brazil have typically used one- or three-month lags. The British indexed guilts are even less well-indexed: they use eight-month lags (see Hetzel 1992).

22 Hetzel (1992) suggests that the U.S. Treasury issue nominal and indexed bonds of identical maturities and the Fed use the "yield gap" as a market indicator of inflationary expectations. In Chile, the UF has become so dominant (because of its intrinsic merits as an inflation-free unit of value) that it has driven off non-indexed paper from the market, except for maturities of less than 90 days in which indexation is not allowed.

224 Money and Markets in the Americas

course, very relevant in the decision not to apply them in Chile. But an additional argument was that the existence of the UF made the demand for narrow monetary aggregates even more unstable. In effect, in Chile the opportunity cost of holding money is not as connected to the expected rate of inflation as it is to the expected change in the UF. The fact that this is determined by the always volatile one-month inflation rate makes nominal interest rates and the demand for money fluctuate very significantly from month to month (Fontaine 1991). This fact also explains why a monetary policy directed to stabilize nominal interest rates would also be very destabilizing in Chile.

On the other hand, the targeting of real interest rates is highly consistent with the intermediate goal of regulating the rate of growth of real aggregate expenditure. The basis for this is the perception that changes in real rates of interest exert a powerful influence on private expenditure in investment and consumption. The channels of influence can be many: intertemporal substitution effects, wealth effects through stock and bond prices, real exchange rate effects and expectational effects. Of all these channels probably the most important is the last one. Changes in real interest rates are a very efficient way monetary authorities can use to convey information about the way they see the current state of the economy, future trends in inflationary pressures and balance of payments conditions, and the resulting adjustments in the monetary policy stance. In principle, this can also be done by announcing changes in monetary targets, but their interpretation and evaluation seems much harder than that of a relative price change, real interest adjustments.[23]

Real interest rate targeting has to be understood as a practical way to implement a feedback policy rule aimed at regulating the rate of expansion of aggregate expenditure. This requires the target to be flexible, that is, the central bank to stand ready to adjust it any time real aggregate expenditure is perceived to be deviating from the projected course. This is not easy to do for at least three reasons.

---

23 This differs from Bernanke and Mishkin's (1992) observation that central banks tend to rely more on monetary targets when they want to convey a tougher anti-inflationary message. Real interest rates have proved in Chile an even better means of transmitting such a message.

First, as mentioned above, monetary authorities have to act on the basis of perceptions or expectations regarding real sector figures; they simply cannot wait until all the hard data is collected and processed. So here there is a great deal of "art." In Chile, something I have found very useful is basing such perceptions and expectations on deviations of the money supply (M1) from an estimate of the demand for money over the previous one or two quarters. So here monetarism can be again of much help.

Second, in an open economy, capital movements make it increasingly difficult to manage interest rates. Changes in interest rates cause large capital movements in precisely the opposite direction to the intentions of the central bank (see Fontaine 1994). This has been the experience not only of Chile, but of most Latin American economies in recent years. But despite this, the Chilean evidence shows that interest rates can be sustained significantly above international levels in a relatively open financial market. The counterpart of this in Chile has been a massive accumulation of international reserves in the hands of the central bank, whose monetary impact has been carefully sterilized. This activity has a financial cost for the central bank that certainly has to be taken into consideration. Alternatively the problem can be faced by allowing some temporary appreciation of the real exchange rate, although an excessive one would go against the central bank's objective of maintaining a sustainable current account deficit. A final option is to introduce capital controls to stem capital inflows. All three options have been applied in Chile and have succeeded in their immediate purpose, although at a non-negligible cost.

The third difficulty in managing interest rates is more of a political nature. Precisely because central bank induced changes in interest rates convey a very clear message, they tend to be politically very sensitive. Monetary authorities may then tend to try to avoid or postpone interest rate increases or decreases. A rigid real interest rule is, of course, the worst economic solution.

This brings us back to the issue of "bounded discretion." The conduct of the Chilean monetary policy since 1985 has been essentially an exercise in bounded discretion. Monetary authorities have been conveniently isolated from political pressures operating as an independent central bank. Their objectives have been clearly stated in terms of price stability, and they have directed their behaviour according to a set of sensible and well-known criteria or, conceptually, a feedback rule. Political independence, well-defined objectives, and transparent criteria for policy have provided a good framework for monetary stability.

Has Chilean monetary policy truly been monetarist? Throughout Latin America Chilean economic policy has frequently been attacked as extremely monetarist. The above discussion, I think, shows that Chilean monetary policy has not adhered strictly to a monetarist rule, but has relied on significant doses of (bounded) discretion. Monetarism, however, has been very present in inspiring a tenacious fight against inflation and as a guide for intelligent discretion.

The future of monetarism

In the previous section we argued that a central bank exerting what we called "bounded discretion" can indeed make a positive contribution for price stability. These said "boundaries" were thought as a set of criteria restricting the monetary authorities so as to minimize the well-known risks associated with discretion. We mentioned that, as in Chile, the independence of the central bank was a crucial precondition.

Central bank independence has become an objective of most stabilization plans in Latin America. Its popularity stems from the relative success of the three long lasting experiences, the U.S. one, the Swiss one and the German. Several studies have suggested that economies with an independent central bank tend to show less inflation (a notable exception is Japan).[24] Chile instituted an independent central bank in 1989. It has since been followed by Argentina, Colombia, Mexico, New Zealand, and Venezuela. Several other countries have plans for following suit. Central bank independence, it seems, is going to reign in the near future.

The foundation of the concept is no other than the two century-old one of the division of power (Fontaine 1989). It is very dangerous to concentrate both fiscal and monetary powers in the executive branch of

---

24 See Cukierman (1992).

government. Without an independent central bank, the goal of price stability typically is sacrificed to more mundane objectives. Granting the central bank independence from the political process creates the necessary checks and balances, which the separation between the executive and legislative branches does in other fields. Of course, as in the latter case, central bank independence creates some coordination problems and conflicts. But those seem a reasonable price to pay to avoid the (inflationary) abuse of an excessive concentration of power.

Central bank independence is no panacea. It's "Achilles' heel" is the problem of incentives. Do independent central bankers face the right incentives to follow stabilization policies? Mere independence, defined as the absence of subordination to political authorities, is unlikely to eliminate a set of wrong incentives. Independent monetary authorities are elected in a way that reduces their dependence on political authorities and, more importantly, prevents their being removed for political reasons. In practice, there are different degrees of independence, but the critical test is whether monetary authorities are free to disobey political authority. An independent central bank must be free not to follow any instruction or suggestion from political authorities.

But, is this enough? Will monetary authorities, left at their will, voluntarily choose to follow the tough anti-inflationary discipline? Experience shows that when they have a clear legal mandate to achieve and maintain price stability they are less prone to seek other objectives. After all, the central bank authorities are typically selected—and rather carefully—from among well- trained and experienced economists who end up seeing their personal future very much linked to having done a good job with respect to inflation. The prestige of the institution is also important. When price stability becomes the sole mandate of central banks their bureaucracies become a powerful internal lobby against any deviation from it, because they fear this could deteriorate the image of the institution and their own future careers. Of course, these motivations may not be strong enough to overcome an explosion of populism such as that seen in many Latin American countries in the 1970s and 1980s.

One can think of other incentives, such as making central bankers accountable for any deviations from price stability. In Chile some ideas were floated in that direction, but in the end the German-Swiss-U.S. model of essentially no formal accountability prevailed. In New Zealand, a new and interesting solution was found: to link the permanence of the central bank chairman to the fulfilment of the inflation target, set formally a year in advance by the Parliament. So far it is working (annual inflation being below the target of 2 percent), but it is too early to judge. I very much like the New Zealand solution. An alternative one, that I favoured for Chile, is to make the compensation of the highest authorities of the central bank a constant nominal sum fixed at the beginning of their terms.[25] Many other solutions can probably be found. To me this is a crucial field for innovation: the future will be characterized by independent central banks, but the search for the right incentive structure for such independent central banks is not at all concluded.

Since even the best solution found is likely to be of a second-best nature, I cannot finish this chapter without devoting a few lines to an alternative arrangement: the privatization of central banking. This of course is a very appealing idea for free-market economists as myself. Central banks are, after all, an intellectually uncomfortable state-owned enterprise, a triumph of pragmatism over doctrine. When F.A. Hayek (1978) presented his novel views on the subject, they sounded a bit like science fiction. But since then the likelihood of applying them has increased. For example, one could argue that a solution for the monetary chaos in Russia could be to do away with the state monopoly over the issuing of money. The problem though is that the implications of such a revolution are not yet fully explored and understood. The risks of substituting a private monopoly for the state monopoly, due to certain natural monopoly characteristics of money, may be important. The "time inconsistency" problem may also be present with private issuers of money. Therefore, it is clearly too early to leap into this unknown water.

However, I think some of the spirit of the proposal can be captured within the present state-controlled framework by introducing more freedom in the financial markets. Three ideas in this direction are: first,

---

25 RI proposed this policy when I was a member of the committee in charge of preparing the draft law for the Chilean central bank. It did not fly.

abolish exchange controls and authorize the free circulation of foreign monies for the payment of goods and services, including taxes. The "dollarization" of Latin American economies has been for long a spontaneous defense against inflation, strongly resisted by central banks and the IMF. Currency substitution can be a powerful constraint on central banks. The standard practice of empowering central banks with the authority to impose exchange controls is therefore problematic.[26]

A second reform would be to minimize central bank regulations on the private issuing of money substitutes. Most banking legislation establishes certain restrictions such as minima maturities, maxima interest rates (at least for current accounts), and reserve requirements to bank deposits. All these limit the capacity of commercial banks to compete with central banks in the production of close substitutes of money. Nonbank competitors are often even more discouraged because of the well-known externalities associated with financial crises.

A final proposal, and one that in Chile has proved successful, is the facilitation of the issuing of CPI-indexed securities and deposits. In Chile, as explained above, UF-denominated financial assets have become the best hedge against inflation and an effective source of currency substitution. This feature substantially reduces the scope for imposing a high inflation tax (money demand becomes more elastic). And, to the extent that it facilitates the indexation of prices, it also may discourage politically induced business cycles. Indexation has to be encouraged by legislation because it does not seem to be a spontaneous solution. Despite its advantages, financial indexation is a rare specie in world economic history. This probably has to do with the fact that for it to work a credible institution has to compute and publish the relevant index or indices, banks must be allowed to issue deposits so denominated, and tax and commercial legislation must be modified to give indexed financial assets the same treatment as nonindexed ones.

To recapitulate, monetarism has won the debate in changing public opinion on the importance of price stability, on the responsibility of monetary policy in preserving price stability, and on the need to shape

---

26 The Chilean central bank continues to have and exert strong powers in this field.

monetary policy according to rules that minimize central bank discretion. Starting from this "monetarist consensus", specific proposals take separate routes. Theoretically inclined monetarists have tended to favour replacing central banks with fixed rules, in the form of either a fixed-quantitative rule or a fixed-price (or exchange rate) rule. I do not think those rules work well in the real world. Other economists have taken the more radical course of advocating the privatization of money, an interesting but yet too risky alternative. For policy-oriented economists as myself, this theoretical debate is extremely useful, although it cannot be asked to deliver practical solutions. Rather this debate gives the policy maker useful insights and guidance for implementing policies according to his own instincts and the concrete circumstances he faces. In my view, monetarism provides a most useful orientation, but cannot be asked to provide a list of specific practical proposals.

Thus, in the future I see monetary policy being implemented by independent central banks with an undisputable commitment to price stability. I see them operating in an open and free financial environment, facing strong competition from private and foreign near monies. And I see the conduct of monetary policy bounded by well-defined criteria, of hopefully a monetarist orientation, but in the end preserving some room for discretion. Such bounded discretion is not free of risks, mistakes, and abuses, as any other human creation. The ability to avoid those pitfalls is what distinguishes a good, artful, central banker from a not so good one.

References

Angell, W. (1992) "Commodity Prices and Monetary Policy: What Have We Learned?" *Cato Journal* (Spring/Summer): 185-92.

Bernanke, B., and Mishkin, F. (1992) "Central Bank Behaviour and the Strategy of Monetary Policy: Observations from Six Industrialized Countries." NBER *Working Paper No 4082*. Cambridge, Mass.

Cagan, P. (1956) "The Monetary Dynamics of Hyperinflation." In M. Friedman (ed.) *Studies in the Quantity Theory of Money*. Chicago: University of Chicago Press.

Cukierman, A. (1992) *Central Bank Strategy, Credibility, and Independence: Theory and Evidence*. Cambridge, Mass.: MIT Press.

De la Cuadra, S., and Valdes Prieto, S. (1990) "Myths and Facts about Financial Liberalization in Chile: 1974-82." *Documento de Trabajo No 128*. Santiago, Chile: Pontificia Universidad Católica de Chile.

Dorn, J. A. (1992) "Money, Macroeconomics, and Forecasting." *Cato Journal* 12 (1) (Spring/Summer): 7-21.

Dornbusch, R., and Edwards, S. (1992) "The Macroeconomics of Populism." *Journal of Development Economics* 32 (2) (April).

Fontaine, J. A. (1989) "Banco Central: Autonomia para Cautelar la Estabilidad." *Cuadernos de Economía* 26 (77) (April): 65-74.

Fontaine, J. A. (1989) "The Chilean Economy in the Eighties: Adjustment and Recovery." In S. Edwards and F. Larrain (eds.) *Debt, Adjustment and Recovery*. Oxford: Basil Blackwell.

Fontaine, J. A. (1991) "La Administración de la Política Monetaria en Chile: 1985-89." *Cuadernos de Economía* 83 (1991).

Fontaine, J. A. (1993) "Transición Económica y Política en Chile (1970-1990)." *Estudios Públicos* (Autumn): 229-79.

Fontaine, J. A. (1994) "External Investments by Pension Funds: Macroeconomic Consequences." Paper presented to *Mandatory Pension Funds: Funding, Privatization and Macroeconomic Policy*, conference organized by Instituto de Economía, Universidad Católica, Santiago.

Friedman, M., and Schwartz, A. (1963) *A Monetary History of the United States*. Princeton: Princeton University Press.

Friedman, M. (1968) "The Role of Monetary Policy." *American Economic Review* 58 (March): 1-17.

Goodhart, C. (1989) "The Conduct of Monetary Policy." *Economic Journal* 99 (June).

Harberger, A. (1963) "The Dynamics of Inflation in Chile." In C. Christ (ed.) *Measurement in Economics: Studies in Mathematical Economics and Econometrics*. Calif.: Stanford University Press.

Hayek, F. A. (1978) *Denationalisation of Money: The Argument Revisited*. Hobert Paper 70. London: Institute of Economic Affairs.

Hetzel, R. (1992) "Indexed Bonds as an Aid to Monetary Policy." Reserve Bank of Richmond *Economic Review* 78 (September/October): 13-23.

Hetzel, R. (1993) "A Quantity Theory Framework for Monetary Policy." *Federal Reserve Bank of Richmond Economic Quarterly* 79 (3) (Summer).

Kydland, F., and Prescott, E. (1977) "Rules Rather than Discretion: The Inconsistency of Optimal Plans." *Journal of Political Economy* 85: 473-91.

Little, I. (1982) *Economic Development: Theory, Policy and International Relations*. New York: Basic Books.

Lucas, R. (1976) "Econometric Policy Evaluation: A Critique." *Carnegie-Rochester Conference Series on Public Policy* (1976): 19-46.

Lucas, R. ([1977] 1981) "Understanding Business Cycles." Reprinted in R. Lucas, *Studies in Business Cycles*. Oxford: Blackwell.

McCallum, B. "Targets, Indicators, and Instruments of Monetary Policy." (1990) In W. Haraf, and P. Cagan. *Monetary Policy for a Changing Financial Environment*. Washington, D.C.: American Enterprise Institute.

McCallum, B. (1993) "Discretion versus Policy Rules in Practice: Two Critical Points. A Comment." *Carnegie-Rochester Series on Public Policy* 39: 215-20.

Poole, W. (1970) "Optimal Choice of Monetary Policy Instruments in a Simple Scholastic Macro Model." *Quarterly Journal of Economics* (May): 197-216.

Rosende, F. (1993) "La Autonomía del Banco Central de Chile: Una Evaluación Preliminar." *Cuadernos de Economía* 30 (91) (December): 293-326.

Sargent, T. (1990) "Elements of Monetary Reform." In W. Haraf and P. Cagan (eds.) *Monetary Policy for a Changing Financial Environment.* Washington, D.C.: American Enterprise Institute.

Simons, H. (1936) "Rules versus Authorities in Monetary Policy." *Journal of Political Economy* 44 (February): 1-30.

Stockman, A. (1992) "Setting a Framework for Monetary Policy." *Cato Journal* 12 (1) (Spring/Summer): 274-53.

Taylor, J. (1993) "Discretion versus Policy Rules in Practice." *Carnegie-Rochester Series on Public Policy* 39: 195-214.

CHAPTER 14

Monetary Systems and Inflation in Developing Countries

Steve H. Hanke and Kurt Schuler[1]

The problem

MOST DEVELOPING COUNTRIES ARE PLAGUED by relatively high and variable rates of inflation. Among the 126 developing countries monitored by the International Monetary Fund, average inflation was 20.2 percent a year from 1971 to 1983 and 43.5 percent a year from 1984 to 1993. In the same periods, the variability of inflation, as measured by the absolute value of the standard deviation, was 14.1 percent and 34.8

---

1 Steve H. Hanke is Professor of Applied Economics at The Johns Hopkins University and Chief Economist of Friedberg Commodity Management. Kurt Schuler is a Post-Doctoral Fellow at The Johns Hopkins University. They have advised governments in Argentina, Venezuela, and El Salvador, as well as in Eastern Europe, on the role of a currency board in bringing about monetary stability.

percent, respectively. For 1994, average inflation was 48.0 percent for developing countries (IMF 1995: 135).

High inflation is associated with low economic growth. In the periods 1971 to 1983 and 1984 to 1993, the 42 developing countries with the highest growth rates of gross domestic product had average growth of 5.8 and 7.4 percent a year and average inflation of 12.0 and 11.5 percent a year, respectively. The 42 developing countries with the lowest growth rates, on the other hand, had average growth of 4.0 and 1.4 percent a year and average inflation of 26.4 and 53.5 percent a year in the same periods, respectively (IMF 1994: 55). To put the numbers into perspective, consider that with the growth rates of 1984-1993, high-growth countries will double their GDPs in a decade, while the low-growth countries will need almost half a century.

Furthermore, the growth rates are absolute, not adjusted for growth in population. Using a slightly different basis of calculation, the World Bank estimates that gross national product per person actually declined in Africa, the Middle East, and Latin America from 1980 to 1993. The average rate of growth for all low- and middle-income countries (i.e., developing countries) in the period was 0.9 percent a year, which reflects the impact of the rapidly growing East Asian economies in the average. In high-income (developed) countries, GNP per person grew an average of 2.2 percent a year in the same period (World Bank 1995: 162-63). Most developing countries have fallen further and further behind developed countries since 1980.

The story told by the raw data is confirmed by a recent study by Stanley Fischer (1993). Employing regression techniques and using data from 94 developing countries for the period 1962 to 1988, Fischer concludes that inflation reduces economic growth by reducing investment and the rates of growth in productivity. His analysis also strongly suggests that a relatively low rate of inflation is a prerequisite for sustained economic growth.

High inflation is not the only way in which developing countries lower the quality of their currencies. Most restrict convertibility (see IMF 1995) and a number have resorted to currency confiscation (Mas 1994). Because of the low quality of most currencies, international trade is transacted only in 15 to 20 of the more than 150 currencies in existence.

These high-quality currencies are the convertible currencies of the major developed countries. Because the currencies of most developing countries are inconvertible or only partly convertible, international trade in developing countries depends heavily on using convertible currencies provided by developed countries. Developing countries use these currencies as units of account and means of payment.

Among the high-quality currencies the U.S. dollar still plays a singular role. It is the vehicle currency in spot and forward exchange transactions across any pair of other currencies. For example, foreign-exchange traders do not sell Mexican pesos for French francs directly; rather, they sell pesos for U.S. dollars and then use the dollars to buy francs. The dollar's role as a vehicle currency is also evident in its continued dominance in Eurocurrency markets, where the main players are international banks. Under the Bretton Woods system of pegged exchange rates, the dollar had a semiofficial role as the key currency of the world monetary system. Today, although the Bretton Woods system has been defunct for more than 20 years and most major currencies float against one another, the dollar unofficially remains the key currency. It is the currency governments usually use for intervention in foreign exchange markets.

Besides being the key currency of foreign exchange markets, the dollar is an unofficial internal currency of many developing countries. More than half of all dollar paper currency in circulation is estimated to be held outside the United States. The larger denominations are used as more reliable stores of value than local-currency bank deposits in many countries, even though paper currency pays no interest. Use of dollar paper currency outside the United States deprives other governments of revenue that they could earn from seigniorage if they issued currencies trusted by their people, and results in a flow of resources from relatively poor countries to the United States.

The currency board alternative

The low quality of the currencies of most developing countries leads one to ask why the quality is low and whether developing countries would not be better off simply using the dollar or another high-quality currency issued by a developed country.

In all but a few developed and developing countries, currencies are issued by central banks. Modern-style central banking in developed countries dates back to the mid-1800s, although some developed countries did not establish central banks until the early 1900s. (Previously most developed countries had competitive issue of notes by private banks, known as free banking; for case studies see Dowd 1992). Originally most of those central banks were somewhat restrained from inflation by the gold standard. With the final breakdown of the Bretton Woods system in 1973, the gold standard ceased to be a restraint. However, after a bout of high inflation in the 1970s, developed countries seem to have learned how to avoid the worst consequences of the post-Bretton Woods system.

Central banks in developing countries have not learned the same lesson. It is therefore worth remembering that central banking in most developing countries dates only from the 1950s or later. Before then many developing countries had currency boards. Under a currency board system, local currency, which is fully backed by foreign assets, is issued by a currency board, and is freely convertible into a reserve (anchor) currency or gold at a fixed exchange rate. The reserve currency is one chosen for relatively good expected stability and convertibility, such as the U.S. dollar. The government of a country with a currency board lacks arbitrary, discretionary control with regard to its monetary policy and its exchange-rate policy. In a currency board system, changes in the supply of local currency are determined entirely by the market forces determining the free flow of reserve-currency assets into and out of the currency board.

The currency board system provides a way for a country to import the relatively credible and stable monetary policy of the reserve-currency country. That is an especially attractive proposition for developing countries, where monetary policy has too often destabilized the economy. Milton Friedman (1974), who has long been the foremost advocate of floating exchange rates for developed countries, has written:

> For developing countries, the case against using monetary policy primarily as an instrument for short-run stabilization is far stronger than for developed countries. The crucial problem for developing countries is to achieve sustained growth, not to

smooth short-run fluctuations. In addition, such countries seldom have financial markets and banking institutions sufficiently sophisticated to permit what has come (most inaccurately) to be called "fine-tuning" of monetary policy [266].

For most such countries, I believe the best policy would be to eschew the revenue from money creation, to unify their currency with the currency of a large, relatively stable, developed country with which they have close economic relations, and to impose no barriers to the movement of money or of prices, wages, or interest rates. Such a policy requires avoiding a central bank [277].

The record supports Friedman's policy conclusions. Orthodox currency boards have existed in more than 70 countries. In all cases, currency boards have produced stable currencies that have kept inflation below 20 percent a year, and typically much lower than that. No currency board has ever devalued against its reserve currency. The currencies of all orthodox currency boards have been fully convertible into their reserve currencies, except in the few cases when the main issuing office of the currency board has actually been overrun by an enemy army (Hanke, Jonung, and Schuler 1993: 80-3, 172-80; Schuler 1992). Currency board systems generally performed much better than the central banking systems that replaced many of them. Where currency boards still exist—in Hong Kong, Gibraltar, Bermuda, the Cayman Islands, the Faroe Islands, the Falkland Islands—they continue to provide high-quality currencies. (Singapore has a note-issuing body called the Singapore Currency Board, but has not been a true currency board system since 1973. Since then the Singapore dollar has had a floating exchange rate.)

In the past few years, central banks in Argentina (since 1 April, 1991), Estonia (since 10 June 1992) and Lithuania (since 1 April 1994) have adopted currency board-type rules. These currency board-like systems have drastically reduced inflation, stabilized exchange rates, and allowed much fuller convertibility of the currency. Before the introduction of their currency board-like systems, annual inflation was roughly 2,000 percent in Argentina, 1,000 percent in Estonia, and 400 percent in Lithuania. In 1994, inflation was 4.1 percent in Argentina; it was 47.8 percent in Estonia, and 72.2 percent in Lithuania, whose price levels are still catching up to those of their reserve countries.

Problems with criticisms of the currency board system

Despite the practical success that currency boards have enjoyed, they have recently attracted new criticism after being neglected for three decades. (Elsewhere [Hanke, Jonung, and Schuler 1993: 37-40, 63-73, 136-42] we have responded to older criticisms, which focused mainly on the operation of the money supply in a currency board system, the alleged colonialism implicit in the currency board system, and flexibility in monetary policy.) Recent criticisms of currency boards have suffered from three flaws. Some criticisms have been purely semantic quibbles arising from misunderstandings of the currency board system. Other criticisms have been inappropriate comparisons, made on the basis that actual currency boards work less well than ideal central banks. But the choice in monetary policy is not between an actual currency board and an ideal central bank; it is between an actual currency board and an actual central bank. That is why the historical record of currency boards and central banks in developing countries is so important for evaluating their potentials as monetary institutions conducive to economic development. Still other criticisms have been merely hypothetical, arising from far-fetched assumptions that have not applied in fact to currency boards. Again, the historical record is important, because it helps to distinguish objections that apply in practice from objections that apply only on economists' blackboards.

What a currency board is

To reply to criticisms of the currency board system that are of a semantic character, it is desirable to have a fuller description of what a currency board is. Table 1 does so by contrasting important features of a typical currency board with those of a typical central bank. Note that the features are not those of ideal or unusually good actual currency boards and central banks. They are the features of typical actual currency boards and central banks. If the characterization of a typical central bank

Table 1: A Typical Currency Board versus a Typical Central Bank

Typical Currency Board	Typical Central Bank
Usually supplies notes and coins only	Supplies notes, coins, and deposits
Fixed exchange rate with reserve currency	Pegged or floating exchange rate
Foreign reserves of 100 percent	Variable foreign reserves
Full convertibility	Limited convertibility
Rule-bound monetary policy	Discretionary monetary policy
Not a lender of last resort	Lender of last resort
Does not regulate commercial banks	Often regulates commercial banks
Transparent	Opaque
Protected from political pressure	Politicized
High credibility	Low credibility
Earns seigniorage only from interest	Earns seigniorage from interest and inflation
Cannot create inflation	Can create inflation
Cannot finance spending by domestic government	Can finance spending by domestic government
Requires no "preconditions" for monetary reform	Requires "preconditions" for monetary reform
Rapid monetary reform	Slow monetary reform
Small staff	Large staff
Hard budget constraints	Soft budget constraints
Smaller economic shocks	Larger economic shocks
No balance of payments problems	Balance of payments problems
Liberal financial system	Financial repression
Low inflation	High inflation

does not reflect your experience, you probably live in a developed country. Central banks in developing countries comprise more than 80 percent of all central banks in existence, however, so the typical central bank is that of a developing country. For them the features we describe are typical, as can be confirmed by examining such publications as *World Currency Yearbook* or the IMF's *International Financial Statistics* and its *Annual Report on Exchange Arrangements and Exchange Restrictions.*

To begin at the top of the list in Table 1, a typical currency board *usually supplies notes and coins only*, whereas a typical central bank also supplies deposits. Some past currency boards have accepted deposits, however. The deposits of a currency board are subject to the same reserve requirement as its notes and coins (100 percent or slightly more).

A typical currency board maintains a truly *fixed exchange rate with the reserve currency*. The exchange rate is permanent, or at most can be altered only in emergencies. The exchange rate may be set by the constitution that describes the legal obligations of the currency board. No currency board has ever devalued against its reserve currency.[2] A typical central bank, in contrast, maintains a pegged or floating exchange rate rather than a truly fixed rate. A pegged exchange rate is constant for the time being in terms of a reserve currency, but carries no credible long-term guarantee of remaining at its current rate. A floating exchange rate is not maintained constant in terms of any reserve currency. The exchange rate maintained by a central bank is typically not permanently binding even if set by law, and can be altered at the will of the central bank or the government. When a typical central bank suffers heavy political or speculative pressure to devalue the currency, it devalues. Allegedly fixed exchange rates maintained by central banks have in reality typically been pegged exchange rates.

As reserve assets against its liabilities (its notes and coins in circulation), a typical currency board holds low-risk securities in the reserve

---

2   The Eastern Caribbean Currency Authority in effect devalued the Eastern Caribbean dollar 30 percent when it switched from the pound sterling to the U.S. dollar as its reserve currency in 1976. We are unable to determine the reason for the devaluation, since the currency board had foreign reserves exceeding 100 percent of its notes and coins in circulation.

currency; it may also hold bank deposits and a small amount of notes in the reserve currency. It holds *foreign reserves of 100 percent* or slightly more of its note, coin, and deposit liabilities, as set by law. Many currency boards have held a maximum of 105 or 110 percent foreign reserves to have a margin of protection in case the reserve-currency securities they held lost value. A typical central bank, in contrast, holds variable foreign reserves: it is not required to maintain any fixed, binding ratio of foreign reserves to liabilities. Even where a minimum ratio exists, a typical central bank can hold any ratio in excess of that. For example, a central bank required to hold at least 20 percent foreign reserves may hold 30, 130, or even 330 percent foreign reserves. A typical central bank also holds domestic-currency assets, which a typical currency board does not.

A typical currency board has *full convertibility* of its currency: it exchanges its notes and coins for the reserve currency at its stated fixed exchange rate without limit. Anybody who has reserve currency (or approved assets payable in the reserve currency, such as low-risk securities) can exchange it for currency board notes and coins at the fixed rate; anybody who has currency board notes and coins can exchange them for reserve currency at the fixed rate. A typical central bank, in contrast, has limited convertibility of its currency. Central banks in most developed countries and in a few developing countries have fully convertible currencies, but most central banks have inconvertible or partly convertible currencies. They restrict or forbid certain transactions, particularly purchases of foreign securities or real estate.

A currency board does not guarantee that deposits at commercial banks are convertible into currency board notes and coins. Commercial banks are responsible for holding enough notes and coins as vault cash to satisfy their contractual obligations to their depositors to convert deposits into notes and coins on demand. Commercial banks are not required to hold 100 percent foreign reserves like the currency board, nor 100 percent currency board notes and coins against deposits. Therefore, M0 is backed 100 percent by foreign reserves in a currency board system, but broader measures of the money supply such as M1, M2, and M3 are not. Nor does a currency board have any direct role in determining exchange rates with currencies other than the reserve currency.

Commercial banks trade them at market-determined exchange rates, which may be fixed, pegged, or floating against the reserve currency and hence against the currency board currency.

A typical currency board has a *rule-bound monetary policy*. A currency board is not allowed to alter the exchange rate, except perhaps in emergencies, nor is a currency board allowed to alter its reserve ratio or the regulations affecting commercial banks. A currency board merely exchanges its notes and coins for reserve currency at a fixed rate in such quantities as commercial banks and the public demand. When the demand for money changes, the role of a currency board is passive. Market forces alone determine the money supply through a self-adjusting process. A typical central bank, in contrast, has a partly or completely discretionary monetary policy. A central bank can alter at will, or with the approval of the government, the exchange rate, its ratio of foreign reserves, or the regulations affecting commercial banks. It is not subject to strict rules like a typical currency board.

A typical currency board is *not a lender of last resort*, that is, it does not lend to commercial banks or other enterprises to help them avoid bankruptcy. Commercial banks in a currency board system must rely on alternatives to a lender of last resort. A typical central bank, in contrast, is a lender of last resort.

A typical currency board *does not regulate commercial banks*. Banking regulations in a typical currency board system are relatively few, and are enforced by the ministry of finance or an office of bank regulation. A typical central bank, in contrast, often regulates commercial banks. Perhaps the most common form of regulation is imposing reserve requirements on commercial banks. The required reserves, which are held mainly in the form of deposits at the central bank, typically exceed the prudential reserves that commercial banks would hold if no reserve requirements existed.

The activities of a typical currency board are *transparent*, because a currency board is a very simple institution. It is merely a sort of warehouse for reserve-currency assets that back its notes and coins in circulation. The activities of a typical central bank are opaque. A central bank is not a warehouse; it is a speculating institution whose effectiveness depends on the ability to act secretly sometimes.

Because a typical currency board is rule-bound and transparent, it is *protected from political pressure*. It is protected by implicit rules of political behaviour, or, better yet, by an explicit constitution. A typical central bank is politicized. Some central banks, such as the German Bundesbank and the U.S. Federal Reserve System, are politically independent in the sense that their governors, once appointed, have sole control of the monetary base and cannot be fired by the executive or legislative branches of government during the governors' fixed terms of office. Even the most politically independent central banks sometimes yield to strong political pressure, though. The Bundesbank, which is justifiably regarded as the paragon of central bank independence, lacked sufficient independence to resist the government's exchange-rate policy during the German monetary reunification of 1990. The government imposed an exchange rate of 1 East German mark per West German mark despite the desire of the Bundesbank for a rate closer to the market rate of 6 East German marks per West German mark. The result was an increase in the inflation rate in Germany followed by a painful policy of high interest rates by the Bundesbank to restrain further inflation.

A typical currency board has *high credibility*. Its 100 percent foreign reserve requirement, rule-bound monetary policy, transparency, and protection from political pressure enable it to maintain full convertibility and a fixed exchange rate with the reserve currency. An appropriately chosen reserve currency will be stable; therefore, the currency issued by the currency board will be stable. A typical central bank, in contrast, has low credibility. A few exceptionally good central banks, which exist mainly in developed countries, have high credibility, but most do not. Because a typical central bank has discretion in monetary policy, is opaque, and is politicized, it has the means and the incentive to break promises about the exchange rate or inflation whenever it wishes.

A typical currency board *earns seigniorage* (income from issue) *only from interest*. The currency board earns interest from its holdings of reserve-currency securities (its main assets), yet pays no interest on its notes and coins (its liabilities). Gross seigniorage is the income from issuing notes and coins. It can be explicit interest income or implicit income in the form of goods acquired by spending money. Net seigniorage (profit) is gross seigniorage minus the cost of putting and maintaining notes and coins in circulation.

A typical central bank also earns seigniorage on its notes and coins in circulation *and* on the deposits that commercial banks hold with it and its loans. The deposits, like notes and coins, usually pay no interest. But a more important source of seigniorage for a typical central bank is inflation. A typical currency board cannot create inflation because it does not control the ultimate reserves of the monetary system. Like any system of fixed exchange rates, a currency board system may *transmit* inflation from the reserve country, but a currency board cannot *create* inflation because it cannot increase the monetary base independently of the monetary authority of the reserve country. A typical central bank, in contrast, can create inflation at its discretion by increasing the domestic monetary base.

A typical currency board *cannot finance spending by the domestic government* or domestic state enterprises because it is not allowed to lend to them. A typical central bank finances spending by the domestic government and domestic state enterprises.

A typical currency board *requires no "preconditions" for monetary reform.* Government finances, state enterprises, or trade need not be already reformed before the currency board can begin to issue a sound currency. A typical central bank cannot issue a sound currency unless the 'fiscal precondition' exists, that is, the government no longer needs to finance budget deficits by means of inflation. Once a government starts to depend on central banks for financing deficits, it usually has trouble stopping.

A typical currency board is conducive to *rapid monetary reform*. For example, the Lithuanian and Argentine currency board-like systems were implemented within three weeks of the laws that established them. Monetary reform with a typical central bank takes much longer.

A typical currency board needs only a *small staff* of a few persons who perform routine functions that are easily learned. A typical central bank needs a large staff trained in the intricacies of monetary theory and policy. The central banks of large countries have thousands of employees; for example, the Central Bank of Russia has more than 45,000 employees. Even the central banks of many small countries have hundreds of employees.

A typical currency board tends to impose *hard budget constraints* on economic agents, that is, it does not finance government budget deficits or provide subsidized credit. Economic agents, including the government, are forced to live within their earnings plus the amounts lent to them voluntarily at market rates of interest. A typical central bank tends to allow soft budget constraints, that is, through the inflation tax it finances government budget deficits or provides subsidized credits. By doing so, it diverts resources from more productive to less productive parts of the economy.

Currency board systems and central banking systems both experience economic shocks, but the source and extent of the shocks differ. A typical currency board system tends to experience *smaller economic shocks*. A currency board cannot be an independent disturbing element in the economy because it has no discretionary monetary policy. A currency board can transmit shocks that originate in the monetary policy of the reserve country, but the reserve currency will be one chosen for its expected stability, and therefore should cause fewer monetary shocks than would result if the country with a currency board instead had a central bank. As for economic shocks that originate elsewhere than from monetary policy, such as from changes in the price of oil, they are typically less important and in any case difficult to offset by monetary policy. A typical central bank, in contrast, tends to experience larger economic shocks. The sudden declines in living standards caused by high inflation in central banking systems, evident recently in Russia, Brazil, Ivory Coast, Jamaica, and other countries too numerous to mention, have no counterpart in currency board systems. The high inflation and low economic growth that most developing countries have experienced since the Bretton Woods era suggest that they would have done better not to have central banks.

A typical currency board system experiences *no balance of payments problems* because its full convertibility with the reserve currency allows for capital inflows to finance deficits in the current account. Also, because a currency board has no discretionary monetary policy, prices and asset holdings adjust "automatically" in accord with market forces.

A typical central banking system, in contrast, experiences balance of payments problems because its currency has restricted convertibility and because the central bank often expands the money supply too fast to maintain the pegged exchange rates that half or more of all central banking systems currently have. We discuss this more below.

A typical currency board is conducive to a *liberal financial system* burdened with few regulations to prevent it from operating efficiently. Most currency board systems have had no reserve requirements, no restrictions on branch banking, and no barriers to entry by foreign banks. Combined with full convertibility into the reserve currency, these features have promoted inflows of foreign capital and financial expertise. Large foreign banks have established branch networks that have offered safe places for the deposit of funds. Under the currency board system, Hong Kong, Bermuda, and the Cayman Islands have developed into international financial centres. A typical central bank, in contrast, creates "financial repression." It restricts financial freedom so that it can grant subsidized credit to the government and favoured sectors of the economy. Most central banking systems impose reserve requirements, which are a tax on banking activity; some still restrict branch banking by requiring lengthy procedures for opening or closing branches; and most have barriers to entry by foreign banks. Consequently, their financial systems tend to be backward, bureaucratic, and weak.

Finally, a typical currency board transmits *low inflation* because its reserve currency is stable. As we mentioned, no orthodox currency board system has ever had inflation exceeding 20 percent a year, and inflation has typically been lower. A typical central bank creates high inflation, as shown by the figures we cited at the beginning of this essay.

Semantic criticisms

Being aware of the differences between a typical currency board and a typical central bank enables us to see that many of the recent criticisms of the currency board system are purely semantic. In particular, they often assume that a currency board is merely a type of central bank, so that it is prone to all the problems that typically afflict a central bank. An orthodox currency board, however, is an alternative to a central bank. Where there is only one issuer of currency, an orthodox currency board exists instead of a central bank. The semantic criticisms do to some extent apply to currency board-like systems, because such systems do not abolish some features of central banking that conflict with the orthodox currency board system, especially the role of the central bank as a lender of last resort. But as we have stressed, the currency board-like systems are not orthodox currency board systems, and we think that currency board-like systems are less desirable than orthodox currency boards.

One semantic criticism is the claim that the exchange rate of a currency board is no more credible than the exchange rate of a central bank (Liviatan 1993: 65). It arises from confusion about the difference between the fixed and pegged exchange rates. The main difference between a fixed exchange rate and a pegged exchange rate is credibility. A declaration by a typical central bank that it maintains a fixed exchange rate is not credible because the monetary rule of a fixed exchange rate conflicts with discretionary monetary policy. At least since 1914, almost all central banks that have claimed to maintain fixed exchange rates, including exceptionally good central banks, have in reality maintained pegged exchange rates. Almost all central banks depreciated their currencies against gold or silver during the First World War, the Great Depression, the Second World War, and the breakup of the Bretton Woods system in the early 1970s. Most central banks with pegged exchange rates have also depreciated their currencies individually at other times (for chronologies see Pick and Sédillot 1971 and *World Currency Yearbook*).

In practice a pegged rate is typically a depreciating exchange rate, involving devaluation or foreign-exchange controls to accommodate soft budget constraints. As compensation for the risk of depreciation of a pegged exchange rate, lenders and investors demand higher real rates of interest than would exist with a truly fixed exchange rate (Walters 1990: 14-15). It may take years for a typical central bank to achieve substantial credibility for a pegged exchange rate. In the meantime, high real interest rates to defend a pegged exchange rate create high costs, which are particularly painful to capital-intensive industries and export industries that compete against foreign counterparts based in countries with more credible monetary authorities. A central bank maintaining a pegged exchange rate typically expands the monetary base faster than its foreign reserves. Consequently, the domestic price level tends to increase. Imports temporarily become less expensive and exports decrease because they become more expensive in world markets. The central bank loses foreign reserves as people buy more imports and as currency speculators bet that the loss of foreign reserves will induce the central bank to depreciate the currency. To avoid losing more foreign reserves and to revive exports, the central bank imposes foreign-exchange controls. Alternatively, the central bank devalues the currency, re-pegging it at an exchange rate sufficiently undervalued that for awhile the central bank can safely continue to inflate.

Because a currency board has 100 percent foreign reserves and allows full convertibility with its reserve currency, it is credible and can maintain a truly fixed exchange rate at lower cost to the economy (especially in terms of real interest rates) than a pegged exchange rate maintained by a central bank.

Still another largely semantic criticism is that the fear that the real exchange rate in a currency board system may become overvalued, making domestic industry uncompetitive in world markets and requiring a devaluation to restore competitiveness. Some observers of the Argentine and Estonian currency board-like systems have recently made this criticism (e.g. Liviatan 1993: xv).

The real exchange rate measures the prices of nontraded goods such as labour and land compared to the prices of traded goods for which world markets exist, such as wheat and airplanes. Arbitrage tends to keep prices of traded goods the same the world over, after allowing for costs of taxes, transportation, and various types of trading risk. Accordingly, changes in the prices of traded goods tend to be the same in a currency board country as in its reserve-currency country. Since Argentina, Estonia, and Lithuania established their currency board-like systems, prices of traded goods have increased at rates close to those in the United States (Argentina and Lithuania's reserve-currency country) and Germany (Estonia's reserve-currency country). Prices of nontraded goods have increased faster, however. In Buenos Aires many goods are now as expensive as in New York City. In Estonia and Lithuania prices have not yet reached such high levels, but consumer price inflation was in double digits in 1994, versus just 4.1 percent in Argentina.

The rapid increase in the prices of nontraded goods in all three currency board-like systems has already made unprofitable some formerly profitable kinds of production. But that is precisely what happens in economic development. The currency board-like systems are undergoing rapidly what developed countries underwent more slowly. Developed countries have lost market share and jobs to developing countries in industries such as textiles and shoes, but they have more than offset the losses by expanding in industries such as medical research and computer programming. In the currency board system of Hong Kong, many companies have shifted their manufacturing operations to southern China in the last several years, but Hong Kong has developed new capabilities as a centre of finance, advertising, research, and communications. In the currency board-like systems, the shift may be even faster for a few years because the currency was previously an important barrier to the efficient use of resources, and now the barrier has been greatly lowered.

Rather than being a problem, an appreciation in the real exchange rate is to be expected in a currency board system. Because an orthodox currency board does not have an active monetary policy, it cannot deliberately create an overvalued exchange rate by intervening in foreign-exchange markets, as a central bank sometimes can. Prices in a currency board country may become expensive, but that does not indicate an overvalued exchange rate or a need for devaluation any more than high prices in New York City compared to Mississippi indicate that New York City should establish its own currency and devalue to remain competitive with Mississippi. In Argentina, consumer price inflation and the appreciation of the real exchange rate has slowed over time as the economy has adjusted to the beneficial sudden stability of the currency. Argentina has been able to withstand a large appreciation of the real exchange rate because productivity has increased by 50 percent since the currency was stabilized (Moffett 1994). We expect the same to happen in Estonia and Lithuania. Because they began with still more distorted structures of prices than Argentina they are taking longer to reach the single-digit inflation rates typical of older currency board and currency board-like systems.

Nor does a currency board system experience difficulties with its balance of payments. In a monetary system with a fully convertible currency there is no need to do so. Within the common currency area formed by the currency board country and the reserve-currency country, people may change their habits of spending, but the changes cause no financial difficulty. Prices in the two countries adjust to reflect the relative strength of flows of payments and investment. The exchange rate remains the same. Outside the common currency area exchange rates may fluctuate, but they impose no constraints on the balance of payments. Changes in the balance of payments may affect exchange rates, but will not affect the convertibility of the currency in the currency board country. Because foreign exchange is not rationed by exchange controls, a deficit of foreign exchange is no more likely than a deficit of wheat in a regime of free trade. Foreign exchange may be in lesser supply at some times, but exchange rates will adjust to reflect this.

So far as we know, no currency board system has ever experienced difficulties with its balance of payments. The three recent currency board-like systems initially restricted capital-account transactions, but they too have experienced no difficulties with their balance of payments. In this connection it is worth mentioning that currency board systems have in the past had current-account deficits for years on end without experiencing difficulties with their balance of payments. They have been able to secure capital-account financing sufficient to offset current-account deficits, because their currency board systems and other institutions made them good places to invest. Hong Kong and Singapore, for example, had current-account deficits for decades at a time while enjoying strong economic growth (Schuler 1992: 159, 178-79, 204-8).

Criticisms using inappropriate comparisons

Other criticisms of the currency board system rely on standards that are not suited to the task at hand. The most frequently made economic criticism of the currency board system is that by eliminating discretionary power in domestic monetary policy (including the power to alter the exchange rate) it eliminates potentially beneficial monetary flexibility (Fieleke 1992: 21-3; Fratianni, Davidson and von Hagen 1992: 42-3).

In analyzing the validity of the criticism it is necessary to ask why the monetary authority should have discretionary power. Advocates of discretionary policy assume that the benefits of discretion outweigh its costs. For developing countries there is an easy way to test the assumption: compare their monetary and economic performance with that of developed countries. A monetary policy with no discretion, such as a currency board system or dollarization, results in a country having an inflation rate close to that of the reserve country (with the caveats made above) and the same degree of convertibility as the reserve country. There is a case for discretionary monetary policy in developing countries if it results in lower inflation, greater convertibility, higher economic growth, or something else such as higher employment compared to rule-bound policy. As the statistics we cited at the beginning of the chapter indicate, developing countries have done much worse with discretionary monetary policy than they would have with completely rule-bound policy linking their currencies to the currency of a suitable developed country.

If anything, monetary policy in developing countries has been characterized by indiscretion rather than by discretion. Central banks in developing countries have used their monetary and regulatory powers to create massive inflations, restrict the convertibility of their currencies, divert credit to favoured economic sectors, hold deposit interest rates to be held below the rate of inflation, and restrict competition in banking.

Therefore, rather than being a restraint on trustworthy discretion in monetary policy, a currency board in practice is a restraint on monetary indiscretions. The rule-bound nature of a currency board tends to protect an economy from the destabilizing effects of discretionary monetary policy and tends to force wages and prices to be flexible. The case for establishing a currency board as a monetary rule is much the same as the case for establishing a constitution that limits the powers of government. The experience of constitutions is far from perfect, but it does support the claim that a constitution is typically more effective than no constitution at constraining the powers of a democratic government. A currency board is a form of monetary constitution that prevents the domestic government from abridging economic freedoms by levying a high inflation tax not desired by the public. Because a currency board cannot finance budget deficits of the domestic government, the currency board system establishes an implicit low-inflation fiscal constitution. Critics of the currency board system as a monetary constitution should state whether by the same logic they favour abolishing written political constitutions.

A related issue to the debate over rules versus discretion in monetary policy is the origin of undesirable economic shocks. If undesirable shocks originate predominantly from monetary events in *other* countries or if discretionary monetary policy can consistently soften the effects of real shocks, there is another argument for discretionary policy (cf. Havrylyshyn and Williamson 1991: 8, 39; Liviatan 1993: 4). If undesirable shocks originate predominantly from the effects of discretionary monetary policy at home or if discretionary policy cannot consistently soften the effects of real shocks, there is another argument against discretionary policy.

We know of no systematic examination of the issue for developing countries, but the study by Fischer (1993) and the raw data on inflation and economic growth suggest that discretionary monetary policy at home is the most important correctable source of undesirable shocks. All high inflations and hyperinflations, and the economic dislocations that have followed, have been caused by discretionary monetary policies that increased the supply of money, not by real shocks to an unchanged supply of money. Observation also suggests that discretionary monetary policy can do little to soften the overall effects of real shocks, although it can redistribute the effects. The oil price shock of the 1970s, for example, was not noticeably milder in countries that had floating exchange rates than in those that retained pegged or fixed exchange rates to anchor currencies. Eliminating monetary shocks by means of currency boards is therefore very desirable.

Purely hypothetical criticisms

The currency board system has also been criticized on grounds that are purely hypothetical. Hypothetical criticism is useful for discussing what could go wrong with a system that has not been well tested. With a system that has been well tested, however, criticism should meet a more exacting standard. A well-tested system yields historical experience that should guide us in determining which of the many potential criticisms have a basis in reality. Criticisms that do not take such historical experience into account are what Ronald Coase (1988) in another context has termed "blackboard economics": objections that result from spending too much time devising theories on blackboards and not enough finding out how things really work.

One criticism is that the currency board system is politically impossible (Schwartz 1992: 18-19, 22-3). When the objection is made by an experienced politician as a judgment of circumstances at a particular time it deserves respect. Even then it should not foreclose discussion of the currency board system, because what is politically impossible one year can become possible the next. But for economists to use the alleged political impossibility of a proposal as an excuse for ignoring it is to presume expertise they do not have and to ignore the expertise they have.

Economists can expand the boundaries of what is thought to be politically possible. Particularly during troubled times, drastic reforms are politically possible because they are more popular than muddling further into trouble with old policies. The politicians who established the currency board-like systems of Argentina, Estonia, and Lithuania gained popularity because the systems quickly reduced inflation. In fact, the currency board-like systems became so popular that they gained support from across the political spectrum. Note that they were established by quite different governments: former fascists in Argentina, a coalition in Estonia considered right-wing by local standards, and former communists in Lithuania.

Another purely hypothetical criticism of the currency board system is that it requires a balanced government budget to be already in place (Liviatan 1993: xx, 9, 31). The objection has the order reversed. Because a currency board does not buy domestic assets, it cannot be a source of compulsory finance for the government budget. The government can still engage in noninflationary deficit finance if it can find willing domestic or foreign lenders. In practice, though, the currency board system reduces the overall scope for deficit finance.

On the other hand, it also tends to increase real tax revenue, especially in countries suffering from high inflation, by promoting economic activity and reducing the loss of real tax revenue from inflation. Although Estonia and Lithuania had budgets that were balanced or nearly balanced when they established their currency board-like systems, Argentina did not. The total deficit of the public sector was 12.4 percent of GDP in 1989 (World Bank 1993: 182). The pressure for noninflationary finance created by the currency board-like system has enabled the government to eliminate the deficits. The Argentine economy has since 1991 experienced strong, sustained growth for the first time in many years.

The objection that a currency board system requires a balanced budget implies that it takes a long time to establish a currency board. Yet in Argentina and Lithuania the currency board-like systems began operating less than three weeks after the laws establishing them were passed. Estonia also began operating its currency board-like system very soon after establishing it.

Another purely hypothetical criticism of the currency board system is that it is susceptible to financial panics because it lacks a lender of last resort (Rostowski 1993). This criticism is based on no analysis of the actual occurrence of financial panics in currency board systems compared to central banking systems. Failures by commercial banks have been minor in orthodox currency board systems, although several large banks have failed in the currency board-like system of Estonia, as a result of bad debts inherited from the period of Soviet central banking. In orthodox currency board systems no large commercial bank has ever failed, and losses to depositors from the few small commercial banks that failed have been tiny (Schuler 1992: 191-3). Since the founding of the first currency board in 1849, there have apparently been no cases in which commercial banks in currency board systems have relied on central banks as lenders of last resort. For example, British overseas commercial banks in currency board systems apparently never relied on the Bank of England as a lender of last resort. Currency board systems, and even the recent currency board-like systems, have performed well without lenders of last resort.

Two important sources of stability for commercial banks in currency board systems have been interbank lending markets and international branch networks. Illiquid banks borrow reserves from more liquid ones, as they do in many central banking systems. Borrowing need not be limited to the domestic market; commercial banks can also borrow abroad and in Eurocurrency markets. By eliminating exchange risk with the reserve currency, the currency board system facilitates access of commercial banks to foreign financial markets. The currency board system also encourages foreign commercial banks to establish branches in the currency board country, in effect importing their stability.

The experience of developing countries suggests that central banks have more often been the cause than the cure of financial instability. By creating financial repression they have often undermined the stability of local commercial banks. The most dramatic example of this recently has been the troubles of commercial banks in former socialist countries, which have been "solved" only at the price of high inflations that have wiped out the real value of previously accumulated savings deposits.

Another purely hypothetical criticism of currency boards is that they are appropriate for small economies that are open (have much foreign trade), such as Hong Kong, but not for large economies that are closed (have little foreign trade) (Liviatan 1993: 7, 28). The criticism implies that a floating exchange rate would encourage greater economic stability than a fixed rate.

Currency boards have been successful in small, open economies such as Hong Kong and large (populous), closed economies such as Nigeria and British East Africa, which initially had little trade with the outside world. Currency boards have opened previously closed economies by providing sound currencies that encouraged trade. Furthermore, Hong Kong, with a GDP of about US$100 billion as of 1995, has a larger economy than, for example, Poland, Ukraine, Pakistan, Egypt, Venezuela, and all but a few other developing countries.

A final criticism of currency boards that is merely hypothetical is that they require initial foreign reserves that are much larger than the existing foreign reserves possessed by many countries (Bofinger 1991, Havrylyshyn and Williamson 1991: 40). This neglects the possibility of establishing temporary arrangements to handle the problem, such as borrowing foreign reserves and repaying them later from seigniorage. (We have developed plans for such arrangements for countries considering currency boards or currency board-like systems.) Furthermore, the currency board-like systems of Argentina, Estonia, and Lithuania began with adequate foreign reserves without foreign borrowing. At the time of their currency reforms, they, like a number of developing countries today, had small real supplies of domestic currency because inflation had induced people to hold foreign currency or other more stable assets instead. The developing countries where currency boards would yield the biggest improvement over current monetary arrangements tend to be those with the smallest real supplies of domestic currency in relation to their size. The experience of the currency board-like systems has been that once people have confidence in the domestic currency, they will convert assets into domestic currency and build up their real cash balances to levels that are more typical of low-inflation countries.

Conclusion

Currency boards are not perfect. They have potential defects that we have analyzed elsewhere (Hanke, Jonung, and Schuler 1993: 109-14). But the defects of central banks in developing countries are typically much worse. Perpetuating central banking in developing countries will perpetuate the high inflation and economic decline that they have recently suffered. The currency board system offers a proven way of achieving low inflation and economic growth.

References

Bofinger, P. (1991) "Options for the Payments and Exchange-Rate System in Eastern Europe." *European Economy*, special ed. no. 2: 243-61.

Coase, R. (1988) *The Firm, the Market and the Law*. Chicago: University of Chicago Press.

Dowd, K. (ed.) (1992) *The Experience of Free Banking*. London: Routledge.

Fieleke, N. S. (1992) "The Quest for Sound Money: Currency Boards to the Rescue?" Federal Reserve Bank of Boston, *New England Economic Review*, November-December: 14-24.

Fischer, S. (1993) "The Role of Macroeconomic Factors in Growth." National Bureau for Economic Research Working Paper 4565, December.

Fratianni, M.; Davidson, L. S.; and von Hagen, J. (1992) "Proposal for Monetary and Fiscal Reforms in the Baltic Republics." *G-7 Report*, Summer: 37-50.

Friedman, M. (1974) "Monetary Policy in Developing Countries." In David, P. A., and Reder, M. W., eds., *Nations and Economic Growth: Essays in Honor of Moses Abramovitz*. Chicago: University of Chicago Press.

Hanke, S. H.; Jonung, L.; and Schuler, K. (1993) *Russian Currency and Finance: A Currency Board Approach to Reform*. London: Routledge.

Hanke, S. H., and Schuler. K. (1994) *Currency Boards for Developing Countries: A Handbook*. San Francisco: ICS Press.

Havrylyshyn, O., and Williamson, J. (1991) *From Soviet Disunion to Eastern Economic Community?* Washington: Institute for International Economics.

IMF. International Monetary Fund (1995) *Annual Report on Exchange Arrangements and Exchange Restrictions*. Washington, D.C.: International Monetary Fund.

IMF. International Monetary Fund. *International Financial Statistics*, various issues.

IMF. International Monetary Fund (1994, 1995) *World Economic Outlook*, May.

Liviatan, N. (ed.) (1993) "Proceedings of a Conference on Currency Substitution and Currency Boards." World Bank Discussion Paper 207.

Mas, I. (1994) "Things Governments Do to Money: A Recent History of Currency Schemes and Scams." Unpublished manuscript, University of Chicago, April.

Meltzer, A. H. (1993) "The Benefits and Costs of Currency Boards." *Cato Journal* 12 (Winter): 707-10.

Moffett, M. (1994) "For Argentina, a 'Miracle' Has Its Limits." *Wall Street Journal*, 24 October: A10.

Pick, F., and Sédillot, R. (1971) *All the Monies of the World: A Chronicle of Currency Values*. New York: Pick Publishing.

Rostowski, J. (1993) "Problems of Creating Stable Monetary Systems in Post-Communist Economies." *Europe-Asia Studies* 45 (3): 439-55.

Schuler, K. (1992) "Currency Boards." Unpublished Ph.D. dissertation, George Mason University.

Schwartz, A. J. (1992) "Do Currency Boards Have a Future?" Institute of Economic Affairs, Occasional Paper 88.

Walters, A. (1990) *Sterling in Danger: The Economic Consequences of Pegged Exchange Rates*. London: Fontana/Collins.

World Bank (1993) *Argentina: From Insolvency to Growth*. Washington: World Bank.

World Bank (1995) *World Development Report 1995*. Oxford: Oxford University Press.

World Currency Yearbook, various issues.

Comments on Selgin, Fontaine, and Hanke/Schuler

John G. Greenwood[1]

THE UNIFYING THEME OF THE THREE PRECEDING PAPERS is their common view that free, private markets combined with sound money would achieve far more for the prosperity of the people of the Americas than the present pervasive mix of extensive intervention in or regulation of markets combined with inflationary financing by governments. As a way of organizing my comments I shall start out by commenting on Selgin's paper since he deals mainly with market regulation and only tangentially with sound money, then move to Fontaine's paper, and finally to the Hanke/Schuler paper since these two papers focus mainly on mechanisms for achieving sound money and only implicitly on the desirability of free, private markets.

---

1   The author is Chairman and Chief Economist at G.T. Capital Management, Inc. In 1983 he proposed a currency board for stabilizing the Hong Kong dollar. The plan was adopted and is still in effect today.

Bank Regulation

George Selgin's paper concentrates largely on regulatory matters, though applied to a banking and monetary topic. He shows conclusively and convincingly that NAFTA's arrangements for cross-border investment in and access to banking services are a definite second-best. His central point is that "real free trade in banking [would give] consumers the right to choose, not only between domestic and foreign bank owners, but between domestic and foreign bank regulatory regimes." In other words, until there is at least some competition among the regulators in the United States, Canada, and Mexico, free trade in banking cannot be expected to materialize.

The main argument used by opponents of free trade in banking is that bank transactions involve externalities, so that systemic problems can occur, triggered by political or other shocks. Selgin argues that these systemic problems are often the result of prior regulatory mistakes such as deposit insurance and the prohibitions or restrictions (in the United States) on interstate banking.

While I have much sympathy with his theoretical arguments, I think there is absolutely no chance of banking regulations being drastically changed or abandoned in favour of a totally laissez-faire approach. Progress is being made toward easing restrictions on interstate banking, but a radical overhaul of U.S. banking laws is not imminent. I therefore wonder whether it might not be more fruitful to argue for a convergence of the bank regulatory systems of the United States, Canada, and Mexico by other means as a springboard for further deregulatory steps later on.

This is analogous to the argument for free trade areas or customs unions within the GATT. Since agreement is so difficult to obtain on a global, multilateral basis, while progress can at least be achieved on a piecemeal basis, it is better to take a few small steps forward than to wait indefinitely for the opportunity to make a single giant leap forward. In the trade case, provided that no external barriers are raised and provided that all participant countries move to the lowest common external tariffs, the costs of trade diversion will be small while the potential for trade creation can be significant, as in the NAFTA case.

Applied to trade in banking services, this argument implies the adoption of the lowest common standards in regulatory matters, rather than harmonization upward to the highest standards—a proposition that would make most central bankers cringe. So what is to be done? The answer is to focus on one or two areas of banking activity and aim for a unified, trilateral approach in that area. Just as the Cooke Committee of the Bank for International Settlements championed minimum standards of capital adequacy for banks in member countries, and eventually achieved agreed measures and standards for bank capital, North America needs a comparable initiative in bank supervision and regulation.

The optimal structure would be a trilateral board or commission with a mandate to propose and pursue implementation of standards and regulatory mechanisms which best serve the interests of bank customers—depositors and borrowers—in all three countries. In individual countries this kind of regulatory framework has been achieved in telecommunications, in the supply of gas and electricity, and other recently privatized industries. The same kind of framework ought to be possible in banking—either on a national level or on an international level.

Rules versus discretion as a means of achieving sound money

Turning to Juan Andres Fontaine's paper, this is an argument for central banking based on rules, but with some discretion permitted—a mechanism which the author calls "bounded discretion." In other words, this is a call for rules with enough flexibility to allow some fine tuning. Before discussing the feasibility of such an arrangement I propose to comment on a secondary theme of his paper.

The sources of inflation

Fontaine makes the point that public deficits—excess spending by the public sector—are not the sole cause of excess money creation. Excess spending by the private sector can also be a cause of the problem. As an example, he details the case of Chile in 1979-81 when excessive private sector spending led to current account deficits that ultimately precipitated the abandonment of the fixed exchange rate. The underlying problem was that a fixed exchange rate combined with large capital inflows caused a sharp rise in the monetary base which in turn fuelled domestic demand.

The standard, textbook way to present this analysis is to break down the components of the assets corresponding to the monetary base into three elements: claims on government, claims on the private sector, and foreign assets. Excessive and unsterilized growth of any of these three components will produce excess money growth and inflation. All of this is unexceptionable.

But Fontaine goes further. He argues for complete elimination of the fiscal deficit, and the prevention of private sector "excess spending" by restraining such spending within the limits of potential income plus sustainable foreign financing. Neither of these arguments is very satisfactory. With respect to fiscal deficits, noninflationary financing of public sector deficits is entirely feasible for relatively long periods of time, though obviously this is a matter of degree. With respect to restraining private sector spending, it is a tautology to say that restraining nominal spending within the limits of potential real income will prevent inflation. Moreover, foreign financing will only be forthcoming if the projects are deemed to be financially viable by the lenders.

The historical record of the debt crisis of the early 1980s shows that large-scale borrowing from international banks by Latin American countries was accompanied by monetary expansions in several countries, with the result that nominal incomes and inflation accelerated, current account balances deteriorated, exchange rates depreciated, and lenders took flight. This ended with a moratorium. No government agency can prevent foreign lenders from taking unwise risks. However, if the demand for real money balances is reasonably stable, the optimum solution is to encourage the inflow of foreign capital (preferably long-term equity capital rather than short-term debt), and then to restrain the growth of private sector incomes through a policy of restraining monetary growth, which brings us back to the question of a monetary rule.

The search for monetary rules

Fontaine points out that quantity-based rules or price-based (i.e., fixed exchange rate-based) rules both have their problems. Where quantity-based rules have been attempted, instability of the demand for money, or the lack or controllability of the particular aggregate chosen (M1 or M2) have both undermined the experiment. Even when central banks have tried to control the monetary base (MO), Fontaine says that it has been difficult in practice to sterilize external shocks (such as inflows of foreign exchange) or domestic shocks (such as variations in the Treasury's balance at the central bank). It is for these reasons that some economists have proposed freezing the monetary base altogether. But even this proposal could work only if (1) there was a completely clean float so that there was no need for the central bank to offset inflows or outflows, and (2) the central government's accounts were maintained at the commercial banks and not with the central bank, so that the central bank is not faced with the daily problem of offsetting the impact of government revenues or expenditures on the monetary base.

As a result of these and other problems, an emerging compromise among central bankers and academics appears to be along the following lines. Assign the central bank a single objective (preferably a stable overall price level), ensure transparency in the procedure for reviewing the achievement of that objective, and accountability of the governor or chief executive of the central bank to the legislature or executive. However, and this is essentially Fontaine's argument, central bankers should be allowed discretion in their choice of instruments for the achievement of that objective.

In the face of these difficulties for quantitative rules, Fontaine turns to consider fixed price rules, i.e., fixing the foreign exchange rate. Here again he claims there have been practical problems in implementation which have proved insuperable. Since these problems are exactly the same as those facing a currency board with a fixed exchange rate I shall deal with them in the next section.

The currency board as a means of achieving a fixed price rule

Steve Hanke and Kurt Schuler's paper argues the case for currency boards as a means of achieving monetary stability in developing countries such as Eastern Europe and Latin America. There are several countries in Latin America which during the past decade have suffered chronic high inflation—Brazil, Guatemala, Guyana, Nicaragua, Peru, Uruguay, and Venezuela. Some of these have experienced chronic high inflation with periods of hyperinflation (i.e., a 50 percent increase in prices per month) for the past decade or more. In some instances numerous attempts have been made to slay the dragon of inflation. Brazil is currently in the midst of its sixth attempt at stabilization in eight years. Why has the problem been so hard to fix? Is there a surefire solution? If currency boards offer a surefire solution to the stabilization problem, as Hanke and Schuler argue, then all these countries are obvious candidates for currency board arrangements.

Since I endorse the Hanke-Schuler view that currency boards would fix the problem for many if not all of these countries, I want to use this opportunity to examine two key issues relating to currency boards. The first concerns the necessary conditions for the successful implementation of a currency board. Are there any conditions in which a currency board cannot be introduced? The second issue relates to the mechanism of a currency board itself. Does it in fact operate in a way that is consistent with the preservation of a passive, nondiscretionary, rule-based monetary authority?

In order to ensure the successful implementation of a currency board solution in a country experiencing chronic inflation and currency depreciation there would appear to be a minimum of three necessary conditions to be met, and a fourth condition, which, if it is not met, will probably prevent the currency board being introduced at all.

First, a necessary condition for adoption of a currency board is access to foreign exchange reserves to back the currency at the outset. This is a non-trivial problem given the size of the note issue in many countries, sometimes amounting to 10 percent of the GNP. Some countries like Brazil are in the fortunate position of having substantial foreign exchange reserves (about US$30 billion or about 7 percent of GDP), and others may be able to negotiate a foreign currency loan for the sole purpose of backing the currency, but there may be countries where this is simply not possible. In that case the country needs to build up a foreign exchange reserve ahead of the adoption of a currency board. This can be done either through deliberate undervaluation of the currency for a period of time, or via sale of domestic assets for foreign exchange. Note that a country does not need 100 percent owned foreign exchange reserves from the start; it can start with a combination of owned reserves and borrowed reserves.

Second, it is necessary to chose an exchange rate at the start of the currency board regime that is not too far from the equilibrium rate. In cases where fixed exchange rates have been adopted which have proven to be clearly out of line with purchasing power parity, severe inflationary or deflationary pressures have seriously undermined political support for the system. In the case of Hong Kong, the currency had depreciated by nearly 40 percent (from HK$6.7 to HK$10 per US$) during the preceding currency crisis of May-September 1993. However, domestic prices and wages had by no means fully adjusted to the depreciation, having only increased in HK$ terms by 15-20 percent over the previous year. The authorities therefore sensibly chose an exchange rate (HK$7.80 per US$) which clawed back some of the depreciation.

The rate was neither too high to lack credibility or imply significant deflationary pressures and downward price adjustments, nor so low that it would validate large price increases in the aftermath of the fixing of the rate. Even so the stabilization program was followed by substantial capital inflows which led to rates of narrow money growth of 40 percent on a year-on-year basis. Fortunately this potentially damaging rate of money growth was fully absorbed by an increase in the real demand for money (or a decline in income velocity). Theoretically, under the currency board system (or indeed any fixed exchange rate system) domestic prices adjust to the nominal exchange rate. But as a practical matter there are limits beyond which the rate poses risks to the acceptability of the system.

Third, the economy must have sufficient flexibility of prices (including wages) and sufficient mobility of resources to enable the difficult transition phase after implementation to be navigated, and to enable the economy to adjust to subsequent external shocks such as sudden changes in the terms of trade. Hong Kong of course is famous for the flexibility of its wages and prices—both upward and downward—so this did not present a problem during or after the stabilization of October 1983, nor has it done so subsequently. The economy is characterised by small firms (80 percent of the labour force is employed by firms with less than 20 employees), which has meant that labour union membership is small, and partly because the territory is small, job mobility is high.

However, in several Latin American cases the same wage and price flexibility has not been evident. In the aftermath of the Chilean stabilization of 1981, for example, the indexing of wages to the CPI proved to be a major problem. At a time when the prices of Chile's products (copper and agricultural products) were falling steeply on world markets, the prices of things that Chile was consuming were rising sharply in the aftermath of large capital inflows at the fixed exchange rate. Similarly, in a case like Brazil's today the high degree of indexation could prove to be a comparable problem. The reason is that during the adjustment phase immediately after stabilization there are not only sudden changes in the overall or absolute level of prices but there is a need for large changes in *relative* prices in addition.

Fourth, and perhaps more critical than all of the preceding three conditions, is the question of whether or not a currency board system can be imposed and survive if there is insufficient fiscal discipline to balance the budget. In the failed attempts of Latin American countries to achieve monetary stabilization, the ability of the government to monetize the budget deficit through central bank funding of the shortfall between revenue and expenditure has typically been the Achilles heel of the whole reform program. Time after time a compliant central bank has been used as a tool of the Treasury to buy government debt or otherwise make loans to the government to make good the deficit. Inevitably this has led to an exploding monetary base and hence an exploding money growth rate. The trump card of the currency board system is that it is impossible for the government to "print money" in the sense of funding a budget deficit through the sale of debt to the monetary authority. Currency boards, having 100 percent of their assets in foreign exchange, are incapable of monetizing the government's deficit.

Conversely, imposing a currency board in a situation where the government has not balanced its budget and has no intention of doing so, cannot be expected to force a solution of the fiscal problem on a reluctant government. Applied to the current situation in Brazil, for example, if a currency board were to be introduced it could well face insuperable credibility problems because the fiscal problem has only been partially fixed. In the worst case scenario a Brazilian currency board could be faced with an internal drain (i.e., the conversion of domestic deposits to domestic cash currency) simultaneously with an external drain (i.e., sales of local currency for foreign currency). Together these two sets of pressure on the system could easily cause the government to abandon the currency board mechanism.

The second issue relates to the mechanics of a currency board. In a strict definition a currency board is an entity that has domestic currency (notes and coin) as its liabilities and foreign currency assets (deposits, bills, or other short-term securities) as the sole counterpart to those liabilities. However, unless there are strong constitutional or other arrangements to ensure the preservation of this simple structure, amendments can easily be made which, over time, can convert the currency board to a discretionary agency conducting monetary policy in an active way.

In Hong Kong, for example, since 1983 several changes have been made (notably in July 1988) to the Exchange Fund, to the point where it now issues bills and bonds of different maturities, it offers a discount window facility to enable banks to cope with overnight shortages of funds, and it can adjust the level of interest rates in the money market by altering the amount that one bank (the Hong Kong and Shanghai Banking Corporation) must maintain with the Exchange Fund. Finally, on April 1, 1993 the Exchange Fund was merged with the office of the Banking Commissioner (responsible for bank supervision), whereupon it changed its name to the Hong Kong Monetary Authority, thus formally acknowledging its status as an effective central bank.

In sum, simple currency board arrangements are not immune from corrupting influences; their mandate and their instruments can be transformed over time. To prevent an institution like a currency board from being undermined by political or other pressures requires not only a strong monetary constitution, but a widespread knowledge and understanding of the benefits of such arrangements among society as a whole.

Chapter 15

A Monetary Constitution for the Americas

Jack L. Carr and Kam Hon Chu[1]

THE PASSAGE OF THE NORTH AMERICAN Free Trade Agreement (NAFTA) has created the world's largest single market, with 370 million consumers and about $6.5 trillion in output. The exploitation of gains from trade should increase income levels in Canada, the United States, and Mexico. The improvement in economic well-being in NAFTA countries should encourage other countries in the Americas to join the free trade area. Exchange in market economies is the main engine of growth. A stable monetary environment is crucial for efficient exchange to take place. Given its responsibility in formulating and conducting monetary policy, the central bank plays a crucial role in providing a stable monetary environment.

---

1   Jack L. Carr is Professor of Economics at the University of Toronto and a Research Associate at the university's Institute for Policy Analysis. Kam Hon Chu is Assistant Professor of Economics at Memorial University of Newfoundland.

The various functions of a central bank can be broadly categorized into two aspects: monetary stability and financial system stability. Most, if not all, central banks assume these two responsibilities, which are interrelated. A stable monetary environment is conducive to financial stability and stability in financial institutions which have a crucial role to play in money creation is conducive to monetary stability. For reasons which will be explained in the following sections, a monetary constitution which takes the form of rules establishing and limiting the power of the central bank appears to be the best way to achieve both monetary and financial system stability. In this paper, we discuss how these objectives of the monetary authorities can be achieved if an appropriate monetary constitution or arrangement is chosen.

Monetary stability

Why monetary stability?

Before we discuss how monetary stability can be achieved it is important to understand why a stable monetary policy is important. In the first instance a stable monetary policy can be defined as a low and stable growth in the money supply. Since "inflation is anywhere and everywhere a monetary phenomenon," a low and stable growth in the money supply will lead to a world with low or zero inflation and low variability in inflation.[2] Figures 1 and 2 show that the relationship between inflation and the rate of growth of money for the post-World War II period for a broad category of countries and for industrialized countries. Monetary stability in turn leads to price level stability and hence price level predictability. In a modern economy short-, medium- and long-term contracts where one party promises to deliver goods and services to another party and in return receives monetary compensation are an important part of exchange in an economy. Labour contracts involve

---

2 For most countries there is a strong positive correlation between the mean and variance of inflation. The argument about to be advanced assumes that low variability of inflation is what is desirable. Empirically this will also mean low rates of inflation.

the exchange of labour for money over one-, two-, or three-year periods. Supply contracts for various goods can last for 10 or 20 years. Debt contracts can last for 20 or 30 years (and in the case of perpetuities can have an infinite duration).

To enter into future contracts economic agents have to be able to predict with reasonable certainty the purchasing power of money (i.e. they have to be able to predict the price level). High and volatile price levels and inflation rates increase price level unpredictability, increase the transactions costs associated with contract formation, eliminate the gains from these efficiency enhancing contracts, and reduce the level of economic performance in an economy. In Canada in the 1970s high and volatile inflation rates eliminated to a large extent the long-term capital market.[3] When hyperinflation exists, all long-term contracts disappear. Prices play a crucial role in market economies. Prices transmit information effectively and efficiently to economic agents and provide incentives for agents to be guided by this information. High and volatile inflation makes it costly for agents to distinguish nominal and relative price changes, distorts the information content of prices and results in inefficient resource allocation. A stable monetary environment which leads to price predictability is a necessary condition for efficient exchange. As Hayek (1945) stated, a stable monetary policy provides a stable economic background that enhances the flow of information and thereby promotes efficiency.

Even anticipated inflation is costly to the society by creating an inflation tax on money. Money facilitates exchange and frees up resources for other productive activities. Rising prices represent a tax on money and encourage economic agents to devote substantial amount of time and resources to economize on the use of money. A recent study by Lucas (1994) on U.S. inflation estimates that the annual zero inflation dividend from reducing inflation from 5 percent to 0 percent would yield an annual benefit of approximately US$15-30 billion, or 0.25-0.5 percent of GDP. There is empirical evidence that a reduction in inflation increases not only the level of output but also the rate of growth of

---

3 In the early 1970s, a 25-year mortgage was the norm in the housing market. By the end of the 1970s, 5-years was the maximum term for a mortgage.

output. Motley's (1994) empirical results for OECD countries suggest that steady state output growth would increase by 0.5 to 0.75 percentage points if inflation could be reduced from 10 percent to 5 percent.[4] This benefit associated with disinflation may appear to be negligible in the short run but it would accumulate into substantial increases in the level of income over the long run. Although the results of these empirical studies can be subject to criticisms, they reinforce a common belief among economists that price stability and low (if not zero) inflation will bring substantial economic gains to the society.[5]

There is abundant evidence to show that high monetary growth rates lead to high inflation rates (see Figure 1; also Barro and Lucas 1994). The evidence is so clear cut that policymakers in high inflation countries should understand perfectly what is causing inflation. The crucial question is not whether money is causing inflation but why some countries consistently have high rates of money growth. Given the inferior performance of a number of Latin American countries in combatting inflation, there is an obvious need for a monetary policy that brings about price stability. The best way to achieve that goal is to adopt a monetary constitution for the Americas.

The choice of a monetary constitution

To achieve the goal of monetary stability, there are at least four possible types of monetary constitutions or monetary arrangements:[6] (1) free-market money, with no governmental role; (2) governmental money

---

4   It should be noted that Motley's empirical results show that reducing inflation in OECD countries from 5 percent to 0 percent would have negligible effect on the long-run growth rate.

5   Economists who argue against a policy of price stability generally argue that the transitional costs of achieving price stability is too high. Two points should be considered with regard to the transitional cost argument. First, these transitional costs can be minimized through the adoption of a "credible" low inflation policy. In the second place, the costs of fighting inflation are transitory whereas the cost of high and volatile inflation are substantial and permanent.

6   These four regimes are considered by Buchanan and Brennan ([1981] 1991).

Figure 1: Inflation and Money Growth in 83 Countries, Post-World War II Period

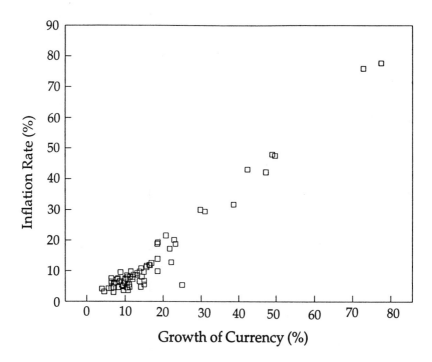

Source: Barro and Lucas (1994).

issue, with competitive entry; (3) pure commodity money, with governmental definition of value; and (4) fiat money, with constitutional constraints on issuance.[7]

The first two regimes essentially advocate free banking or competitive supply of money, but the role of the government differs. There has been revived interest in free banking in the last two decades and a number of studies, both theoretical and empirical, arguing for the

---

7   The third and fourth regimes may not be as separate as they first appear. A gold standard almost always includes paper money and can be viewed as a paper money standard constrained by the operation of a monetary rule.

Figure 2: Inflation is a Monetary Phenomenon: Industrial Countries, 1971-1990

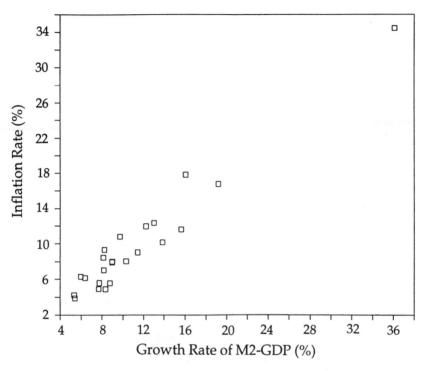

Source: *International Financial Statistics.*

feasibility of free banking.[8] Nevertheless, for political and practical reasons, it is highly unlikely, at least in the foreseeable future, that the monetary authorities would voluntarily surrender their controlling positions. By the same token, it is unlikely that they would constrain their control over the money supply by returning to the gold standard. Therefore, we focus on discussing the issues related to a regime in which the government (or central bank) issues fiat money but is constrained by constitutional rules.

---

8   See, for example, Klein (1974), Hayek (1978), and more recently White (1984), Selgin (1988), and Dowd (1992).

Rules versus discretion

Theoretical Literature

In a fiat money regime, the central bank controls the money supply. Should the central bank control the money supply according to some predetermined rule or should it use its discretion in the conduct of monetary policy? Disputes on questions like these and related issues have existed for a long time and can be traced back at least to 1820s when adherents of the Currency School in Britain advocated the use of policy based on rules whereas adherents of the Banking School advocated the use of discretionary policy.[9] Henry Simons (1936) and Milton Friedman (1959, 1962) argued for the superiority of a rules-based approach to monetary policy rather than discretion. According to Friedman, the long and variable lags of countercyclical monetary policy are more likely to destabilize rather than stabilize the economy. In their seminal work, Friedman and Schwartz (1963) provide historical evidence showing that the Federal Reserve has frequently been a source of economic instability.

A major criticism of a rules-based approach is the argument that discretion should be superior to a rule because discretion can always encompass the rule. With discretion, the policymaker can consider each episode separately and for each particular episode where the rule is superior then the policymaker would adopt the rule for that episode. In such a scenario, discretion should perform at least as well as, if not better than, a rule. Why tie the policymaker's hands with a rule? In answering such a critique Friedman (1962: 240) compares this issue to the First Amendment guarantee of an individual's right of free speech in Bill of Rights to the U.S. Constitution:

> Is it not absurd, one might say, to have a general proscription of interference with free speech? Why not take up each case separately and treat it on its own merits? . . . One man wants to stand up on a street corner and advocate birth control; another communism, a third, vegetarianism; and so on, ad infinitum.

---

9   See, for example, Schwartz (1989) for an overview of the debates, and Fetter (1965) for more detailed elaborations.

Why not consider each case on its own merits? Why tie the policy-makers hands? Friedman gives the following answer:

> It is immediately clear that if we were to take up each case separately, a majority would almost surely vote to deny free speech in most cases and even in every case. . . . But now suppose all these cases were grouped together in an bundle, and the populace at large was asked to vote for them as a whole: to vote whether free speech should be denied in all cases or permitted in all alike. It is perfectly conceivable, if not highly probable, that an overwhelming majority would vote for free speech; that, acting on the bundle as a whole, the people would vote exactly the opposite to the way they would have voted on each case separately [240].

And then apply this logic to a monetary rule, Friedman argues that

> Exactly the same considerations apply in the monetary area. If each case is considered on its merits, the wrong decision is likely to be made in a large fraction of cases because decision-makers are examining only a limited area and are not taking into account the cumulative consequences of the policy as a whole. On the other hand, if a general rule is adopted for a group of cases as a whole, the existence of that rule has favourable effects on people's attitudes and beliefs and expectations that would not follow even from the discretionary adoption of precisely the same on a series of separate occasions [241].

For Friedman the adoption of a credible rule affects agents expectations differently than if the same policy was reached through a series of separate decisions. Friedman recommends a constant money supply growth rule designed to yield zero inflation. Such a rule would credibly signal to economic agents the central bank's intention to provide a regime of stable and predictable price levels.

The case for rules over discretion was greatly strengthened with the seminal work of Kydland and Prescott (1977), which shows the possible existence of the now well-known time inconsistency problem of optimal plans in a dynamic economic system in which agents possess rational expectations. A policy which forms part of an optimal plan formulated at an initial date is said to be dynamically inconsistent if it is no longer optimal at a later date even though there is no arrival of new information in the meantime. More importantly, they show that given the current situation a discretionary policy selected optimally by the policymakers will not maximize the social objective function; while economic welfare can be improved by relying on some policy rules. Their inflation-unemployment example demonstrates that discretionary policy results in excessive inflation without any reduction in unemployment.

This then novel, counter-intuitive idea is further elaborated in a game-theoretic framework by Barro and Gordon (1983).[10] Although this model is quite well known, let us here consider it again to illustrate the basic ideas. In their model, the central bank sets the inflation rate to minimize a social loss function. If the central bank can precommit itself to choose a zero inflation, it can achieve a second-best outcome. Alternatively, the central bank can use discretionary policy. If the government is able to manipulate expectations and fool the public, it can attain an outcome better than the precommitted solution by reneging from its initially announced policy of zero inflation. However, given rational expectations, the central bank cannot fool the public systematically or repeatedly without losing its reputation or credibility. Over the long run, inflation will be higher than it would be if the central bank could precommit to a zero inflation monetary policy. Consequently, the precommitted solution is better than the short-sighted, discretionary solution. Since the Barro-Gordon work, the literature has proliferated. There are subsequent extensions by Backus and Driffill (1985), Barro (1986a), and Vickers (1986), to name just a few. (See the surveys by Barro 1986, Blackburn and Christensen 1989, and Fischer 1990.) While more recent work has introduced the notions of asymmetric information, signalling and different equilibrium concepts in the framework, the key question remains essentially unchanged: how can commitments be sufficiently well enforced to resolve the inflationary bias from the dynamic inconsistency problem?

In summary, recent developments in the rules versus discretion literature conclude that a rules-based approach leads to zero inflation (if commitment to the rule can be sufficiently enforced) whereas discre-

---

10 Dynamic consistency is equivalent to the notion of subgame perfection in a game-theoretic framework.

tion leads to costly inflation without any gains in employment and output.

Empirical Evidence

Where are we going to find evidence in favour of a monetary rule? In the post World-War II period, the only OECD central bank to follow a monetary rule is the Swiss National Bank (see Rich 1987). However, the operation of the gold standard in the pre World-War I period was essentially a monetary rule under which money supply was controlled to keep the money price of gold constant. In this monetary regime, there were periods of inflation. However, there is evidence of stable prices over a long period of time. In England the price level in 1930 was approximately the same as it was in 1660. In the United States the price level in 1940 was just 30 percent higher than at the founding of the nation in 1776 (McCallum 1989: 246-48). With the abandonment of the monetary rule of the gold standard, the price level in England in 1990 was more than 25 times higher than in 1930, and the price level in the United States in 1985 was five times higher than the price level in 1946. This evidence shows that discretionary policy resulted in higher inflation rates than the rules-based approach of the gold standard.

The discretionary monetary policy in Canada in the post-World War II period is of particular interest. Canada had a system of fixed exchange rates during the 1960s and, hence, lacked the ability to follow a monetary policy independent of the United States. Since Canada adopted floating exchange rates in 1970, let us consider the discretionary monetary policy followed by the Bank of Canada from 1970-90 and compare it to the monetary policy in Canada under the gold standard.

The Province of Canada went on the gold standard in 1853. Canada became an independent country in 1867, remained on the gold standard until 1914, temporarily went off the standard during World War I, came back on the standard in 1926, and permanently went off gold in 1933. Hence, the 1870-1910 period represents a 40-year era in which Canada was on the gold standard. Table 1 shows that during this period inflation averaged 0 percent per year and output grew at 4.2 percent per year.

After the Second World War Canada had a discretionary monetary policy. Many Canadian policymakers, like U.S. policymakers, believed monetary policy could be used to fine tune the economy, help eliminate the business cycle, and achieve full employment. In fact, many Keynesian macroeconomists believed that with the new Keynesian macroeconomic knowledge, policymakers had the ability to eliminate the business cycle. During the 1960s in Canada, domestic monetary policy was restrained by the dictates of fixed exchange rates. True Canadian discretionary

Table 1: Inflation and Output Growth in Canada 1870-90

Period	Inflation	Output Growth
1870-1910	0.0%	4.2%
1950-70	3.0%	4.9%
1970-90	6.6%	3.7%

Notes:
1. All figures are annual average.
2. Inflation is measured by GDP price deflator.
3. Output is measured by real GDP.

Sources:
1. For data from 1926-90 see Statistics Canada, *Canadian Observer: Historical Statistical Supplement, 1991/92* (No. 11-210).
2. For data from 1870-1925 see Altman (1992, Table 1, Series B).

monetary policy can be observed in the period 1970-90. In this period money supply growth was high and volatile. Table 1 shows that inflation was high (averaging 6.6 percent per year) and volatile, and so were interest rates. This period did not witness the death of the business cycle. Significant downturns occurred at the beginning of the decades of the '70s, '80s, and '90s. Average growth in output was 3.7 percent (and only 2.8 percent in the decade of 80s), less than the 4.2 percent observed in the gold standard period. The high money growth rates of the discretionary monetary policy period in Canada fuelled high inflation rates but failed to stimulate growth of output.[11]

The experience of Canada indicates that discretionary policy entails costs and no benefits. Discretionary policy has an inflationary bias and

---

11 Evidence from the new growth literature indicates high and volatile monetary policy lowers rates of growth of output rather than increasing them (see Motley 1994).

does not result in increased economic activity. The Canadian evidence firmly supports the adoption of a monetary rule.

Types of Rules

The above theoretical analysis and empirical evidence indicate clearly that a rules-based approach is superior to discretion in maintaining monetary stability. The question now is what kind of monetary rule is required to achieve this goal? From time to time monetary economists and practitioners have proposed various monetary rules. On a purely theoretical basis, a feedback rule is preferred to a simple rule. However, the optimality of a feedback rule depends on the strong assumption that the structure of the economy is known and hence an optimal feedback rule can be designed. In reality, economists should humbly admit that little is known about the "true" structure of the economy, not to mention that there are from time to time structural or regime changes. Moreover, a feedback rule may have the potential problem of instrument instability, which can be costly and undesirable as it may result in a breakdown of the existing economic relationships. Against the shortcomings of a feedback rule, a simple rule is usually preferred in practice. Simple monetary rules include a constant (k percent) money growth rule, a nominal interest rate rule, an exchange rate rule, a price level targeting rule, a nominal income rule, and a compensated dollar rule. It is not the place to discuss here the pros and cons of each rule in detail. We argue that the simple k percent money growth rule is the most appropriate one and is consistent with the spirit of a monetary constitution. Potential problems with this rule include the problem of defining money, the difficulty of controlling its growth, and the instability of the velocity of money. If one assumes that the structure of the economy is inherently stable and evolves gradually over time, the definition of money and the stability of velocity should not be detrimental to the implementation of the k percent money supply growth rule.

All other simple rules also implicitly assume that the structure of the economy is stable. While the central bank is unlikely to control the money supply on a day-to-day basis, it is technically feasible, as experience reveals, for the central bank to control the money supply within the announced target over the short, medium, and long run. As far as controllability is concerned, the k percent money supply growth rule should be preferred over the nominal GNP rule or the price level rule, as both the price level and output are not directly controllable by the monetary authority. More importantly, the k percent money supply growth rule is simpler and easier than the other two rules for the public to monitor the conduct of monetary policy and, hence, the accountability of the central bank under a monetary constitution.

Under the other two rules, it is more difficult to judge whether the source of monetary instability is due to the mistakes of the central bank in implementing monetary policy or to supply shocks causing price shocks. The nominal interest rate rule and the exchange rate rule also have the desirable property of making the central bank accountable for its policy decisions. However, it is well known that the nominal interest rate is an ambiguous and misleading indicator and pegging the interest rate can be destabilizing rather than stabilizing. For a small open economy, pegging the exchange rate is a simple and easy to implement monetary rule, but this rule can be risky for the economy as its monetary stability will to a large extent depend on the decision of the central bank of the key currency. This begs the question that what kind of monetary rule to govern the behaviour of the central bank of the key currency.

A Credible Rule

In February 1991, the Canadian Government and the Bank of Canada jointly announced a series of targets for reducing inflation and reaching price stability in Canada. The targets were specific numbers that were announced for year-to-year increases in the Consumer Price Index:

- 3 percent by the end of 1992;
- 2.5 by the middle of 1994;
- 2 percent by the end of 1995; and
- thereafter, the objective is further reduction in inflation until price stability is secured.

The Bank of Canada has more than met these targets.[12] However, these targets are agreements between the executive branch of the Fed-

---

12 In January 1988 the Bank of Canada adopted a goal of zero inflation. Unfortunately inflation rose after the adoption of this goal and this hurt the

eral Government and the Bank. The targets can be changed by a simple change in the agreement. In fact, in Canada, the Bank of Canada ultimately has to follow the directives of the Government. If the Government ultimately wants a change, the Bank of Canada must follow the change.[13]

With a new Federal Government appointing a new governor of the Bank of Canada there was a new statement by the Government and the Bank:

> High levels of economic growth and employment on a sustained basis are the primary objectives of monetary and fiscal policies. The best contribution that monetary policy to these objectives is to preserve confidence in the value of money by achieving and maintaining monetary stability... the government and the Bank of Canada have agreed to extend the inflation targets from 1995 to 1998 and to maintain the objective of holding inflation inside the range of 1 to 3 percent (mid-point 2 percent) during that period [Bank of Canada 1994: 85].

Some Canadian commentators interpret the new joint statement as a modest backing away from the goal of price stability. In the statement it is clear that the Liberal government of the 1990s has a different view of monetary policy than the Liberal government of the 1970s. In the 1970s the Liberal government believed economic growth could be fuelled by expansionary monetary policy. Today the Government believes that a monetary policy which achieves price stability provides the best environment for high economic growth and employment.

Although the Government of Canada and the Bank of Canada have the correct objective of price stability, it is also clear that there is insufficient enforcement to make such a rule credible. The key question is how to achieve credible precommitment. Precommitment is, however, easier said than done. If the gain from acting opportunistically outweighs the cost of failing to precommit, there is always a temptation

---

Bank of Canada's credibility.

13 Technically, the governor of the Bank of Canada has two choices if a formal government directive is issued: either follow the directive or resign.

for the government to produce the discretionary outcome. Several solutions to the time inconsistency problem have been suggested in the literature. One of these suggestions is to require the government to post bonds which will lose their values if it fails to follow the precommitted outcome. While this bond solution theoretically sounds sensible, it is unclear what the bond is in practice—although it has been suggested that we can view such a bond as the government's reputation or a punishment at the next election (say being not reelected) if the government fails to carry out its promised plan. A more concrete suggestion is to have a government debt structure such that the government is a nominal creditor and it will be subject to capital losses if it implements inflationary monetary policy.[14]

Another possible solution is to have the monetary policy or rules fixed by constitutional law which is costly to change. An example is an overlapping generation model constructed by Kotlikoff, Persson, and Svenson (1986) in which the optimal policy is enshrined in a law saleable to the younger generation. If this social contract is violated by the old generation, it becomes valueless and cannot sell it to the younger generation. However, it is unclear what such a law or social contract exactly is in the real world.

It is clear that a central bank goal by itself or agreement of a goal between the central bank and the government is insufficient to have a credible monetary rule. In Canada the agreement between the Bank of Canada and the government was not credible. If such a policy were credible the contractionary monetary policy followed at the beginning of the 1990s would not have created such economic dislocation. During the constitutional debates in Canada in the 1990s, it was suggested that the Bank of Canada Act be modified to make price stability the sole goal of the central bank.[15] Such a policy would be more credible than the

---

14 See Lucas and Stokey (1983) and Persson, Persson, and Svensson (1987).

15 As we discussed previously, for a number of observers this is the wrong kind of rule. Friedman (1962) argues that such a rule gives too much leeway to monetary authorities. However, Barro (1986b) argues for the superiority of price over quantity rules and the stabilization of a general price index. Hall (1980) suggests a monetary rule which would stabilize nominal GNP.

simple agreement between the government and the central bank. The most credible policy would be a constitutional amendment which mandated the central bank to follow a monetary rule.[16]

A related solution is to have an independent central bank by legislation.[17] Central bank independence, as some recent studies argue, helps achieve price stability. For example, the empirical study by Alesina and Summers (1993) indicates that there is a negative correlation between central bank independence and inflation.[18] The theoretical argument for an independent central bank is based on the notion that public opinion and political pressures may result in destabilizing shifts in monetary policy.[19] The political business cycle hypothesis by Nordhaus (1975) postulates that governments have a vested interest in creating business cycles so that they are in a favourable position at the date of election. More recently, Alesina (1988) surveys both theoretical and empirical works in support of the political business cycle hypothesis. The seminal work by Woolley (1984) shows that the Federal Reserve is far from being politically independent and is sensitive to a wide range of political influences from the president, Congress, bankers, and economists. With legal independence, central banks can be immune from political pressures

---

16 An independent bank with a separate constitutional existence and constitutionally constrained to follow a monetary rule would in effect be a fourth branch of government, the monetary branch in addition to the executive, legislative, and judicial branches.

17 Friedman (1962) is sceptical that an independent central bank by itself is the solution. For Friedman an independent central bank would result in a dispersal of responsibilities, which promotes shirking of responsibility in times of uncertainty and difficulty, an extraordinary dependence on personalities and undue emphasis to the point of view of bankers. Friedman believes from a political point of view an independent central bank is undesirable.

18 See also studies by Alesina (1988) and Cukierman (1992).

19 For Friedman (1962: 239), the adoption for rules-based monetary policy "would enable the public to exercise control over monetary policy through its political authorities while at the same time preventing monetary policy from being subject to the day-to-day whim of the political authorities."

to inflate or use counter-cyclical monetary policy.[20] In the extreme case, an independent central bank can be a source to discipline the fiscal authorities.

It should be stressed that central bank independence is unlikely a panacea for monetary instability. Many of the countries which have statutory independence for their central banks—such as Austria, Argentina, Germany, and New Zealand—have experienced either hyperinflation or periods of high inflation in their history. The citizens of these countries probably realized both the economic and political costs of inflation were considerably high. The formation of an independent central bank by legislation was a consequence of previous monetary mismanagement rather than a preventive measure. The empirical finding of a negative correlation between central bank independence and inflation can be due to anti-inflationary bias in the objective functions of central bankers rather than to the effectiveness of central bank independence in curbing inflation. Success in achieving monetary stability requires coordination between monetary and fiscal policies. Having an independent central bank alone is not sufficient, particularly when we do not have adequate knowledge about the incentives facing central bankers. In theory, economists usually assume that the central bank acts on behalf of the society to maximize a social welfare function or minimize a social loss function. This is not necessarily the case in the real world. The objective function of the government, as Cukierman and Drazen (1987) argue, should be viewed as a reflection of the political pressures on the government rather than a social welfare function. No matter what the actual objective function of the central bank is, the existence of an independent central bank can also potentially be a source of conflicts of interest and coordination failure, thus resulting in monetary instability. Therefore, it is obvious why a monetary constitution is necessary to govern the behaviour of the central bank.

A monetary constitution alone is unlikely to be sufficient, a fiscal constitution may also be necessary. An expansionary fiscal policy might

---

20 Central bank independence does not guarantee a central bank immune from political pressure. Debelle and Fischer (1994) argue that the Russian central bank is independent and yet has chosen a hyperinflationary policy.

ultimately put pressure on the monetary authorities to inflate. This is particularly the case if the monetary authorities are not independent of the fiscal authorities. It is important to distinguish between *de jure* independence and *de facto* independence. Take the U. S. Federal Reserves System, for example. It was originally set up as an independent agency of the federal government. It is legally an agent of the Congress, but it is not controlled by the Congress or the president. In reality, however, evidence indicates that the Fed's operations have not been independent of or immune from influence from the administration.[21] We also do not find a monotonic negative relationship between legal independence of central bank and inflation, although those countries which have the most independent central banks, like Switzerland, Germany, and Austria, also have the lowest inflation rates over the period under study. From Figure 3, it can be seen that there is a strong correlation between money supply growth and the growth in government expenditures.[22] This suggests that to keep inflation under control, a control of the money supply should also be accompanied by a control in the growth of government expenditure in order to make the policy credible. Therefore, in the ideal case, both fiscal and monetary constitutions are desirable and necessary to achieve the goal of monetary stability.

A monetary rule for the Americas

The theoretical analysis is clear. A credible rule is superior to discretion. Discretion results in high inflation without output gain. The limited empirical results examined in this paper supports the theoretical anal-

---

21 Havrilesky (1994) argues that the executive branch of government systematically signals its policy desires to Fed officials, who may respond particularly at times when Congress intensely challenged the budgetary authority, regulatory domain and monetary policy autonomy of the Federal Reserve System.

22 If Iceland is excluded from our sample, we can also find a positive correlation between the size of government deficits as a percentage of GDP and money supply growth. The correlation, however, is not as strong as the one between government expenditures growth and money supply growth.

Figure 3: Money Supply and Government Expenditure: Industrial Countries, 1971-1990

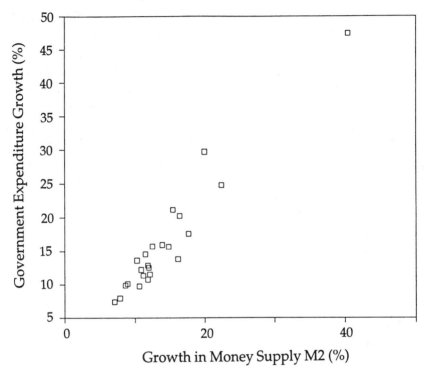

Source: *International Financial Statistics.*

ysis. If a rule is superior to discretion, why is a monetary rule not adopted by all countries? It is hard to find any country following an enforceable rule. Why are Brazil, Argentina, Bolivia, Uruguay and Chile the world leaders in post-World War II inflation? One answer is to argue that these countries are unaware of the long-run harmful effects of expansionary monetary policy. This may be the case at certain times, but it is hard to believe governments never learn. It is difficult to believe models where economic agents are rational but governments irrational.

Our modern theoretical results are from game theoretic models in which in general the monetary authority maximizes an objective function where inflation (or deflation) is bad and monetary surprises which temporarily increases output and reduces unemployment is good. For the models to be analytically tractable, this objective function is simple but it may in fact miss crucial aspects of government and central bank behaviour.

Perfectly expected inflation may be preferred at certain times by certain governments. In underdeveloped economies with informal markets where sales and income taxes are costly to collect, the inflation tax may be preferred. In wartime the excess burden of a temporary inflation tax may be substantially less than the excess burden of a temporary income tax. In addition, in most countries the tax system is not inflation neutral, and higher inflation results in higher effective income tax rates without any need for parliamentary or congressional approval.

Certain vested interests may gain from unexpected increases in inflation. For example, farmers with long-term debt, would gain from unexpected inflationary increases. If political parties with support from these groups form governments, new inflationary policies may be adopted. The game theoretic models assume agents are rational and, at least, on average actual and expected inflation rates are equal. However, these models have difficult times handling regime changes. In an unstable political environment, regime changes may be commonplace. And when regimes change, inflationary policies may be adopted as a means of redistributing income to supporters of the party in power.

The efficiency of the tax system is not the only consideration that influences governments. Tax incidence is another primary consideration. The game theoretic models completely ignore the question of tax incidence. The incidence of an inflation tax may be substantially different from the incidence of an income tax. In countries with highly unequal income distributions and a progressive income tax system, income taxes fall disproportionately on higher income individuals. The inflation tax may be closer to a proportional tax, placing equal tax burden on all income groups.[23] Countries with unequal income distributions may consistently have higher inflation rates.

---

23 The incidence of the inflation tax depends on the income elasticity for the demand for high-powered money. With a unitary elasticity, the inflation tax

Latin American countries, which have relatively unequal income distributions, have the highest inflation rates, while countries like West Germany and Switzerland, which have relatively equal income distributions, have the lowest inflation rates.[24] Table 2 shows that the top inflation country Brazil has a Gini coefficient for the post-World War II period of 0.58, whereas Switzerland has a Gini coefficient of 0.34 and West Germany 0.38.[25] The average Gini coefficient for the top six inflation countries is 0.49 (no data for Bolivia) and for the bottom six inflation countries is 0.35 (no data for Malta). The average Gini coefficient for the top six inflation countries is significantly higher than the average Gini coefficient for the bottom six countries.[26] Latin American countries exhibiting political instability, constant regime changes, and underdeveloped economies with unequal income distributions[27] may knowingly adopt high inflation.

---

will be a proportional tax. The income elasticity will depend on the availability of substitutes to high-powered money to the various income groups. A case can be made that high income groups in countries with high inflation have access to substitute currency (i.e., U.S. dollars). Foreign monies tend to be used in higher-valued transactions which are made by high income people rather than lower-valued transactions in which low income people make most of their transactions.

24 The traditional explanation for Latin American countries having high inflation rates is the high cost of collecting sales and income taxes. If this is the main explanation for high inflation rates in Latin American countries, it is hard to understand why inflation rates are higher in Latin American countries than in the underdeveloped countries in Africa. It is hard to believe collection costs of income taxes are higher in Latin American countries than African countries. Cukierman, Edwards and Tabellini (1992) argue that current governments in Latin American countries may deliberately maintain an inefficient tax system in order to constrain the revenue collecting capacities of political opponents who may form future governments.

25 We have collected Gini coefficients for 71 countries since the 1950s and computed the averages for each country. The figures range from the lowest of 0.27 for Belgium to the highest of 0.68 for Ecuador.

26 The t-statistics for the difference of means is 3.56.

27 Unequal income distribution and political instability may be related.

Table 2: Gini Coefficients of Selected Countries

Country	Early '50s	'55-'65	mid-'60s	'65-'75	'75-'85	'85-latest	Avg.
Brazil	—	0.5896	—	0.6093	0.5388	0.5688	0.5766
Argentina	0.413	0.435	—	0.4113	—	—	0.4198
Bolivia	—	—	—	—	—	—	—
Peru	—	0.6123	—	0.5941	0.363	0.4172	0.4967
Uruguay	—	—	—	0.4968	0.36	—	0.4284
Chile	—	—	—	0.5065	—	0.5122	0.5094
USA	—	0.3865	0.4018	0.4171	0.3828	0.3536	0.3884
Belgium	—	—	—	—	0.2652	—	0.2652
Singapore	—	—	—	—	0.3804	0.3974	0.3889
Malta	—	—	—	—	—	—	—
Switzerland	—	—	—	—	0.3232	0.3568	0.3400
Germany	—	0.5219	—	0.3939	0.3188	0.2998	0.3836

Note
—not available

Sources
1. Jain (1975).
2. Sundrum (1990).
3. World Bank, *World Development Report*, 1993.
4. United Nations, *National Accounts Statistics: Compendium of Income Distribution Statistics*, 1985.

Does the foregoing analysis mean that high inflation cannot be eliminated from high inflation countries or that high inflation countries will *never* adopt a monetary constitution? We do not believe this to be the case. To advocate policy reform, it is important to understand the reasons why a current policy is in place. Without understanding the rationale of current policies, successful reform will be unlikely.

The foregoing analysis indicates that political instability which leads to constant regime changes will make it difficult to enact reform. Wide dispersions in income will make reform difficult. In addition, underdeveloped economies with informal markets will make reform difficult. Stable economic growth is necessary to achieve political stability. Strong economic growth is the greatest alleviator of poverty and maldistribution of income in a country. Policies such as free trade, which open markets and provide for strong stable growth, will make the Americas more conducive to the adoption of a monetary constitution. The adoption of a monetary constitution will itself provide a stable monetary environment that will permit strong and stable economic growth and hence relieve any political pressure to follow inflationary policies. "Such a rule seems to be the only feasible device currently available for converting monetary policy into a pillar of a free society rather than a threat to its foundations" (Friedman 1962: 243).

Financial system stability

In addition to monetary stability, central banks also have responsibility to ensure an efficient and stable financial system. Central banks are often called upon to act as a lender of last resort and to bail out failing financial institutions. Hence financial system stability is important to the maintenance of monetary stability. In Canada, as well as a number of other countries, there is a government regulation of the financial system which we believe threatens the stability of the financial system. This government regulation is the imposition of federally mandated non-risk rated deposit insurance.

Deposit insurance was not introduced in Canada until 1967.[28] Despite the Great Depression, there were no bank failures in Canada from 1923 to 1967. Even in 1967 when the Canadian Deposit Insurance Corporation was formed, there were no bank failures or bank panics in Canada. In 1965, an Ontario Trust company (i.e. a nonbank financial intermediary), the British Mortgage and Trust Company, experienced

---

28 The analysis in this section is essentially taken from Carr, Mathewson, and Quigley (1994).

financial difficulties. Another trust company, York Trust and Savings Corporation lost 11 percent of its deposits in 1966. This run on York Trust represented the investors' rational response to a badly managed company. There was no general crisis resulting from the withdrawal of deposits from the chartered banks or trust and mortgage loan companies in 1966. Of the 61 trust and mortgage companies, only six experienced a net withdrawal of funds in 1966. The remaining companies grew rapidly that year; they experienced a 31.8 percent increase in their liabilities. What happened in 1966 was that depositors transferred their funds from badly managed trust companies to well-managed loans and trust companies.

The trust industry, which represented to a large extent small (high risk) financial intermediaries, feared that depositors would withdraw funds from their institutions and place them in large (low-risk) banks. We believe that in response to political pressure from these small higher risk financial institutions the government enacted non-risk rated deposit insurance. The insurance was made compulsory for the federally regulated banks and optional for the provincial regulated trust companies. All the provincial regulated trust companies joined the scheme.

A number of economists believe that in a banking system with a "first-come-first-serve" rule for deposit payment and with imperfectly informed depositors, that the banking system is suspectable to runs and panics. To eliminate banking panics and provide for a stable financial system, these economists believe that deposit insurance is necessary and efficient.[29]

However, in Canada, prior to deposit insurance, the financial system was stable. The enactment of deposit insurance encouraged the entry of risky financial institutions and provided incentives for existing financial institutions to engage in riskier activities. Depositors no longer monitored financial institutions. As long as the institution was insured

---

29 Friedman and Schwartz (1963, p.434) argue that the U. S. deposit insurance was "the most important structural change in the banking system to result from the 1933 panic, and indeed in [their] view the structural change most conducive to monetary stability since state bank note issues were taxed out of existence immediately after the Civil War."

and as long as deposits were within the limits of coverage of the scheme, depositors only cared about the interest rate paid on their deposits. New riskier institutions entered after the creation of deposit insurance.

In the 18-year period before deposit insurance net entry of Ontario or federal trust companies was 12, while in the 18-year period after deposit insurance net entry was 31. In the 18-year period before deposit insurance no banks or trust companies failed, whereas in the 18-year period post-deposit insurance 17 Ontario or federal trust companies failed of which 14 were incorporated after 1967. There has now been chartered bank failures in Canada. Canada now has a system with substantial financial institution failure and with substantial loss for the federal deposit insurer. The evidence is consistent with the private-interest hypothesis that deposit insurance was enacted to protect small, high-risk trust and loan companies from the competition of large, low-risk banks. Contrary to the efficiency hypothesis, deposit insurance has led to financial system instability.

The Canadian experience points to the risk to financial system instability imposed by non-risk rated deposit insurance. Deposit insurance in the Americas should either be eliminated or substantially reformed. The elimination of deposit insurance should be both *de facto* and *de jure*. Just as in the case of monetary stabilization, the central bank also confronts a time-inconsistency problem in stabilizing the financial system—there is a temptation for the central bank (or some other government agency) to bail out problem financial institutions. Such a policy implicitly guarantees deposits. Expecting implicit deposit insurance from the central bank, depositors do not have incentives to monitor financial institutions. This in turn provides an incentive for the latter to undertake excess risk. If the central bank can tie its hands and precommit to no bailout of financial institutions, in this case as in the case of monetary stability, financial institutions will make their portfolio choice based on the correct risk-return tradeoff.

Lessons can be learned not just from Canada. Argentina had both explicit deposit insurance and a high degree of implicit government support for insolvent banks up to 1991. But in 1991 and 1992, as part of a package of reform designed to end hyperinflation and monetary instability, deposit insurance was first severely limited in scope and subsequently abandoned. The Argentine authorities have gone to some length to stress their commitment not to bail out insolvent institutions in the future.[30] With the limited data there is, it appears the Argentine financial system is more stable in the post-deposit insurance era than it was in the pre-deposit insurance era. The Argentina experience shows that monetary and financial stability are interrelated. As such the reform or elimination of deposit insurance schemes should be seriously considered in any monetary constitution for the Americas.

Conclusion

It is now clear that a monetary constitution is desirable for the Americas in order to promote both monetary and financial stability. With regard to monetary stability, both recent theoretical developments and empirical evidence, for both Canada and other countries in the world, strongly suggest that rules are superior to discretion. Discretionary monetary policy results in higher inflation but no gains in output and employment. In contrast, a monetary rule can lead to zero inflation if the central bank can precommit and this precommitment is enforceable. The credibility or reputation of the central bank in implementing the rule-based monetary policy plays a crucial role in maintaining monetary stability. The more credible a zero-inflation monetary policy is, the lower the transitional costs to price stability; and a monetary constitution will make monetary policy credible. At the same time, to enhance credibility and avoid coordination failures, a fiscal constitution restraining growth of the government sector is also necessary. In addition, policies which open markets will lead to larger output growth, more developed markets, greater political stability and less income inequality and as a result provide the appropriate incentives for governments to adopt monetary constitutions. Monetary constitutions insure price stability and price

---

30 For more details see Miller (1993). Argentina banned the central bank from rescuing troubled financial institutions except short-term loans on good security. Apart from legislation, the central bank is required to hold gold and foreign currency reserves at least equal to the monetary base. This requirement might be violated if the central bank were to bail out depositors in a major bank failure.

level predictability which provide a stable economic background that enhances the flow of information and promotes economic efficiency.

To achieve financial system stability, reforms of the current non risk-rated deposit insurance are urgently needed. The role of the central bank as a lender of last resort needs to be specified explicitly so that the central bank will not be tempted to provide implicit deposit insurance to depositors when their financial institutions become insolvent. As in the case of monetary stability, it is desirable to have legislated rules for the conduct of this specific role of the central bank.

What we have discussed and proposed above is definitely not entirely novel. Some of the key arguments for legislating rules for monetary policy have been advocated by renowned economists, such as Simons and Friedman, many years ago. Nevertheless, policymakers usually, for one reason or another, ignore the advice and lessons we have learned from history. In order to prevent them from acting opportunistically and hence resulting in costly inflation, it is time we had a monetary constitution to govern the behaviour of the central bank in its conduct of monetary policy in order to achieve and maintain both monetary and financial system stability.

References

Alesina, A. (1988) "Macroeconomics and Politics." In S. Fischer (ed.) *NBER Macroeconomics Annual*, 13-52. Cambridge: MIT Press.

Alesina, A., and Summers, L.H. (1993) "Central Bank Independence and Macroeconomic Performance: Some Comparative Evidence." *Journal of Money, Credit and Banking* 24(2): 151-62.

Altman, M. (1992) "Revised Real Canadian GNP Estimates and Canadian Economic Growth, 1870-1926." *Review of Income and Wealth* 38: 455-73.

Backus, D., and Driffill, J. (1985). "Inflation and Reputation." *American Economic Review* 75(3): 530-8. Bank of Canada (1994) "Statement of the Government of Canada and the Bank of Canada on Monetary Policy Objectives." *Bank of Canada Review*, Winter 1993-94: 85-6.

Barro, R.J. (1986a) "Reputation in a Model of Monetary Policy with Incomplete Information." *Journal of Monetary Economics* 17(1): 3-20.

Barro, R.J. (1986b) "Recent Developments in the Theory of Rules versus Discretion." *Economic Journal* 96, Supplement: 23-37.

Barro, R.J., and Gordon, D. (1983) "Rules, Discretion and Reputation in a Model of Monetary Policy." *Journal of Monetary Economics* 12(1): 101-21.

Barro, R.J., and Lucas, R.E. (1994) *Macroeconomics.* Toronto: Irwin.

Blackburn, K., and Christensen, M. (1989) "Monetary Policy and Policy Credibility: Theories and Evidence." *Journal of Economic Literature* 27(1): 1-45.

Brennan, G., and Buchanan, J.M. (1981) *Monopoly in Money and Inflation.* London: Institute of Economic Affairs.

Calvo, G. (1978) "On the Time Consistency of Optimal Policy in a Monetary Economy." *Econometrica* 46(6): 1411-28.

Carr, J., Mathewson, G.F., and Quigley, N.C. (1994) *Ensuring Failure.* Toronto: C.D. Howe Institute.

Crow, J. (1992) "What to do about the Bank of Canada?" *Bank of Canada Review*, June 1992: 3-10.

Crow, J. (1994) "Central Banks, Monetary Policy and the Financial System." *Bank of Canada Review*, Winter 1993-94: 57-69.

Cukierman, A. (1992) *Central Bank Strategy, Credibility, and Independence: Theory and Evidence.* Cambridge: MIT Press.

Cukierman, A., and Drazen, A. (1987) "Do Distortionary Taxes Induce Policies Biased Towards Inflation? : A Microeconomic Analysis." Working Paper. Tel Aviv University August, 1987.

Cukierman, A., Edwards, S., and Tabellini, G. (1992) "Seigniorage and Political Instability." *American Economic Review* 82(3): 537-55.

Debelle, G., and Fischer, S. (1994) "How Independent Should a Central Bank Be?" Mimeo. MIT.

Dowd, K. (1992) *The Experience of Free Banking.* London: Routledge.

Edwards, S. (1993) "The Political Economy of Inflation and Stabilization in Developing Countries." NBER Working Paper No. 4319.

Fetter, F.W. (1965) *Development of British Monetary Orthodoxy, 1797-1875.* Cambridge: Harvard University Press.

Fischer, S. (1990) "Rules versus Discretion in Monetary Policy." in B. Friedman and F. Hahn (ed.) *Handbook of Monetary Economics Vol. II.*, 1155-84. Amsterdam: North Holland.

Friedman, M. (1959) *A Program for Monetary Stability.* New York: Fordham University Press.

Friedman, M. (1962) "Should there be an independent Monetary Authority?" in L.B. Yeager (ed.) *In Search of a Monetary Constitution*, 219-43. Cambridge: Harvard University Press.

Friedman, M., and Schwartz, A. (1963) *A Monetary History of the United States, 1867-1960.* Princeton: Princeton University Press.

Harvrilesky, T. (1994) "Outside Influences on Monetary Policy." *Contemporary Economic Policy* 12(1): 46-51.

Hall, R.E. (1980) "Monetary Policy for Disinflation." Reminder prepared for the Federal Reserve Board, October 1980.

Hayek, F. (1945) "The Use of Knowledge in Society." *American Economic Review* 35(4): 519-30.

Hayek, F. (1978) *Denationalization of Money.* London: Institute of Economic Affairs.

Jain S. (1975) *Size Distribution of Income: A Compilation of Data.* Washington D.C.: World Bank.

Klein, B. (1974) "The Competitive Supply of Money." *Journal of Money, Credit and Banking* 6(4): 423-53.

Kydland, F.W., and Prescott, E.C. (1977) "Rules rather than Discretion: the Inconsistency of Optimal Plans." *Journal of Political Economy* 85(3): 473-91.

Lucas, R.E. Jr. (1994) "On the Welfare Costs of Inflation." Mimeo. University of Chicago.

Lucas, R.E. Jr., and Stokey, N. (1983) "Optimal Fiscal and Monetary Policy in an Economy without Capital." *Journal of Monetary Economics* 12(1): 55-93.

McCallum, B.T. (1989) *Monetary Economics: Theory and Policy.* New York: MacMillian.

Miller, G.P. (1993) "Politics of Deposit Insurance Reform: the Case of Argentina." Federal Reserve Bank of Chicago, Conference on Bank Structure and Competition. Forthcoming.

Motley, B. (1994) "Growth and Inflation: A Cross-Country Study." Mimeo. Federal Reserve Bank of San Francisco.

Nordhaus, W.D. (1975) "The Political Business Cycle." *Review of Economic Studies* 42(2): 169-90.

Parkins, M. (1987) "Domestic Institutions and Deficits" in J.M. Buchanan et. al., (ed.) *Deficits*, 310-37. Oxford: Basil Blackwell.

Persson, M., Persson, T., and Svensson, L.E.O. (1987) "Time Consistency of Monetary and Fiscal Policy." *Econometrica* 55(6): 1249-73.

Pollard, P.S. (1993) "Central Bank Independence and Economic Performance." *Federal Reserve Bank of St. Louis Review*, July/August 1993: 21-36.

Rich, G. (1987) "Swiss and United States Monetary Policy: Has Monetarism Failed?" *Federal Reserve Bank of San Francisco Economic Review*, May/June 1987.

Schwartz, A (1989) "Banking School, Currency School and Free Banking School." in J. Eatwell, et. al. (ed.) *The New Palgrave: Money*, 41-9. New York: W.W. Norton.

Selgin, G. (1988) *The Theory of Free Banking: Money Supply Under Competitive Note Issue.* New Jersey: Rowman and Littlefield.

Simons, H.C. (1936) "Rule versus Authorities in Monetary Policy." *Journal of Political Economy* 44: 1-30.

Swinburne, M., and Castello-Branco, M. (1991) *Central Bank Independence: Issues and Experience.* IMF Working Paper. Washington, D.C.

Statistics Canada, *Canadian Economic Observer: Historical Statistical Supplement, 1991/92.* Ottawa: Statistics Canada.

Sundrum, R.M. (1990) *Income Distribution in Less Developed Countries.* New York: Routledge.

United Nations (1985) *National Accounts Statistics: Compendium of Income Distribution Statistics.* New York, N.Y.

Vickers, J. (1986) "Signalling in a Model of Monetary Policy with Incomplete Information." *Oxford Economic Papers* 38(3): 443-55.

White, L.H. (1984) *Free Banking in Britain: Theory, Experience and Debate, 1800-1845.* Cambridge: Cambridge University Press.

Woolley, J. (1984) *Monetary Politics.* Cambridge: Cambridge University Press.

World Bank (1993) *World Development Report.* Washington, D.C.: World Bank.

Part IV:
Future Policy
Directions

CHAPTER 16

The Future of the Dollar as an International Currency

Lawrence B. Lindsey[1]

A LTHOUGH THE PRECISE MIX OF SUCCESSFUL POLICIES varies slightly from country to country, the world has learned some key lessons. Widespread prosperity cannot be engineered from the central planner's rulebook. Higher real incomes do not flow from the ink of the currency printing press. Restricting the free flow of goods and investment may protect the few, but at enormous cost to the many. These rules are not new; they would not have surprised Adam Smith or David Ricardo. Indeed, as Margaret Thatcher used to remind Britain and the world so many times, "There is no alternative."

---

1   The author is a Governor of the U.S. Federal Reserve Board.
        This article is adapted from a speech given at the Cato conference, "Monetary Arrangements in the Americas After NAFTA," held in Mexico City on May 25-26, 1994.

Indeed, it is important to remember the context of Margaret Thatcher's words. The fundamental soundness of these policies is not unique to developing nations, but to all economies. It is true that highly developed economies have a large stock of wealth which temporarily may be consumed to avoid the stark consequences of pursuing unsound policies. Politicians may therefore buy time when they pursue wrong-headed notions before reality comes home to roost. For less developed nations, by contrast, time is of the essence and the consequences of not getting it right are more dire. But rich or poor, in the final analysis economic policies are unforgiving in their consequences.

One aspect of sound economic policy is of special importance, namely, the positive role a currency can play in the international arena. In particular, I wish to consider the future of the dollar as an international currency. I must preface my conclusions by saying that the future of the dollar depends on which policies are pursued over the long term by the United States government and central bank. For in a very real sense, the international position of a currency is one of the most sensitive indicators of the efficacy of the policies being pursued.

The reason for this is that international currency markets are among the most competitive in the world. International contracts of all kinds can easily be written in any currency. The attractiveness of a currency for this purpose depends crucially on whether or not it is attractive as a medium of exchange. Open borders, liquid markets, and the absence of restrictions on capital movements are all essential to this attractiveness. The currency must also hold its purchasing power over the periods for which contracting parties may be concerned.

In the end, the value of a nation's currency depends on confidence in the decision making institutions of the issuing country. This year, as the world celebrates a half century without a global conflagration, a number of countries have had the opportunity to develop sufficient international confidence in the stability of their institutions to have their currencies play an international role. We in the United States cannot, therefore, assume that the international role of the dollar is unassailable. Unlike during the years immediately following the Second World War, our institutions do not have a near-monopoly on global confidence. The position of the dollar in the world must no longer be taken for granted. It must be earned, it is not automatic.

Choice in currencies

As a result of the wide variety of choice in currencies, other nations have less to fear from potential abuse by those issuing the currencies. I know that there is some particular concern throughout the Western Hemisphere of potential risks from a growing hemispheric role for the dollar. I believe such fears are misplaced. In a sense, we are now in a "buyers' market" for international currencies. "Sellers," that is, the issuers of currencies, must offer a quality product in order to attract users and maintain market share.

Ultimately, an indigenous competitor to the U.S. dollar may emerge from within the hemisphere. In that regard, it is almost certainly true that it is in the interests of such nations to pursue policies that increase both domestic and international confidence in their economic institutions. But in the interim, the widespread use of an international currency in the hemisphere, be it the dollar, the mark, the yen, or some other currency holds substantial potential benefits and few risks to the countries of the region. As I already noted, the issuing countries must earn their customers' loyalty.

Constraints on policy makers

Earning a position for a nation's currency in the international arena naturally imposes certain constraints on policy makers. They must act in a manner that is consistent with preserving, and if possible enhancing, faith in the institutions of which they temporarily are in charge. I will turn to some specifics shortly. But first, let me say that although policy makers may feel temporarily constrained by the pursuit of virtuous policies, their countries, and ultimately their own freedom of policy making is enhanced. In short, it may be hard work, but it is worth it.

Benefits and costs of using the dollar as an international currency

I believe that the benefits to the United States of having a leading international role for the dollar are enormous, and go well beyond those that are readily quantifiable. One cannot imagine, for example, New York retaining its role as the world financial capital if the dollar did not retain its leading role as a world reserve currency. New York's role in the U.S. economy should not be underestimated. It is a prime example of why the quantifiable benefits of the dollar's role are but a fraction of the total benefits.

But quantifiable benefits are illustrative. Let us begin by considering the most basic value of a currency to its issuer: seigniorage. The capacity of a country to issue currency means that, in effect, a portion of government spending can be financed by a permanent interest-free loan. Holders of currency exchanged real goods and services in return for what is, to all appearances, little more than a piece of paper. In reality, the value of the currency flows from the services which that piece of paper can provide as a medium of exchange and a store of value. At first blush, the exchange of real goods and services for paper would appear to be as close to the proverbial "free lunch" as an economist could imagine. In practice, the price of the supposedly free lunch is real constraints on policy to convince holders that the currency has value.

An illustration of the amount of benefits seigniorage can provide comes from the experience of the U.S. dollar during the 1980s. By 1981, after two bouts of inflation in less than 10 years and serious concerns about the future of the U.S. role in the world, the ratio of dollars in circulation to U.S. GDP had fallen to just a bit over 4 cents of currency per dollar of GDP. Twelve years later, after a painful disinflation and sustained efforts by the central bank and successive administrations at rebuilding America's international economic credibility, there were slightly more than 5 cents of currency for every dollar of GDP.

The extra penny per dollar of GDP amounted to $64 billion in extra seigniorage resulting from an increased willingness to hold dollars. Total currency in circulation had risen by nearly $200 billion over this period. Most of this increase was used to provide a medium of exchange for a higher level of nominal GDP. The extra $64 billion, roughly the equivalent of half a year of corporation income tax collections, was and continues to be largely held by foreigners outside the U.S. economy.

These extra resources understate the real financial benefits. Most use of the dollar as a store of value is represented by interest-bearing holdings of government paper. While the government and taxpayer does not get the "free lunch" from these instruments that currency provides, the liquidity and convertibility of these instruments, which stems from the role of the dollar as a reserve currency, certainly carries some value. As a result, the yield of these instruments is lower than what they otherwise would be if the dollar did not have its current role. How much is involved is uncertain. But each basis point —one hundredth of a percentage point—off the yield on government paper is worth $350 million annually to the American taxpayer.

Thus, the benefits to the United States of having a major international role for the dollar are quite significant. But, again, there is no free lunch. What, then, are the costs?

First, the United States government and central bank must run a credible anti-inflation policy. An international currency must be credible as a store of value as well as a medium of exchange. Some might argue that an anti-inflation program, far from being costly, is actually beneficial to a nation's economy. I would not disagree. But it should surprise no one familiar with the United States if I reported that the political consensus against inflation is far weaker in my country than in, say, Germany.

Indeed, while international opinion on the recent tightening actions by the Federal Reserve seems divided between those who feel it was appropriate and those who feel it was not enough, some leading members of Congress have denounced last year's tightening as unjustified and excessive. Thus, while we might argue about the benefits to the economy of an anti-inflationary policy, it is clear that some policy makers do find it constraining.

A second constraint on policy makers seeking an international role for their currency is an obligation to keep their capital markets open and their currency readily convertible. I believe that a good portion of the decline in the international role of the British pound was the result of a series of experiments with exchange controls during the 1960s and 1970s. Convertibility is the sine qua non of internationalization of a currency.

There are two very straightforward reasons for this. The first is the conventional notion of liquidity. Exchange controls and other regulatory limits on capital flows limit the usefulness of a currency as a medium of exchange. The second is that exchange controls signal the likelihood of other policy changes which are likely to attack the currency as a store of value. After all, why else would a government restrict its own citizens from taking money abroad or from holding other mediums of exchange, but to make their capital captive to national policies? Nor would it make any sense to impose controls if those likely policies were actually going to enhance the value of either the capital or the currency. Thus, capital controls and exchange controls are generally viewed as a strong signal of a currency to avoid.

A third constraint on policy makers in countries with an international currency is the need to promote a generally free trade policy. While less obvious a threat to a currency's value than exchange or capital controls, an interventionist trade policy limits the domestic convertibility of a currency into goods and services. At the very least it creates artificial price differentials between the domestic and overseas use of the currency. It also signals a willingness, if not a preference, by decision makers to bend economic policies to political ends. A sceptical foreign currency holder is likely to find such a willingness a risk factor in determining which assets to hold.

This final point has wider ramifications. Any government with a widely used international currency has a stake in promoting the expansion of world trade and a generally open world economic order. A vibrant world economy becomes, in an economic phrase, a valuable public good. The more vibrant the international economic order, the more demand for the country's currency, and the more benefits which flow to the issuer. The self interest of a country such as the United States, with the widespread use of the dollar, is well served by a world which is generally free of international political conflict, and one in which political disagreements are not allowed to interfere with the free flow of goods and services. This may mean that policy makers must, from time to time, pursue international policies designed to promote this liberal world order which may be unpopular with key constituencies at home.

In sum, the costs of being the country of issuance of an international currency are low inflation, open capital and exchange markets, a relatively liberal trade policy, and the support of a world order in which trade is unimpeded by political differences. Some might say that these alleged costs are not costs at all. The price of maintaining an international currency is the pursuit of sound policies—ones that should be pursued in any event. But the individual policy maker, faced perhaps with a looming election or the need to appease key constituencies, may not always view things so cleanly. Perceived limitations on policy makers are real to those who must make the decision to promote an international currency, even if such limitations may be in their own country's best, long-run interests.

Dollarization of Latin America

If being the issuer of an internationally used currency is clearly good—what of being the user of such a currency? More to the concerns of this volume, even if the increased dollarization of Latin American economies is good for the United States, is it good for Latin America? Is what is good for the United States necessarily bad for the rest of the hemisphere? There is a simple test that can determine the answer.

The key is whether the dollarization of the hemisphere's economy is being done voluntarily or through coercion. For example, if an occupying army imposed its currency upon the nation it occupied, that would quite clearly be abusive. But that is not the case here. Latin Americans have held U. S. dollars as a store of wealth, a protection against domestic monetary policies that have eroded the value of their currencies. More generally, dollars are not the only alternative currency. Individuals and businesses may, and sometimes do, hold marks or yen. It is thus hard to maintain that dollarization is anything other than a voluntary process.

As a policy matter, therefore, dollarization is placing the same type of constraints on the governments and central bankers of the host countries as maintaining the dollar's attractiveness places on U.S. decision makers. As local currencies are forced to compete with the dollar, domestic economic policies must become less inflationary, more pro-market, and more internationally open. In some sense, therefore, dollarization is a transfer of power from political decision makers to the individual citizens and market participants of the hemisphere's countries. My personal view is that such a transfer is not a zero-sum game, but is of net benefit to the countries involved. As long as dollarization is voluntary, I believe that it is clear that it is a net benefit to the economies involved.

There is also a public goods aspect to increased dollarization which deserves mention. Much, if not most, of the international trade among Latin American nations has never been conducted in the currencies involved, but among third country currencies such as the dollar. Increased dollarization in Latin America therefore increases the possibilities for market development throughout the region.

The risk of mismanagement

Dollarization does hold risks. Not least among them is that the economic fate of the countries using the dollar becomes somewhat tied to a currency controlled by policy makers abroad. Mismanagement of the dollar will therefore not only affect the United States, but other countries as well. There is no obvious way to hedge such a risk. But, there are two mitigating realities that should be borne in mind. First, there are, and will continue to be for the foreseeable future, international alternatives to the dollar. As long as such alternatives exist, the widespread use of foreign currency within an economy is of lesser concern because the particular currency used can be fairly readily changed. Second, increased dollarization of the hemisphere's economy places reciprocal obligations and constraints on United States decision makers. A larger international role for the dollar means that the consequences of pursuing unsound policies viewed internationally as unsound are potentially larger, and the rewards for pursing internationally sound policies are similarly enhanced.

Conclusion

Like the traditional economic theories of exchange—that both buyer and seller are beneficiaries, dollarization may well prove to be beneficial for all economies concerned. The only lost alternatives are inflationary, interventionist, or protectionist policies. Speaking frankly though, that kind of loss can only be viewed as a social gain.

Chapter 17

NAFTA: A Bridge to a Brighter Future

Michael Wilson[1]

In 1558, Thomas Gresham, the founder of the Royal Exchange, is said to have cautioned Queen Elizabeth about the need to restore the purity of the realm's coinage. In Gresham's words, "bad money drives out good." Of course, "bad" or "good" money is not exchanged in a vacuum, and what has come to be known as "Gresham's law" is applicable to more than the physical integrity of coinage. With the benefit of 450 years of experience, Gresham's counsel should instruct the policies and practices that affect today's monetary relations. In effect, "bad trade and economic policy drives out the good."

---

1   Michael Wilson is Chairman of Michael Wilson International and former Minister for International Trade for Canada. He was Chairman of the Economic and Trade Policy Committee and was directly involved with the Canada-U.S. Free Trade Agreement and had responsibility for the NAFTA negotiations.

   This chapter is drawn from a speech by Michael Wilson delivered at the Cato Conference on "Monetary Arrangements in the Americas After NAFTA," held in Mexico City on May 25-26, 1994.

I am confident that the course we in North America have set for our economic futures, particularly as this is reflected in the North American Free Trade Agreement (NAFTA), will contribute to "good" money and trade and economic policy in North America and should, in the long term, serve to improve the value of our coinage.

The globalization of trade

In thinking about NAFTA, one should consider the overall globalization of trade that is now taking place with the emergence of multinational enterprises (MNEs) and the integration of international economic systems. These developments have important implications for policy makers and market players alike. The globalization process has been a powerful element in our economic life in recent years, and has been termed a "virtuous circle"—uniting new technologies, integrating financial markets, and internationalizing business. It is a process that has encouraged the unprecedented growth in the volume of our manufactured goods and commercial services trade. Over the past decade we have been the beneficiaries of growth in trade that has outperformed world output. We have also witnessed the increased role of services activities in our national economies. In 1992 services trade constituted an estimated 21 percent of total world exports of $4.6 trillion.

If we look at foreign investment trends, global foreign direct investment (FDI) outflows have far outpaced both exports and output. In the period 1982-87, the average annual outflow of global FDI was (U.S.) $67 billion. The outflow in 1992 had reached $171 billion. The flow of FDI between 1985 and 1992 grew at a nominal annual average rate of 34 percent—far exceeding that of merchandise exports at 13 percent and nominal GDP growth of 12 percent.

Recent estimates of the stock of global FDI exceed $2 trillion, with investment being concentrated heavily in the service industries and in the industrialized world. As for global portfolio capital outflows, these averaged $63 billion in the period 1981-85; in 1992 outflows were estimated at $244 billion.

In Canada FDI increased at an average growth rate of 7 percent in the 1980s and had more than doubled over the period to (CDN) $140 billion by 1993. Canadian foreign direct investment abroad (FDIA) increased fourfold over the same period—from $27 billion to $114 billion by 1993.

As to the influence of technology, even those of us who drive in the slow lane on the information highway recognize the extent to which technological advances have helped businesses operate more effectively within an international context. Certainly, the growth and development of financial markets and their increasing integration have advanced in lockstep with improved communications and data management.

Together, these elements of globalization represent a powerful force in our economies. They are also beneficial. Policy today must recognize their existence; at a minimum to accommodate them; ideally to encourage them.

This was the international context faced by NAFTA negotiators. In the regional context, the increased exposure of the domestic economy to international economic conditions was making certain traditional domestic structures and some industries both less relevant and less competitive. This set real parameters on the objectives of the negotiation. We were also breaking new ground, since these parameters would take us past what other trade agreements had achieved.

Policy makers recognized the need for an effective policy framework; one that would encourage, guide, and facilitate industry adjustment and foster competitiveness in the manufacturing industries. Moreover, it was increasingly apparent that the service industries, and the financial services industry in particular, had to be part of a comprehensive policy fix.

Regionalization as a policy response

For more than half a century, Canada's trade and economic policy making has embraced multilateral attempts to move to more open markets. It has done so (in its best moments) on the premise that measures that distort the efficient allocation of resources are likely to lower national and global welfare, while the removal of such barriers among many nations is likely to raise them. The GATT has been the primary force in this effort.

Yet, the integration of national economies—and the interdependence of producers, consumers, and governments internationally—has more recently served to intensify what might be considered a natural process of regionalization. With respect to Canada, the United States, and Mexico, the close economic ties between the three countries are borne out in the trade and investment figures. The policy response adopted in North America focused on the development of a regional trade and investment arrangement first exemplified by the Free Trade Agreement (FTA) between Canada and the United States and later by NAFTA.

The North American Free Trade Agreement

From the beginning, Canada's negotiating strategy for NAFTA was premised on two important, overarching objectives: (1) to ensure NAFTA was firmly rooted in and complementary to the multilateral GATT framework of rules and disciplines, and (2) to retain and enhance the benefits provided under the terms of our Free Trade Agreement with the United States. We succeeded, and transformed the FTA into a more comprehensive trilateral trade agreement more consistent with the dynamic pattern of globalization I described earlier. NAFTA is an impressive framework for trade and economic cooperation in North America. It provides new rules and disciplines that will encourage business exchanges that today generate three-way trade and investment flows estimated at close to $500 billion.

NAFTA's market access provisions effectively eliminate tariffs and import licenses on all manufactured goods. This has been a standard pattern for trade agreements for years. Where NAFTA made a major advance was in the recognition that international flows of capital and knowledge are now at least as important as the flow of goods.

Improved rules for investment and services will significantly expand business opportunities in previously closed sectors—particularly Mexico's automobile and parts industry, and in financial services, trucking, energy, and mining sectors. The agreement includes many other important provisions, including intellectual property protection, procurement, and the development and administration of product standards. Of obvious significance, NAFTA's trade remedy and dispute settlement provisions represent a strengthening and improvement over those of the FTA. Specifically, in dealing with trade remedy measures of countervail and antidumping, experience has confirmed that the FTA/NAFTA dispute settlement mechanism has no equivalent outside North America and has served participants well.

A fair and effective means to deal with disputes is essential. Our experience with the FTA suggests that the size and breadth of the economic relation makes disagreements among NAFTA partners virtually inevitable. In part, and particularly for Mexico, these will be driven by the enormous adjustment challenge NAFTA will occasion as Mexico's economy is opened further to competition.

Let me be frank about adjustment—living with clearer and more exacting rules of the game as well as with the shock wave that increased competition brings to the domestic economy presents major challenges. But, in placing economic relationships on a more solid, open, and rules-based footing, trade agreements, and specifically NAFTA, can provide no end of opportunity. What trade agreements cannot do in themselves is produce the products at the right price the world will buy. The benefits of trade liberalization come fast and best to those firms and workers prepared to adjust and take advantage of opportunities that free trade offers.

Our FTA experience demonstrates all too clearly that sometimes wrenching adjustment is required to move people and companies to the point where they are equipped to participate in global markets and ready to take on the competition at home and abroad. There is no question that the FTA severely challenged Canada's capacity to adjust to these changes. Nor do I believe there is any question that this adjustment was necessary. The fact is, that adjustment has worked to help Canada's export-oriented goods and services firms compete, to the point where our export success has led Canada out of the recent recession. I can only sympathize with the responsibility and very real challenge that these changes force upon managers and politicians in moving the course forward.

The Free Trade Agreement

Although the FTA built on the underlying multilateral framework of the GATT, it went further and faster than multilateral negotiations had been able to take us. Of particular importance, the FTA established the first comprehensive set of principles governing services trade. With respect to the provision of services, it made national treatment, the right of establishment, the right to sell across borders, and transparency all part of the rules of the game. These four provisions are all interrelated and are necessary to allow service providers to benefit from access to foreign markets.

Financial services are critical to this process and very sensitive. They have been the subject of specific sectoral negotiations, in the FTA, NAFTA, and the Uruguay Round. While prospects are in sight for significant liberalization, a number of remaining barriers inhibiting access remain.

In addressing only specific irritants, the FTA gave us a series of specific liberalization commitments. It failed to establish comprehensive principles for each country to adhere to in financial services and investment. There were also problems of "turf". The financial services chapter covered only bilateral trade in banking and securities but not insurance. This was covered in the nonfinancial services chapter. In the United States, the Treasury is responsible for banking and securities. Commerce is responsible for insurance. The result was that only insurance benefitted fully from the principles-based liberalization under the FTA and from binding dispute settlement provisions.

Under the FTA, Canada exempted U.S. financial firms from certain laws that limited aggregate foreign ownership of federally regulated financial institutions. But Canada maintained the 10 percent individual ownership limitation for both U.S. and Canadian equity investors in domestic banks. There were additional liberalizing concessions by both Canada and the United States, but these were admittedly modest. A comfort level of sorts was achieved as both parties undertook to continue to provide existing rights and privileges to the other party's institutions. Perhaps most importantly, both parties undertook to extend the benefits of any further liberalization of the rules governing the financial markets and institutions. The text of the agreement summed it up best in providing that the provisions were intended as a first step in establishing "freer" trade in financial services and "not intended to be construed as representing the mutual satisfaction of the parties concerning the treatment of their respective financial institutions."

In sum, while the U.S.-Canada FTA liberalized trade in goods in a comprehensive manner in tune with clear adjustment requirements within the two economies, the new areas in the agreement (investment, services, and particularly financial services) were dealt with on a more piecemeal basis. The FTA did not, in any systematic way, significantly encourage further domestic rationalization, competition, and integration in the service industry. This outcome undoubtedly was influenced by the fact that the FTA was negotiated during a time when Canada's regulatory framework was undergoing substantial reform and during what continues to be an ongoing debate in the United States concerning the permitted activities of financial institutions.

Since that time, regulatory reform in Canada has liberalized Canadian financial institutions considerably. There are still some services banks are not allowed to provide. Many also would like to see the deposit insurance system revised and the complex mix of federal and provincial regulations rationalized. But the process has achieved a lot and is ongoing. There will be another review of Canadian federal reforms in 1997 and every 10 years thereafter. Future reforms should enhance the international competitiveness of Canada's financial institutions.

The United States has not progressed as far. Policy makers in the United States continue to examine the justification for and viability of the separation of commercial banking and other financial services as part and parcel of ensuring the continued health and competitiveness of U.S. financial institutions.

Meanwhile, the industry is not standing still. Volatile markets and rapid technological advancement have encouraged banks to explore the limits of their legal powers—to engage in bank and nonbank activities. Financial conglomerates have emerged through a process of acquisition and consolidation and many U.S. institutions have become affiliated with large nonfinancial enterprises.

All said, many of the same factors which have blurred the distinctions within Canada's financial services sector have influenced the evolution of the U.S. financial services sector. But the policy response in the United States has been far short of what is needed to keep the industry modern and competitive and, quite frankly, as open as the sector is in many other countries.

Liberalization of financial services

Going into the NAFTA negotiations, it was clear to us in Canada that as we addressed the investment, services, and financial services issues, maintenance of Canada's international competitiveness required a policy landscape that supported Canada as a prime location for international investment. This seems one of those self-evident motivations for a trade agreement, but it is useful here to recall that Canada had gone from being sceptical of the benefits of FDI in the 1960s and 1970s to become a convert and fully committed to the benefit of international investment agreements by the end of the 1980s. I might add that it took a change of government to implement this process!

By the time NAFTA was negotiated, financial institutions had strengthened their identities as export and investment facilitators as their domestic clients looked further afield for business. With this increased trade, domestic banks and other financial service players are themselves being encouraged to establish a more effective international presence.

NAFTA builds on and improves the FTA arrangements which addressed banking and securities. Canada insisted that it establish principles for trade in financial services as well as a dispute settlement mechanism that was lacking for banking and securities in the FTA. Coupled with the significant reforms introduced in 1990 in Mexico's financial services industry, Mexico's undertakings in NAFTA has established the basis for truly liberalized trade in financial services in North America.

Banks

From the banks' perspective—for Canada, an industry with extensive international operations—NAFTA provides a clear opportunity to expand trade relations in the hemisphere. There were really two major objectives Canada's banking industry identified with in the NAFTA negotiations: (1) to gain entry into the Mexican market (which had been restricted for the last decade to representative offices), and (2) to try and overcome the shortcomings in the Canada-U.S. FTA, both in terms of market access to the United States and with respect to trade principles. The United States is a very important market for Canadian banks. Depending on the bank, between 30 percent and 40 percent of total assets are booked in the United States. This is despite the remaining restrictions on bank powers under Glass-Steagall rules regarding securities and the interstate branching barriers—restrictions that NAFTA did not address.

Canadian banks increasingly are integrating their North American strategy. NAFTA now allows North American banks to bring Mexico into a unified strategy. Recent examples include: (1) the Harris Bank purchase by the Bank of Montreal and their recent acquisition of Suburban Bank in Chicago, and (2) the Bank of Nova Scotia's purchase of a 10 percent share in Grupo Financiero Inverlat, which owns the fourth largest Mexican bank.

Life insurance

The virtual free trade that existed in the life insurance sector between Canada and the United States focused negotiations on preserving the status quo. No Canadian life insurer had established a presence or marketed its product in Mexico at the commencement of NAFTA negotiations in 1991. Mexico's financial sector liberalization in 1990 allowed a 49 percent minority ownership stake in a Mexican life insurer, and some U.S. and European companies already have entered via joint venture arrangements. I hope Canadian insurers follow suit.

Clearly there is great potential in Mexico. Canadian and U.S. life insurers can enter into joint venture arrangements with new or existing Mexican life insurance companies subject to 50 percent share ownership limitations that will gradually be phased up to allow for 100 percent ownership by the year 2000. While full access is not yet a reality, national treatment and equality in competitive opportunity with domestic companies is enshrined in the agreement.

Securities

The impact of NAFTA's financial services provisions on securities trade between Canada and the United States is expected to be limited. On the downside, the legal text contains no bilateral freeze between Canada and the United States on new restrictions on the cross-border provision of securities services. NAFTA cannot be seen as having provided significant liberalization benefits for securities trade between Canada and the United States. But both countries will see opportunities with respect to the gradual liberalization of specific aspects of the financial services industry including the securities sector.

Clearly, in financial services, more liberalization must be achieved. The direction is set. The objectives are understood. But domestic pressures resulted in less progress than that achieved in other parts of NAFTA. Both the industry and policy makers must keep this file open and continually press for domestic policy changes and further opening of markets. There is fertile ground for further reform and a consequent reduction in derogations from NAFTA. If this is not achieved, this key sector will not be able to contribute as fully as it should to the development of trade and investment in the region.

Monetary union

Does NAFTA argue for a monetary union? My answer is "no." For both economic and political reasons, this is simply not on. We have seen from the tensions in the European Union how difficult it is to bring about sufficient convergence in economic policies and performance to support a system of fixed exchange rates. This would be even more difficult when the system encompassed economies as different as the United States, Canada, and Mexico—and possibly other developing nations. Politically, it would not be acceptable. There have been periodic calls to fix the Canadian dollar to the U.S. dollar, or to have us share a common currency. Again, one need only look at the debate in which the European Union engaged respecting monetary union to recognize just how sensitive an issue is the surrender of political and economic sovereignty associated with a common currency. I do not think it a likely subject of any trade agreement involving Canada for the foreseeable future.

Clearly, I am not ruling out increased cooperation, and in this respect would note the recent trinational facility put in place by the United States, Mexico, and Canada to deal with shocks to our respective currencies. This accord underscores the commitment of the three governments to monetary stability in North America, but falls far short of monetary integration.

I do think that one of the best ways to assist in creating a stable monetary environment and one in which exchange rate volatility is less of a concern, is through a common objective of price stability—particularly important given the global move toward lower inflation.

Quo vadis?

The horizon offers reason for optimism. Commitment to the free movement of both goods and capital is entrenched in the framework of several trade arrangements, most notably the Uruguay Round agreements now under the umbrella of the World Trade Organization and NAFTA. This said, the WTO has set itself an ambitious agenda, both in terms of implementing the Round results and in tackling new issues which include the environment, labour standards, and technology policy.

The Multilateral Trade Negotiation's result offers far-reaching liberalization gains including improved and more secure access to important developing country markets, but in no way does it provide Canada, the United States, and Mexico with the degree of comprehensive and preferential access provided under NAFTA.

Laurel wreaths are not yet in order, however, since the NAFTA process is not complete. While countries with aspirations of NAFTA membership deepen their policy reforms, NAFTA members must continue to press their own agenda toward reform. NAFTA working groups have been established to develop solutions to antidumping and subsidy/countervail issues; review of the relation between competition law and trade may see the replacement of the pernicious aspects of trade remedy regimes. Additional negotiations in the area of government procurement and in services, including financial services, are planned. Ongoing liberalization of trade in financial services is particularly important to a successful outcome of NAFTA. It will require removal of remaining impediments limiting foreign ownership, entrenchment of the right of establishment, and the provision of effective market access through the elimination of barriers that impede operations of foreign and domestic financial institutions alike.

NAFTA accession

There can be no doubt of Canada's commitment to ongoing development of economic and trade relations within the hemisphere, a commitment reflected in the NAFTA accession clause. Open regionalism plainly envisages partnerships in Latin America. But it must be clear that accession requires adoption of the agreement's exacting disciplines over the full range of obligations.

NAFTA's accession clause foreshadows the extension of NAFTA and of agreements on environmental and labour cooperation to other Latin American and Caribbean countries. Adherence to NAFTA is only feasible for those countries that have made a major and sustained commitment to market-based economic reform.

A bilateral arrangement, or even a piecemeal approach to liberalization as an alternative to accession, may suit a political or short-term economic imperative. But there are a number of drawbacks. In the case of bilateral negotiations, one cannot underestimate the negotiating disadvantages smaller economies face when sitting across the table from a much stronger economic partner. Smaller countries can quickly find themselves responding to the "elephant's" agenda. I have already noted the contrast in the FTA and NAFTA negotiations. The former was driven by bilateral irritants; the latter negotiation was framed in a series of principles from which countries could negotiate limited derogations. I believe there is far more protection available to smaller countries joining a principles-based NAFTA than exists in entering into a bilateral negotiation with the United States. Inevitably, that bilateral negotiation will be driven by the bilateral irritants as perceived by Congress and the administration.

A piecemeal approach to negotiations will likewise undermine coherence and control over the overall process of reform. I call it death by a thousand cuts. It may seem attractive to engage in negotiations or a series of negotiations limited to specific sectors. Domestically, it can be very divisive, particularly to those sectors that lose out. There are always going to be economic and political gains and losses to any negotiation. Domestic support will more easily be garnered when negotiations involve a comprehensive package of tradeoffs that can be shown to balance the gains and losses.

At the risk of being blunt, one of the strengths of NAFTA, and where it betters a bilateral trade arrangement, is in its greater balancing of interests and power. This advantage over a bilateral trade approach is reflected in both the conduct and in the outcome of negotiations. In a bilateral relation, a dominant U.S. partner sets a powerful challenge to a small country. The United States will abuse its position—not due to any ill will, but simply because of the nature of the U.S. political system.

A multilateral arrangement, with a strongly supported dispute settlement system offers clear advantages. In addition to optimizing resources and broadening the size and depth of the market, it provides a more level playing field for negotiations.

In short, for both raw political reasons, as well as to most effectively advance economic objectives, I strongly encourage those countries in the hemisphere that may be weighing the option of NAFTA or a bilateral arrangement with the U.S. to opt for NAFTA. Let me add that the prospect for NAFTA accession is not universally evident in Latin America. Candidates that initiate adjustments in domestic policy that meet the standard for trade and investment liberalization established under the agreement will be best positioned for accession.

There are those who would ask whether policy reform is worth it. Many countries in the Americas have shaken off the economic stupor of the 1980s which saw regional GDP growth plummet from almost 6 percent in the 1970s to 1 percent between 1985 and 1990. In the transformation, policies that favoured import substitution have been discredited and given way to bold new economic development strategies based on market-based development and trade liberalization. Reforms are far-reaching and have taken hold most effectively in Mexico, Chile, Colombia, and Argentina.

With these reforms, there are welcome signs that growth prospects have taken root. In 1990 Latin American economic growth climbed to over 5 percent, and one analyst has predicted that Latin America's compound annual growth in real GDP in 1990-95 will exceed 4 percent. Prospects are likewise bright for the last half of the decade, with GDP growth predicted to be twice that of North America and Europe and slightly ahead of Asia.

There is no doubt that, apart from trade, patient investment capital is essential to sustained growth. There is every indication that investors are responding to the reform process. Foreign direct investment flows to the five major markets of Argentina, Brazil, Chile, Mexico, and Venezuela rebounded in 1991, more than doubling to $36 billion. The cautionary note is that predictions for a buoyant decade of growth are predicated on Latin American countries staying the course. It is very important for political leaders to continually reinforce their vision of the results of their reform measures and encourage people to look past the inevitable short-term costs of reform.

To some extent the necessary discipline should be reinforced through recent liberalization commitments undertaken in Mercosur; the G-3 negotiations between Mexico, Venezuela, and Colombia; and the bilateral accords between Colombia and Venezuela and Mexico and Chile, respectively. To a certain extent, the obligations undertaken in those agreements will help to lock in domestic reforms. From my vantage point, however, I would like to think that NAFTA and the accession prospect provides an even greater incentive and a more focused discipline.

The process of economic reform and renewal that we have embarked upon in this hemisphere should be pursued in concert with our underlying commitments to global trade liberalization and to the rules-based system supported in regional and multilateral trade and economic arrangements. The process of economic reform and renewal that we have embarked upon in this hemisphere should be pursued in concert with our underlying commitment to global trade liberalization and to the rules-based system exemplified by the GATT and reflected in the NAFTA. This process will contribute to greater competitiveness globally and, in the longer term, should help sustain business confidence, a key requisite of monetary stability.

CHAPTER 18

Problems and Prospects for a Mexican Currency Board

Roberto Salinas-León[1]

> By and large, currency boards have outperformed central banks on price stability.
>
> —*Paul Volcker*

THE DEMANDS FOR A NEW EXCHANGE RATE regime in Mexico to stabilize the sharp volatility in the financial environment following the

---

1   The author is Executive Director of the Centro de Investigaciones Sobre la Libre Empressa (CISLE) in Mexico City and an Adjunct Professor of Political Economy at the Escuela Libre de Derecho. The account of currency boards offered in this paper owes much to the conceptual framework and defense of currency boards articulated in the contribution of Steve Hanke and Kurt Schuler to this volume, "Monetary Systems and Inflation in Developing Countries." I am also grateful to both authors for extensive conversations on the topic.

peso currency collapse has generated a vigorous debate concerning the feasibility of a currency board. Unfortunately, this debate has exhibited a widespread misunderstanding of the aims and claims behind the establishment of such a strict system. The original goal of stabilizing the peso-dollar parity at 4.5 pesos per dollar quickly collapsed in view of the disorder engendered by the devaluation in the macroeconomic scene. An immediate challenge for Mexico's monetary authorities is to fashion mechanisms that can bring about a closer and more stable relation between the local currency and the U.S. dollar. A currency board seems to be an ideal method to achieve this top policy objective.

The reason is simple. A currency board involves transforming Mexico's monetary system into a de facto dollar standard, by guaranteeing that all money in circulation (notes and coins) be fully backed by dollar assets. The system is based on three principles: a fixed exchange rate, full convertibility of the domestic currency with the "anchor" currency, and a monetary law prohibiting the central bank (or board) from expanding the monetary base beyond the stock of available hard currency reserves. Thus, the size of the monetary base depends entirely on the market demand and supply of local money.

The principal virtue of this system is that it practically rules out a devaluation of the local currency vis-à-vis the target currency. This means that if a run on the peso occurred, under a currency board system in Mexico, the worst that could happen would be total "dollarization" of the economy, that is, trading would take place in U.S. dollars while the currency board would hold all pesos in stock. This is so since, under an ideal currency board, each unit of the local currency is backed at a fixed exchange rate by international reserves. Hence, the potential for discretionary monetary policy is virtually null. The government cannot borrow from the board for fiscal purposes, that is, to finance a deficit, in order to expand the bureaucracy and underwrite government spending. This makes boards powerful antidotes against culprits like monetary expansionism, fiscal irresponsibility, and inflation.

A normative monetary framework

In his contribution to this collection, Juan Andrés Fontaine encapsulates the "beauties" of a currency board system. It is, he says, clear, understandable, and publicly announced. It serves as a public commitment to price stability on the part of both the monetary and the fiscal authorities. Any deviation from it is politically and economically very costly: it creates a crisis of confidence that typically forces out from their offices central bank presidents, ministers of finance, and even presidents. It effectively eliminates discretion, and thus [removes] that source of price instability....It is also operationally very simple...[and] serves to foster international trade and finance.[2]

This summary of the virtues of a currency board under a fixed exchange-rate regime underscores the normative importance of transparency and accountability. A currency board solves the problem afflicting traditionally unreliable central bank regimes (and certainly one of Mexico's thorniest problem at the moment): the lack of transparency. The board is fully transparent because it is liable to the real owners of reserves: regular moneyholders. In Argentina, where the system resembles the operation of a currency board, the level of reserves can be identified every 24-hour period. In contrast, in the past several years, the government in Mexico would announce the level of reserves three times a year. This was a source of major speculation.[3]

A currency board is a *rule-bound* system, not a *discretionary* system. It has a clear and specific purpose: to ensure that the domestic currency is fully redeemable in hard currency assets at the selected exchange rate and thereby fulfil its contract with the real owners of reserves, namely, regular members of society. It does not seek to "manage" the main monetary variables. Hence, a currency board system is based on a normative idea of money.

Domingo Cavallo, Argentina's finance minister, explains this normative conception as follows: each unit of currency is an implicit

---

2   See his "Applying Monetarism," this volume.

3   The Bank of Mexico now regularly announces the level of reserves, as part of the requirements imposed by the Clinton bailout package. The condition requires a monthly announcement, although the central bank has been unveiling the data every two weeks. This is a highly welcome change of past practices, but it has yet to be legally institutionalized.

contract between the government and the ordinary holder of currency. The contract is supposed to guarantee that the value of the currency is legally bound to remain stable throughout a specified period of time. So, under this framework, a devaluation breaks this contract and therefore breaks the monetary law. This normative feature of stability has been incorporated into the framework of countries that give maximum priority to money as a stable store of value. In New Zealand, legislation prohibits the central bank from exceeding an annual inflation rate of 2 percent. In Argentina, Cavallo himself acted as the main architect behind the convertibility law, which requires a large majority of legislative votes in order to be changed (or repealed).

Argentina is facing a severe crisis as a result of the fallout of the peso devaluation—the so-called *tequila effect*. Many critics claim that the system will be unable to survive the tide of capital flight that has taken place in the wake of Mexico's financial disaster. Still, it is instructive that the Menem government responded to the liquidity crisis by seeking strong budget cuts rather than by falling prey to the false temptations of a devaluation. In other words, the peso was defended at all costs, despite the electoral pressures to relax monetary policy. Indeed, the re-election of the Menem government can be interpreted as an overwhelming referendum in favour of monetary stability. The system of convertibility helped Argentina bring inflation down from 2,400 percent to 3 percent in three years, and real economic growth has averaged 7 percent per year during that time-frame.

The currency board system has gained credibility in nations facing financial turbulence, a discredited currency, and hyper-inflation. Regions as varied as Estonia, Lithuania, Singapore, Hong Kong, and Argentina have successfully instituted currency boards. Currently Venezuela and Ecuador are considering a currency board system in order to effectively counteract the destabilizing forces of the tequila effect.

Currency boards and central banks

In an address given in 1991, Miguel Mancera, governor of the Bank of Mexico, inveighed against the currency board model on the grounds that it imposes "too strict a degree of discipline" on monetary and fiscal policy, and that it precludes the "proper management" of monetary variables.[4] For advocates of the currency board system, these are precisely the reasons why it should be adopted. The authorities of Mexico's Ministry of Finance have also opposed the model, for the wrong reasons: it would sever all control of the exchange rate by making the large bulk of monetary policy purely passive.

An important issue concerning the currency board alternative is: what would happen to the central bank? If a currency board system were established, the central bank would radically downsize its operations. It would require a much smaller bureau, consisting of a set of members in charge of maintaining full convertibility of the currency. On the other hand, a central bank can also coexist with a currency board as a parallel regulatory entity. The net effect of union or coexistence is the same: monetary policy action would become severely limited.

The prevalence of strict fiscal discipline and sound monetary policy was supposed to be provided by the implementation of an autonomous regime in the central bank, in April 1994, backed by a mandate to preserve the purchasing power of the currency. In other words, it seemed that public policy would be practised consistent with the demands of price stability and exchange rate stability. The peso collapse and the ensuing declarations to escape blame for the crisis revealed two flaws. First, that real autonomy could not be pursued with a monetary regime that left exchange rate policy in the hands of the executive branch. Second, that an autonomous monetary policy was devoid of public accountability. After all, an explicit constitutional mandate to maintain price stability was violated.

Not surprisingly, many voices have demanded change. It is a mistake to think of the currency board option as an impulse to castigate the central bank for broken mandates and unfulfilled promises. Some analysts have erroneously opposed the currency board idea on those grounds. The point is that a resignation of the monetary establishment in the central bank would have little or no long-term effect without a major restructuring of the system. It is not a problem of persons, but of the way institutions work. Indeed, even if some saintly leader were to

---

4   This address was delivered at the Kansas Fed symposium on Trade and Currency Zones in August 1991, and subsequently in Mancera (1991).

assume the executive duties in the current state of the central bank, things would not change much. It is fundamentally a problem of institutionalizing confidence.

A recent and important study in the United States found that the Banco de México ranked 101 out of 108 central banks worldwide in preserving a stable currency (Deane and Pringle 1994: 352-54). This result indicates that Mexico's monetary problem centres on the lack of institutional credibility. According to Steve Hanke, the main appeal of a currency board system is that "it commands instant credibility." It makes the monetary constitution of a country fully transparent and fully accountable, by imposing a *rule-bound lock* on sound fiscal and monetary policy. Thus, it can survive the most unorthodox of discretionary authorities. The post-1994 peso has lost one of the two fundamental functions of money: it is still a medium of exchange, but it has ceased to be a reliable store of value. This renders it "funny" money. A currency board would restore the credibility of the currency by strongly linking it, under a strict framework, to a more reliable currency that can act as a store of value.

Objections to a Mexican currency board

Despite the clarity and transparency of the currency board system, it has come under heavy fire in Mexico by authorities, policy analysts, and members of the financial status quo. It is impossible to include all objections to a currency board, but the most common and important will be addressed.

Some objections are superficial reactions to the strictness of the system—for instance, it is claimed that currency boards began in different historical circumstances (so what? what hasn't?), or that they preclude fighting inflation through discretionary policy (correct, the problem is precisely that monetary discretion has a pathetic record), or that a currency board is just a measure to artificially bring down the peso-dollar parity to 3.5 to 1 (the actual rate is a matter of secondary importance, what matters is that the parity, at 1, or 3.5, or 5, or 12, or whatever, has institutional credibility).

It is also stated that a currency board is "too costly", that the central bank does not have the amount of reserves required to back the monetary base. This is not an objection per se, but a short-term technical obstacle. Permission would have to be obtained from the creditors underwriting the $52 billion package, but the point is that the resources are available. If the exchange rate is fixed at 6 to 1 (or even 5 to 1), then only some $12 billion would be required to underpin the monetary base. Of course, bank deposits cannot be fully backed. If the latter are liquidated and exchanged for foreign assets, then the money supply would contract in the same proportion. The commercial banks then would be forced to offer more attractive premiums.

A standard objection is that a currency board would transform Mexico into a de facto 13th district of the Federal Reserve System, and with Mexico in the dollar zone, there would be a loss of monetary sovereignty in Mexico. This is true, but as economist David Hale (1995: 2) argues, "monetary sovereignty in an era of capital mobility is an illusion." For obvious reasons, the peso has traditional close links to the U.S. dollar. Indeed, even without a currency board, Mexico has already witnessed a spontaneous rush towards dollarization, as investors and savers continue to seek out a store of value. This explains why the peso has traded at patently undervalued levels (as much as 8 pesos per dollar at one point). Hale again explains: "If the peso is to continue a role as a denominator of transactions, it will have to be underpinned by a new central bank regime which explicitly focuses on currency stability and convertibility" (ibid.: 4). A currency board does just that.

Another important objection is that, under a currency board, the central bank could no longer act as a lender of last resort to troubled banks. In light of the precarious situation that Mexican banks face today, amid a high interest-rate environment, this could prove deadly. The response is that there is a crucial tradeoff. If the central bank begins to rescue insolvent commercial banks, it will have to expand internal credit, and the result will be the very factor that reduces real patrimony and contributes to high interest rates: inflation. The establishment of a currency board, by restoring confidence and stabilizing the peso, would encourage a faster transition to lower interest rates and hence diminish the damaged loan portfolios of weakened commercial banks. This risk is unavoidable. However, in the very process of transition, the government could fashion alternate measures through public and private deposit insurance as a means to provide financial support for fragile banks. In fact, no large commercial banks have failed under currency board regimes.

A related objection is that a currency board places too much burden on interest rates as the main variable to offset external shocks. Thus, acute recession becomes unavoidable in troubled times—which is, anyway, precisely what Mexico now suffers. The claim is that a currency board would have collapsed in 1994, just as the fluctuation band did. This is highly speculative, and applies to other regimes as well. The "bet" is that a currency board has a more credible opportunity to offset external shocks than other options, in light of its role under a well-defined monetary constitution. So, in 1994, had Mexico operated under a currency board, it would have forced the central bank to raise interest rates instead of expanding internal credit and let reserves fall below the monetary base. This does not make a devaluation completely inevitable, nor does it preclude abandoning the board system in favour of another option, but it is illuminating to find that in its 150-year history in over 70 nations, currency board systems have never witnessed a balance of payments crisis and have never resulted in a devaluation. The current crisis in Argentina is a litmus test of this claim. It might collapse, but the historical evidence is on the side of currency boards.

A similar objection to currency boards is that they make the economy too dependent on foreign capital flows—that is, they allow the same external vulnerability that brought about the currency crisis in Mexico. This is a serious problem. However, it is a problem in all exchange rate regimes. The solution lies not with the monetary system alone, but with the entire foreign investment regime. It requires greater emphasis to attract direct capital investment, and this is a function of proper public policy. Mexico is an undercapitalized economy and as such will remain dependent on foreign capital flows as long as it continues to seek modernization and greater standards of living. To use a biological analogy, a healthy heart does not remove all illness, but it is clearly a precondition for a healthy body.

A recent study by Argentine economist Carlos Zarazaga (1995) attempts to discredit the currency board model. Many of the objections he levels are sophisticated variations of the foregoing, but they merit close scrutiny to gain a broader perspective on the problems and prospects for the adoption of a Mexican currency board.[5]

Zarazaga claims that "currency boards are no better than wedding rings at keeping everlasting commitments." The regime can be abandoned at any time, particularly in the face of a liquidity crisis. This is true, but so what? Everything and anything can be abandoned. If the leadership of a country decides that price stability is an overblown ideal (such as during the López Portillo administration in Mexico), it can readily abandon anti-inflation policy. Currency boards have an attractive public choice element with respect to the execution of policy: they encourage fiscal discipline and a liberal investment regime. The issue surrounding the choice to abandon the model or not simply reflects the issue of whether stability should be abandoned or not. The rational course is to sustain stability, but this does not necessarily translate into policy initiatives. In short, the claim that currency boards do not work because they can be abandoned proves too much.

A more serious objection is that under a board regime, "a minor Orange County-like liquidity crisis" can generate a massive financial panic overnight. Zarazaga offers Argentina as evidence: despite the currency board model, a financial panic ensued associated with the capital outflow shock occasioned by the tequila effect. Thus, since a currency board is "defenceless against financial crises," the medicine they administer can have devastating side-effects in the form of pro-

---

5   Some of Zarazaga's objections are silly, such as the claim that Hanke and others unwittingly confirm the suspicion that currency boards have functioned because they "were controlled by foreign powers", in view of Hanke's claim that board directors should be foreigners appointed by commercial banks (Zarazaga 1995: 3). If I understand Hanke correctly, the point behind this was to *exercise overkill in transparency*, and the need to keep the exchange rate isolated from political pressures. However, if the rules behind currency boards are followed, the directors are really a matter of secondary concern. In fact, this is the crucial appeal of a board system: it would prevail, even if managed by Keynes, Alan García, or Fidel Castro.

longed credit crunches similar to the Great Depression. This, of course, is a purely hypothetical scenario. In any case, speculation aside, it is untrue that currency boards cannot resort to financial rescue of commercial banks: the function of lender of last resort (as Hanke explained to me, in conversation) can be shifted from the monetary to the fiscal side. Moreover, for the sake of fiscal precaution, a rule may be adopted whereby the board can offer a discount window on the basis of an additional percentage of reserves. This would involve tying the monetary base to over 100 percent in hard-currency reserves.[6]

This too involves excessive reliance on counterfactual speculation. To repeat, anything can happen. A currency board is best understood as a manifestation of conservative risk management in the execution of monetary and exchange rate policy. This is what Zarazoga's apology for discretionary monetary policy misses. In effect, the report in question was written in April, at a time when many critics predicted the collapse of Argentina's system. To substantiate his claims, Zarazoga points out that interest rates skyrocketed 32 percent in mid-March, in order to stem the wave of capital outflows. Zarazoga never mentions that interest rates reached triple-digit levels in Mexico during the same time-frame. Yet, the rise in Argentine interest rates was a natural expectation, given the foreign capital outflow externality. It was an instrument of temporary adjustment. Since then, interest rates have fallen to single-digits once again, amid the renewed expectations of stability and a new round of aggressive liberalization measures—just what one is supposed to expect from the public choice features of currency boards in encouraging proper market-based solutions to external shocks.

In effect, Zarazoga's study underestimates the strategic and normative role of a currency board system. He asks: "If it is true that currency boards can prevent the financial meltdown we observed in Mexico, as

---

6   For Zarazoga (1995: 7-8), such an initiative would mean that the system was no longer functioning as a currency board. This, of course, trivializes the dispute, rendering it a verbal and boring issue. It is not a matter of definition, but a matter of the principles involved behind what is called a currency board. In fact, the name is irrelevant for conceptual purposes.

their advocates claim, then why are we seeing a perhaps worse crisis now in Argentina?" (Ibid.: 10).

It seems completely gratuitous to claim that the Argentinean case is economically worse than the Mexican case. Argentina will still grow at over 3 percent in 1995, with a stable inflation rate of under 3 percent. In Mexico, stagflation has set in and credibility has collapsed. In fact, however, it is estimated that virtually all deposits in Argentina's system will return by the end of 1995. The reason is clear: the stabilizing effect of its rule-bound monetary system. Zarazoga also asks how long can the Argentinean economy continue to take the heat. In fact, the Menem governments re-election constituted a popular mandate for stability—despite recession, despite unemployment, despite the liquidity crunch, and despite the worst fears of critics like Zarazoga.

Indeed, Zarazoga's objections blatantly miss the moral of the peso collapse: the institutional need for a currency regime that rules outs discretionary monetary policy and thereby restores the peso's credibility as a store of value and an internationally accepted financial instrument. To be sure, a rule-bound system that links expansion of the monetary base to foreign reserves risks a meltdown in light of the huge foreign debt incurred via the bailout package. However, this particular problem reflects the need for creative strategies designed to bolster new investment and earmark revenue toward debt amortization—for example, via privatizations and a new round of foreign investment liberalizations.

In sum, there are important obstacles and objections to the establishment of a currency board system. It is not a perfect system, but then neither are the alternative policies of a peg, a floating rate, or a band system. As Fontaine notes, the adoption of a currency board regime is a matter of "cost-benefit analysis" vis-a-vis the specific circumstances surrounding the country under analysis. Mexico seems ripe for such a system. The current state of affairs is more a crisis of *credibility* than a crisis of financial volatility; and this demands shock therapy. In turn, this is what makes the currency board option attractive.[7]

---

7   In fact, other voices have expressed the need for a system based on a basket of currencies, in order to avoid excessive dependence on what is deemed a

Conclusion

Some members of the Bank of Mexico, including Vice-Governor Francisco Gil Díaz, quietly voice their approval of a currency board system as the only viable regime consistent with the institution's mandate to guarantee sound money and price stability. On the other hand, the vast majority of politicians disapprove of a currency board regime. A prominent and oft-cited criticism is made by Francisco Suárez Dávila, chairman of the finance committee in the Chamber of Deputies. He denounces the currency board alternative as "colonialist and fundamentalist." In truth, this is a convenient smoke screen that reflects the failure of the government to follow a normative, rule-bound monetary system.

The issue of exchange rate adjustment transcends the complex models fashioned in the ivory towers of academic universities. It is an issue which centres on the medium of exchange and the real value of a person's patrimony. For this reason, future efforts in Mexico to create a more reliable monetary system must incorporate the normative concepts of *accountability* and *transparency* into the framework governing monetary policy. This is just what a currency board does. It acts as a mechanism to maintain the most important ingredient of sustainable economic growth: price stability.

Unfortunately, the gap between monetary theory and political reality is wide. The proposals for monetary reform along the lines of a currency board have lost momentum. In other words, the "timing" has waned. To be sure, one of the obstacles to a currency board is the ability of the host government to meet its strict financial and institutional prerequisites. Gil Díaz (1995: 18) expresses this dilemma as follows:

---

gradually unstable currency—namely, the U.S. dollar. Others, such as economists working with the centre-right wing party PAN, advocate a system of competing currencies between the peso and a new unit backed by silver (given that Mexico is the world's foremost producer of silver). Such proposals aim to enable consumers to choose between the two currencies to denominate transactions. Space precludes a full treatment of those issues, but the point is clear: there is a popular demand for a mechanism that is able to guarantee monetary strength and currency stability.

Market interventions are counterproductive and may combine with other developments to contribute to a collapse, a problem that could be solved under a currency board. But a board is an unlikely immediate proposition for Mexico given the vast institutional and reserve requirements imposed by such a system. The other possibility is a floating rate and that this is a feasible solution, one only has to look into the recent experience of a small economy managed successfully under such a regime: New Zealand.

The months ahead are supposed to see the unveiling of a new exchange rate regime. Once the level of international reserves consolidates to adequate levels (i.e., in the area of $20 billion), discussions are bound to resurface concerning the plausibility of a currency board. A floating regime is theoretically sound, and supported by the majority of the central bank. Yet, it has failed to restore confidence. As Rogelio Ramírez de la O says (in conversation), the problem with a float is that in it, Mexico continues to sink.

The principal issue derives from the institutional requirements of a sound monetary policy, one able to avoid a speculative onslaught and a generalized rush for a store of value such as the dollar. As Gil Díaz states, a floating regime is viable in the long-term and does not require the strict preconditions of a currency board system. On the other hand, as the experience that Gil Díaz describes makes manifest, such a regime is unlikely to restore credibility in the absence of a mandate that holds the central bank *publicly accountable* for price stability. New Zealand enjoys such a mandate, whereas Mexico does not. It is arguable that if such a mandate were supplemented to the autonomous regime adopted in 1994, it would render Mexico's monetary system credible, transparent, and accountable. Then, the political choice between a board and a floating regime would constitute a distinction without a difference.

Be that as it may, if a currency board is not adopted, it will likely not be due to technical reasons, but to the fundamental political unwillingness to relinquish control of a powerful policy tool: the exchange rate. However, monetary history in the period of 1976-94 has taught what ordinary Mexican citizens know all too well, and far better than the ruling technocracy: that the peso desperately requires transparency, simplicity, and complete depoliticization.

References

Deane, M., and Pringle, R. (1994) *The Central Banks.* New York: Penguin Books.

Gil Díaz, F. (1995) "A Comparison of Economic Crises: Chile in 1982, Mexico in 1995." Paper presented at "The Forum of Managed Futures and Derivatives," Chicago, July 14.

Hale, D. (1995) "Will Mexico Follow the Monetary Path of Chile or Argentina?" Kemper Financial Services, Chicago.

Mancera, M. (1991) "Different Types of Currency Zones." In *Policy Implications of Trade and Currency Zones,* 190-202. Kansas City: Federal Reserve of Kansas City.

Zarazaga, C. E. (1995) "Mexico, Argentina, and Currency Boards." Paper prepared for the Board of Directors of the Federal Reserve Bank of Dallas, April.

CHAPTER 19

The Natural Course
of Trade

Edward L. Hudgins[1]

THE FUTURE OF FREE TRADE IN THIS HEMISPHERE will effect directly any future hemispheric monetary arrangement. Indeed, greater economic integration through trade will drive monetary considerations. But some analysts caution that expanding NAFTA could cause adverse consequences. For example, they fear expansion could lead to trade diversion; that it could result in trade blocs; or that it could cause America to neglect its "natural markets" in Asia in favour of those in Latin America.

While it is theoretically possible that some trade diversion might take place, these criticisms for the most part are not well founded. The case for expanding NAFTA to the entire hemisphere is overwhelming. Consider three reasons that call into question the critics.

---

1   The author is the Director of Regulatory Studies at the Cato Institute and Senior Editor of *Regulation* magazine. He has served as a Senior Economist with the Joint Economic Committee of the U.S. Congress.

The case for expanding NAFTA

First, the nature of free trade areas mandate that market liberals not miss an opportunity to establish them wherever and whenever possible. A free trade area basically is a tax cut for individuals. The U.S. government agrees not to tax its own citizens' purchases of goods from overseas, that is, it lets them import goods and services more freely. And the same, of course, applies to the citizens of other countries that are members of free trade areas. In a sense, trade liberalization takes power out of the hands of bureaucrats, that is, out of the hands of governments. It restores the sovereign right of individuals to trade freely with one another and to dispose of their property as they see fit.[2]

Some Americans who oppose free trade, Ross Perot and Pat Buchanan, for example, say that the United States should not mix or merge it's economy with the economies of Mexico or Chile or Argentina. But this is a collectivist premise that assumes that the U.S. economy is the property of the U.S. government. But it is not. It is the property of millions of property owners, that is, private individuals. Those favouring free markets should never miss an opportunity to restore freedom to the hands of individuals, which would include establishing free trade areas.

A second reason not to fear expanding NAFTA is that the United States can avoid trade blocs by, among other means, making similar free trade area offers to other, especially Asian, countries. If Japan wants to have a free trade area with the United States, the two countries should negotiate one. Actually, the U.S. government has had discussions with Japan about such an arrangement but Japan, frankly, was not interested. That country has not reached the point of economic policy maturity to go this trade route. This is Japan's loss. The Japanese suffer with lower living standards.

But other Asian countries, for example, Singapore, Taiwan and Thailand, have expressed interest in free trade areas. The U.S. government should pursue these arrangements not only for their inherent

---

2   For an overview of NAFTA, see Hudgins (1993).

economic benefits but because such arrangements would help ensure that exclusive trade blocs are not established in Asia or the Americas.

Trade blocs also are unlikely because of the trade liberalization and international trade rules brought about through the General Agreement on Tariffs and Trade (GATT) since its formation after World War II. Tariffs have been cut, on average, from 40 percent in the late 1940s to less than 5 percent today. The imperial preference systems that characterized trade between Britain and its colonials and dominions, and between France and its dependents before World War II, would be extremely difficult to reproduce today. This is because a trading bloc would have difficulty insulating itself from the competition from members of other blocs.

Further, trade integration in the Western Hemisphere is not moving toward a customs union, with common tariffs or other trade barriers that might effectively hinder imports from non-hemispheric countries. Finally, the United States, the hemisphere's and world's economic giant, has substantial trade relations with Japan and Western Europe. This means that Americans would benefit by opening hemispheric markets but would suffer by closing markets elsewhere.

A third reason not to fear expanding NAFTA is that the way for America to discover its "natural markets," at least in part, is to trade freely with countries wishing freer trade, not simply to look at present trade patterns. Consider the error that the United States would make through too shortsighted a trade policy. If we were having this discussion in the early 1960s, some trade analysts might say that America's "natural market" was in Western Europe, not Asia. And at that time more U.S. trade was transatlantic. But in the early 1960s Western European countries were on the verge of expanding many of their destructive welfare state programs. And this also was the time many Asian countries were on the verge of initiating fairly free-market oriented reforms. Using the "natural markets" criteria, the United States would have rejected free trade areas with Asian countries just at the time their economies were about to burst forth with spectacular economic growth.

The U.S. government should be a trade entrepreneur and seek out countries that are engaging in market reforms, the Hong Kongs and

Japans of tomorrow, and offer them free trade areas. These will certainly include Latin American countries.

Crisis in the West

It is necessary now to offer a cautionary note about expanding free trade areas in this hemisphere. But to do this requires a discussion of conditions in the world today. Western Europe, Japan, and the other industrialized democracies, including the United States, are experiencing a slow motion version of what happened in the communist world.[3] The contradictions of the welfare state have produced economic, social, and political crises that can no longer be mitigated by the same kinds of government policies that caused them to begin with. In the Western European countries, half of GDP, on average, is in the state sector, compared to about 35 percent in the United States. Attempts in these countries to help workers through mandated benefits, through generous unemployment compensation, through rules making it extremely difficult to dismiss workers, have in fact produced unemployment twice as high as in the United States. Productivity in Western Europe is lower than that in the United States. Not surprisingly, real purchasing power for Western Europeans is lower than for Americans.

Another problem faced in the West is corruption. This is the problem that many people believe is confined to less developed countries. And critics often will complain about corruption in Mexico and other Latin American countries. This kind of corruption occurs when a bureaucrat or public official exchanges a favour for cash or some other material benefit. In other words, the arbitrary use of power governs rather than the rule of law.

But more destructive of civil societies is a form of corruption that is inherent in the welfare states in the West. By its nature, a welfare state breaks down the separation between government and the private sector and thus between political and economic power. Government is expected to act directly to help this industry or that sector. The public good becomes, in fact, simply interest group driven. This means that policies

---

3   For a more detailed analysis of this theme, see Hudgins (1994).

are often arbitrary, often contradictory. In essence, the rule of law gradually gives way to the rule of particular men and particular powerful interest groups. Politicians trade favours not simply for cash but for other coins of the realm: for political power, for political influence, for prestige. And the buying and selling of favours, at least technically in the West and in the United States, is legal. In other words, corruption is institutionalized and legal.

Exporting goods or exporting failure?

Given the current global economic situation, Western industrialized countries face two options:

1. They can dismantle the welfare and corporate state systems that have caused their problems. The French, Italians, and Swedes among others at least are considering this approach. Many lawmakers in the Republican controlled Congress in the United States claim they wish to adopt this approach as well.
2. They can make minor reforms in an attempt to save their systems. This approach simply will forestall disaster but guarantee that disaster, when it does come, will be far worse than any inconveniences that might result from fundamental reforms.

Unfortunately, many policymakers are opting for this latter approach. And one way to buy time for the failed systems is through managed trade.

The Clinton administration insisted that NAFTA include labour and environmental side agreements and establish international panels to deal with domestic policies in these areas. This approach was an attempt to export not goods and services, but many of America's failed policies to Mexico. Mexican firms, free of the kinds of regulatory baggage that U.S. policymakers refuse to lift from the shoulders of American businesses, could compete effectively and make Americans more acutely aware of the weight of their regulatory burdens. Fortunately, the side agreements are very ineffective.[4] But if the United States ex-

---

4   For a detailed analysis of the probable effects of these agreements, see Taylor

pands NAFTA in this hemisphere, some of its statist policymakers and special interest groups will try to foist regulatory burdens on the prospective Latin American members. Those countries should resist such attempts.

Pollution that harms health and property is undesirable, and Latin American governments should be concerned about this problem. Of course, Latin American leaders should not consider workers in their countries as enemies, just as workers should not fear free markets. Indeed, it was Ludwig von Mises who observed that the poor have the most to gain from free markets since they have the least. They are the ones who need the opportunities that free markets, including free trade, offer. For the sake of their own countries, Latin American leaders would do well to understand that allowing all of their citizens the opportunity to participate in market systems characterized by open entry, not government insulation from competition for the already powerful, will head off social unrest to say nothing of economic problems in the future.

Latin American leaders should vocally oppose attempts to impose American regulatory burdens on their economies as the price for freer trade. But they should adopt a positive strategy as well. Much good scholarly work has been done on free-market ways to protect the public health and the public safety. Ideally, strict protection of private property rights and freedom of contract for all citizens, rich and poor, is the basis of such a regime. Especially important is a system of tort law that enforces reasonable standards of liability, injury, negligence and the like. Latin American countries that do not have the English common law tradition in some ways will find tort reform more difficult. But then again, the United States has lost a good part of this tradition through decades of judicial activism that ignored the Constitution as well as common law.

Latin American leaders should adopt these property and tort-based approaches for protecting health and safety and dealing with pollution in their own countries. They should also counter demands by America that they adopt a command-and-control approach to regulation by

---

(1993).

suggesting that America adopt a market approach. Regulatory competition in this hemisphere would be good for Latin American countries and the United States as well.

But most important is that trade be allowed to take its natural course so that markets expand to create new opportunities and prosperity in the Americas.

References

Hudgins, E.L. (1993) "The Case for NAFTA." National Center for Policy Analysis *Pc¹ ᵣkgrounder* No. 130, 15 November 1993.

Hudgins, E. L. ⠀⠀⠀⠀⠀West at the Crossroads." In *The 1994 Joint Econom⠀⠀⠀⠀⠀⠀⠀⠀onomic Committee, Congress of the Unitec

Taylor, J. (19⠀⠀⠀⠀⠀⠀⠀⠀⠀⠀ccords: Sound and Fury Signifying Littl⠀⠀⠀⠀⠀⠀⠀⠀⠀⠀*lysis No. 198,* 17 November 1993.